# The Golden Book of

# PASTA

# The Golden Book of
# PASTA

First English language edition
for the United States and Canada
published in 2012 by Barron's Educational Series, Inc.

© 2011 McRae Publishing Ltd, London

The Golden Book of Pasta
was created and produced by McRae Publishing Ltd, London
www.mcraepublishing.co.uk

*Publishers* Anne McRae, Marco Nardi

*Project Director* Anne McRae
*Art Director* Marco Nardi
*Photography* Brent Parker Jones
*Texts* Carla Bardi
*Editing* Carla Bardi, Anne McRae
*Food Styling* Lee Blaylock
*Food Preparation* Rebecca Quinn, Michelle Finn
*Layouts* Aurora Granata
*Pre-press* Filippo Delle Monache

*All inquiries should be addressed to:*
Barron's Educational Series, Inc.
250 Wireless Boulevard
Hauppauge, New York 11788
www.barronseduc.com

*Picture credits* p. 18: Leonetto Cappiello (1921) / Poster Photo Archives,
Posters Please, Inc., New York City / © ADAGP, Paris and DACS, London 2011

ISBN-13: 978-0-7641-6559-7

Library of Congress Control Number: 2012935352

9 8 7 6 5 4 3 2 1

Printed in China

### NOTE TO OUR READERS

Eating eggs or egg whites that are not completely cooked poses the possibility
of salmonella food poisoning. The risk is greater for pregnant women, the elderly,
the very young, and persons with impaired immune systems. If you are concerned
about salmonella, you can use reconstituted powdered egg whites or pasteurized eggs.

The level of difficulty for each recipe is given on a scale from
1 (easy) to 3 (complicated).

# CONTENTS

# INTRODUCTION

# INTRODUCTION

Pasta brings a unique combination of virtues to dinner tables in Italy and, increasingly, in many other parts of the world. It is nutritious, versatile, simple to prepare, economical, easy to store, and delicious in so many different ways. Few foods have more to offer.

Nutritionally, pasta is a carbohydrate, providing the energy necessary to fuel muscles and brains. In a healthy balanced diet, between 40–50 percent of daily calorie requirements should be provided by carbohydrates. There are two types of carbohydrates: complex and simple. Simple carbohydrates are found in unhealthy food choices, such as cookies, cakes, chocolate, and sugary drinks. They release their energy into the body too quickly, creating swings in levels of energy and mood that can leave you feeling tired and irritable. The energy in complex carbs is absorbed more gradually, maintaining stable levels of energy and well being. Pasta belongs to the complex carbohydrate group. Less refined whole-wheat (wholemeal) pasta is even better in this sense. In this book we often suggest that you use whole-wheat dried pasta or flour to make fresh pasta, but even where we do not, feel free to use them all the same.

Pasta is a healthy food choice for many other reasons too. It is low in saturated fat, cholesterol, and sodium, all of which should be eaten in moderation to help protect against heart disease. Pasta contains useful amounts of dietary fiber and protein and is a good

source of minerals, such as manganese, selenium, and phosphorus. Pasta, especially the whole-wheat variety, contains useful amounts of a range of B vitamins. With about 360 calories in each $3^1/2$ ounce (100 g) serving, pasta is not particularly fattening.

Beyond the health aspects, pasta is popular because it is the ultimate convenience food. It is cheap to buy and can be stored for months before use. Pasta is easy and quick to prepare: a nutritious pasta salad, for instance, can be whipped up in the time it takes to boil the water and cook the pasta. Fresh tomatoes, garlic, salad greens, cheese, capers, olives, and herbs can be chopped while it cooks. Many pasta sauces can be prepared while the pasta is cooking.

Versatility is another of pasta's virtues. In summer, a cool pasta salad makes a wonderful starter at dinner, a nutritious lunch, or a great barbecue or picnic food. In winter, hearty pasta soups and baked pasta dishes make warming meals for the whole family. Boiled fresh, filled, or dried pasta with meat or vegetable sauces are good all year round on any occasion.

Italy is the largest pasta producer in the world today, with more than 3 million tons produced each year, one-third of which is exported, mainly to Germany, the United States, and France. Not surprisingly, Italians lead the world in pasta consumption, tucking away an average of 62 pounds (28 kg) each per year. What is striking, underlining this versatile food's international appeal, is that many other countries are catching up. Venezuelans and Tunisians consume an average of about 26 pounds (12 kg) each. They are followed by the USA, with 20 pounds (9 kg), and France, Germany, Slovenia, Portugal, Canada, and Brazil at between 14–18 pounds (6–8 kg) per head.

Pâtes
BARONI

# A SHORT HISTORY OF PASTA

Pasta is made with the simplest of ingredients—essentially flour and water—and has alway been a staple of the humble and poor. Because their history is not well documented, the origins of pasta are lost to us. Food historians believe that pasta, or varying forms of pasta including oriental noodles, were probably invented independently, in different parts of the world, wherever cereals were cultivated.

There is evidence of pasta-making in Italy in Etruscan times and a detailed relief in a 4th century BC tomb shows all the equipment needed to roll and cut pasta, including a fluted pastry cutting wheel that looks almost identical to its modern counterpart. But there is no real proof that this Etruscan artisan was making pasta. The Greeks had *laganon*, a product that is thought to be a forerunner of pasta. The Romans cut *laganon* into strips and called them *lagani* (similar at least linguistically to lasagna). Roman *lagani* are the first recorded example of dough that is kneaded and rolled into sheets, but they were cooked in oil or baked in the oven like unleavened bread.

Galeno, a 2nd century Greek doctor, uses another term, *itria*, also of Greek origin, to refer to mixtures of flour and water, of which *lagani* seem to be a variant. We don't know what shape *itria* were, but it is certain that the term was used in medieval times by the Arabs, who played a key role in spreading the early technology for drying pasta to Sicily and the rest of the Mediterranean. The Arab geographer, Al

Idris, uses the term *itriyah* in 1154 to indicate the unleavened strands of pasta produced in large quantities at Trabia, in Sicily, and exported to Calabria and other parts of the Mediterranean. Sicily soon became a major producer of dried pasta, while medieval chronicles reveal that the consumption of fresh pasta had spread to northern Italy.

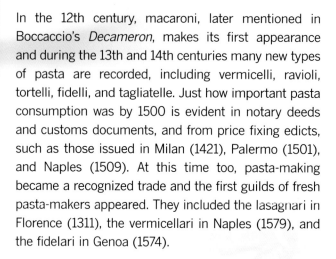

**20**

In the 12th century, macaroni, later mentioned in Boccaccio's *Decameron*, makes its first appearance and during the 13th and 14th centuries many new types of pasta are recorded, including vermicelli, ravioli, tortelli, fidelli, and tagliatelle. Just how important pasta consumption was by 1500 is evident in notary deeds and customs documents, and from price fixing edicts, such as those issued in Milan (1421), Palermo (1501), and Naples (1509). At this time too, pasta-making became a recognized trade and the first guilds of fresh pasta-makers appeared. They included the lasagnari in Florence (1311), the vermicellari in Naples (1579), and the fidelari in Genoa (1574).

In the 15th and 16th centuries recipes for fresh pasta began to appear in cook books and gastronomic treatises. Bartolomeo Scappi (1474) and Cristofero da Messisbugo (1548) both recorded pasta dishes that were often served with sugar and spices. These recipes were aimed at the upper classes, who preferred fresh pasta, especially the stuffed varieties.

With the advent of the first steam machinery, hydraulic presses, and then electricity, dried pasta manufacturing underwent a major revolution. The first machine capable of carrying out all stages of the production process—grinding, kneading, rolling, drying, cooling, and packaging, was patented in 1933. Since then, industrial pasta making has not looked back and pasta production increases each year.

# COOKING &
# SERVING PASTA

**Timing:** One of the most difficult things for the novice pasta cook is knowing when the pasta is cooked. It should be boiled until the outer layers are soft enough to absorb the delicious sauce you have prepared, while the inside is firm enough to pose some resistance to the bite. This is called "al dente."

**Water:** Pasta needs lots of water to cook properly. Allow about 4 quarts (4 liters) for each pound (500 g) of pasta. Never cook even a small amount of pasta in less than 3 quarts (3 liters).

**Salt:** Allow 1 heaped tablespoon of coarse sea salt for each pound (500 g) of pasta. Add the salt after the water has come to a boil, just before adding the pasta.

**Quantity:** As a general guideline, allow about $3^1/_2$ ounces (100 g) per head. If the pasta is a first course, with seconds to follow, you may need less. If you are just serving pasta with a salad, you may need more.

**Cooking:** When the water is boiling, add all the pasta at once. Stir with a wooden spoon so it doesn't stick together. Cover the pot with a lid and bring it back to a boil as soon as possible. When the water is boiling again, leave to cook uncovered, stirring frequently.

**Draining:** Drain the pasta in a colander as soon as it is cooked. Don't leave it sitting in the water as it will continue to cook.

A CATALOG

OF PASTA

# SOUP PASTA

Made from durum wheat flour or, less often, soft wheat flour with eggs, tiny soup pasta shapes were created to substitute the wheat that was traditionally used to give substance to chunky soups and broths. They were probably among the earliest types of dried pasta since they were quick and easy to cook and kept well, making them suitable for trading, even over long distances. In medieval Arabian cook books, the term *fidaws* is used to indicate small pasta, shaped like kernels of grain. These are thought to have originated in the areas of Spain then under Arab rule. The only pasta in use in Spain and other parts of the Mediterranean, soup pasta was not widespread in Italy until the 18th century, although there are a few recipes in cook books and treatises on cooking dating from the 15th and 16th centuries.

Soup pasta is now available in a wide variety of shapes. The smallest are tiny seed or grain shapes which are served in clear vegetable or meat soups (bouillon). The larger shapes, which are often hollow or ridged, are ideal for thicker vegetable soups and broths made with pulses, such as beans, garbanzo beans (chick peas), and lentils. They are widely used in regional Italian dishes.

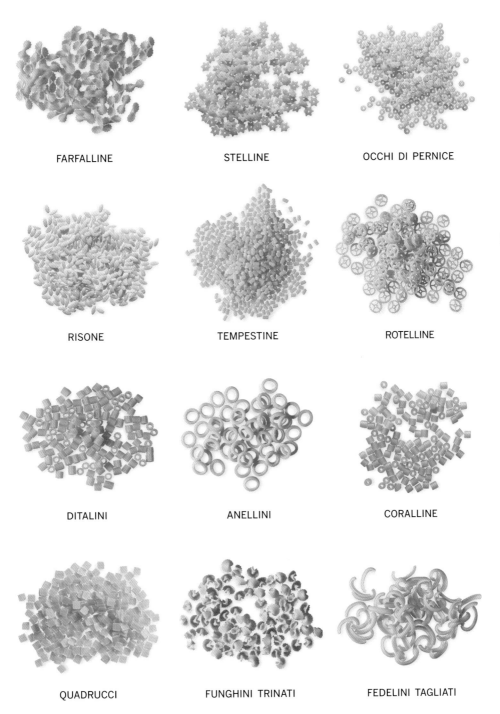

FARFALLINE

STELLINE

OCCHI DI PERNICE

RISONE

TEMPESTINE

ROTELLINE

DITALINI

ANELLINI

CORALLINE

QUADRUCCI

FUNGHINI TRINATI

FEDELINI TAGLIATI

# SHORT PASTA

Most short pasta shapes are produced industrially from durum wheat flour and water. Durum wheat is richer in protein and gluten than other types of wheat. It is a hard, strong wheat and is ideal for pasta-making since it holds its shape and texture during cooking. About 90 percent of all the pasta made today is made of durum wheat and about 65 percent of this figure is made up of short pasta, making it the most popular type with consumers.

Dried pasta's conquest, firstly of Italian tables and then of the global market, is a relatively recent occurrence and it has imposed the Italian way of cooking and eating pasta "al dente" (literally "firm to the bite") on the world. This is the pasta which, from the 18th century onward, established itself in Naples, earning that city the nickname of "the macaroni capital." Short pasta spread to the rest of Italy after the country was unified in 1861.

PENNE RIGATE

PENNE LISCE

PENNONE

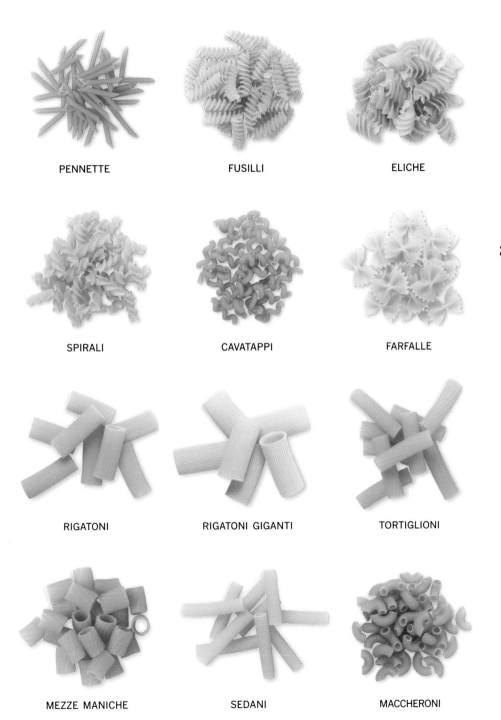

PENNETTE          FUSILLI          ELICHE

SPIRALI          CAVATAPPI          FARFALLE

RIGATONI          RIGATONI GIGANTI          TORTIGLIONI

MEZZE MANICHE          SEDANI          MACCHERONI

## (SHORT DRIED PASTA)

Created to be served with thick, often chunky sauces, short pasta is now available in hundreds of shapes: flat, such as farfalle; twisted, like eliche, fusilli, and gemelli; tubular and obliquely cut like penne, or cut straight like rigatoni; and imaginative, like ruote (wheels), gomiti (elbows), and lumache (snails). Short pasta shapes vary greatly in size, from $1/4$-inch (5-mm) mezze penne to 4-inch (10-cm) cannelloni. Externally, short pasta is either smooth or ridged. Some short pasta shapes are associated with specific regions of Italy: malloreddus, for example, come from Sardinia, while cavatelli, traditionally from the southern region of Molise, are now mainly associated with Puglia (the "heel" of Italy).

MACARONCETTI

CONCHIGLIONE

CONCHIGLIE

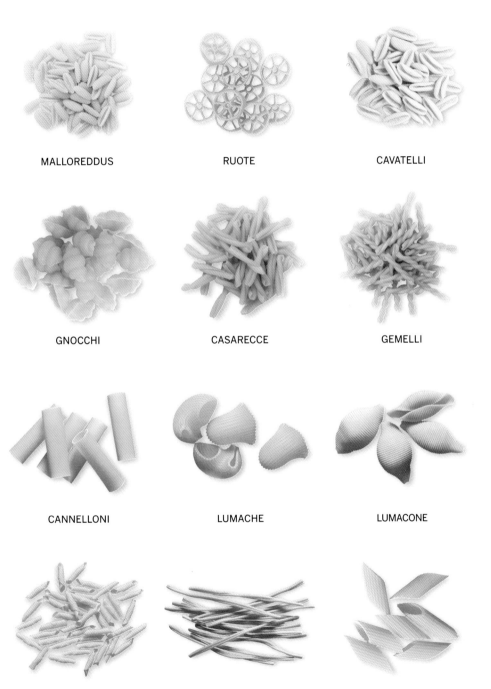

MALLOREDDUS

RUOTE

CAVATELLI

GNOCCHI

CASARECCE

GEMELLI

CANNELLONI

LUMACHE

LUMACONE

GARGANELLI

MACCHERONI AL FERRO

MEZZE PENNE

**REGINETTE**

**FUSILLI LUNGHI**

# LONG PASTA

Long pasta shapes can be either fresh or dried. These two pages feature dried, industrially produced pasta made from durum wheat flour. Long, fresh pasta shapes are shown on pages 36–7.

Without doubt, spaghetti are the most well known long pasta type; in fact they are the most popular of all pasta types. Spaghetti were invented in Naples, and the word first appears in a short poem from 1824 by Antonio Vivani entitled *Macaroni in Naples*. Long and cylindrical in shape, spaghetti were originally thinner, more like modern spaghettini. Later, when served with richer northern sauces, they needed to be thicker and consequently became the fatter spaghetti we know today.

There are several other popular long pasta shapes and they range in diameter from about $1/20$ inch (1 mm) (angel hair pasta) to about $1/2$ inch (1 cm) (ziti). Some long pasta shapes are whole, like spaghetti, while others are hollow, like bucatini and ziti. Linguine, also known as trenette, are slightly flattened. Many long dried pasta shapes are associated with specific Italian regions or cities: bucatini with Rome, for example, ziti with Naples, and linguine with Genoa.

ANGEL HAIR PASTA        SPAGHETTINI        SPAGHETTI

BUCATINI           LINGUINE           ZITI

# COLORED & SPECIAL PASTA

SPINACH SPAGHETTI

MULTI-COLORED PASTA

SPINACH FUSILLI

TOMATO SPAGHETTI

The coloring and flavoring of pasta has distant origins. From medieval times up until the end of the 17th century, saffron was often used to color pasta, with some recipes suggesting the addition of rose water as well. Saffron is still used today in the traditional recipe for malloreddus. Records show that in Renaissance times, pasta was often was cooked in milk until it was very soft and mushy, and then flavored with sugar and sweet spices. Some colored pastas belong to regional traditions. Apart from Sardinian malloreddus, there are also green spinach tagliatelle from Emilia, and garganelli from Romagna, which are flavored with nutmeg and grated lemon zest. Generally speaking, colored or aromatic pasta should be served with simple sauces with an oil, butter, or cheese base, in order not to kill the flavor and to avoid clashing tastes. In recent years whole-wheat (wholemeal) and gluten-free pasta shapes have also become popular.

GLUTEN-FREE PENNE

TOMATO LUMACHE

BUCKWHEAT FUSILLI

TRICOLOR FARFALLE

SPINACH FUSILLI

TOMATO FUSILLI

TRICOLOR FUSILLI

COLORED STROZZAPRETI

SQUID'S INK PENNE

WHOLE-WHEAT RIGATONI

WHOLE-WHEAT PENNE

WHOLE-WHEAT FUSILLI

# FRESH PASTA

We know that fresh pasta became increasingly popular in Italy from the 14th century onward, as more and more small fresh or semi-dried pasta manufacturers, known as *lasagnari, vermicellari,* or *fidelari,* were registered with guilds throughout the peninsula (but especially in northern and central Italy). Experimenting with shapes and fillings, and combinations of these with different sauces, these local artisans created the huge variety of fresh pasta we know today.

Classic fresh pasta, including tagliatelle and pappardelle, is made using soft wheat flour and eggs. See our recipe and step-by-step instructions on pages 242–45. Fresh pasta can also be colored or flavored with spinach, tomatoes, carrots, beets, or herbs, among other ingredients. See our recipe on pages 276–7. Many regions of Italy also have their own fresh pasta types and we have included instructions for many of these as well. Pici, for example, come from southern Tuscany (see recipe on page 248), and pizzoccheri are from the Valtellina in Lombardy (see recipe on page 322), while orecchiette come from Puglia in the south (see recipe on page 326–7).

TAGLIOLINI

TAGLIATELLE (FETTUCCINE)

PAGLIA E FIENO

PAPPARDELLE

MALTAGLIATI

GARGANELLI

BIGOLI

PIZZOCCHERI

PICI

LASAGNA

POTATO GNOCCHI

ORECCHIETTE

# STUFFED PASTA

Exquisite, stuffed pasta shapes are among the best-loved dishes in Italian cuisine. Stuffed pasta has been prized since Renaissance times, and over the centuries the richest array of flavors and textures have been married to the delicacy of fresh pasta, as the infinite variety of different stuffings and regional specialities demonstrate. Agnolotti, ravioli, anolini, cappelletti, tortelli, tortellini, and tortelloni: the repertoire of stuffed pasta is rich and varied and is one of the highlights of Italian regional cuisines.

Most filled pasta types are made by preparing classic soft wheat flour and egg pasta sheets which are then filled and folded into ravioli, tortellini, agnolotti, and so on. We have included detailed instructions on how to make several different kinds in the chapter on stuffed pasta (see pages 342–409).

RAVIOLI

AGNOLOTTI

TRIANGULAR RAVIOLI

39

TORTELLINI

TORTELLONI

CAPPELLACCI

HALF MOON RAVIOLI

ROUND RAVIOLI

ANOLINI

# SHORT
# PASTA

# FUSILLI SALAD WITH GRILLED SUMMER VEGGIES

Put a large pot of salted water to boil over high heat. • Preheat a grill pan over medium-high heat. • Grill the eggplant, bell peppers, zucchini, and tomatoes until tender and marked with brown lines. • Put all the grilled vegetables in a large serving bowl with the mozzarella and sprinkle with the basil, salt, and pepper. Drizzle with the oil. • Cook the pasta in the boiling water until al dente. Drain well and let cool a little in the colander. • Add the pasta to the bowl with the vegetables, toss gently, and serve.

| | |
|---|---|
| 1 | large eggplant (aubergine), with skin, thinly sliced |
| 1 | red bell pepper (capsicum), seeded and sliced |
| 1 | yellow bell pepper (capsicum), seeded and sliced |
| 2 | large zucchini (courgettes), thinly sliced |
| 4 | ripe, "meaty" tomatoes, thickly sliced |
| 8 | ounces (250 g) mozzarella cheese, cut in small cubes |
| 2 | tablespoons coarsely chopped fresh basil |
| | Salt and freshly ground white pepper |
| ⅓ | cup (90 ml) extra-virgin olive oil |
| 1 | pound (500 g) fusilli |

■ ■ ■ *This salad is best if left to cool for 1–2 hours. The flavors of the vegetables will melt into the pasta.*

Serves: 4–6
Preparation: 20 minutes
Cooking: 30 minutes
Level: 1

You could also use: farfalle, conchiglie, rigatoni

# FARFALLE SALAD WITH FETA & GRILLED PEPPERS

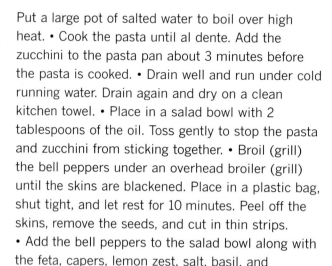

**44**

Put a large pot of salted water to boil over high heat. • Cook the pasta until al dente. Add the zucchini to the pasta pan about 3 minutes before the pasta is cooked. • Drain well and run under cold running water. Drain again and dry on a clean kitchen towel. • Place in a salad bowl with 2 tablespoons of the oil. Toss gently to stop the pasta and zucchini from sticking together. • Broil (grill) the bell peppers under an overhead broiler (grill) until the skins are blackened. Place in a plastic bag, shut tight, and let rest for 10 minutes. Peel off the skins, remove the seeds, and cut in thin strips. • Add the bell peppers to the salad bowl along with the feta, capers, lemon zest, salt, basil, and remaining 3 tablespoons (90 ml) of oil. • Toss well. Serve at slightly chilled or at room temperature.

| | |
|---|---|
| 1 | pound (500 g) farfalle |
| 2 | zucchini (courgettes), cut in small cubes |
| 8 | tablespoons (120 ml) extra-virgin olive oil |
| 1 | large yellow bell pepper (capsicum) |
| 1 | large red bell pepper (capsicum) |
| 5 | ounces (150 g) feta cheese, crumbled |
| 1 | tablespoon salt-cured capers, rinsed |
| | Zest of 1 organic lemon, yellow part only, cut in tiny pieces |
| | Salt |
| 2 | tablespoons coarsely chopped fresh basil + extra leaves to garnish |

Serves: 4–6
Preparation: 20 minutes
    + 10 minutes to rest
Cooking: 20–30 minutes
Level: 2

You could also use: conchiglie, fusilli, cavatappi

# CONCHIGLIE SALAD WITH TUNA, CHERRY TOMATOES & OLIVES

46

Combine the tuna, tomatoes, olives, scallions, celery, carrot, and garlic in a bowl. Drizzle with the oil and season with salt, white pepper, and oregano. Cover with plastic wrap (cling film) and refrigerate for 1 hour. • Put a large pot of salted water to boil over high heat. • Cook the pasta in the boiling water until al dente. • Drain well and let cool under cold running water. Drain again and dry on a clean kitchen towel. • Put the pasta in a serving bowl. Add the tuna mixture and toss well. Garnish with the parsley and basil and serve.

| | |
|---|---|
| 8 | ounces (250 g) canned tuna, drained and crumbled |
| 1 | pound (500 g) cherry tomatoes, halved |
| 1 | cup (100 g) black olives, pitted and coarsely chopped |
| 2 | scallions (spring onions), coarsely chopped |
| 2 | stalks celery, coarsely chopped |
| 1 | carrot, coarsely chopped |
| 1 | clove garlic, finely chopped |
| 1/3 | cup (90 ml) extra-virgin olive oil |
| | Salt and freshly ground white pepper |
| 1 | teaspoon dried oregano |
| 1 | pound (500 g) conchiglie (shells) |
| 2 | tablespoons finely chopped fresh parsley |
| 2 | tablespoons fresh basil leaves |

Serves: 4–6
Preparation: 15 minutes
+ 1 hour to chill
Cooking: 12 minutes
Level: 1

You could also use: farfalle, fusilli, eliche

# SOUP PASTA
# IN BEEF STOCK

48

**Beef Stock:** Stick the onion quarters with the cloves.
• Place all the stock ingredients in a large soup pot
and cover with the water. Bring to a boil over high
heat. • Simmer over low heat for 3 hours. Skim the
stock during cooking to remove the foam that will
rise to the surface, at first abundantly but then
tapering off. • Strain the stock through a fine-mesh
sieve into a large bowl, discarding the vegetables
and bones. The beef can be sliced and served as a
main course, if liked.
**Soup:** Measure out 4–6 cups (1–1.5 liters) of stock.
Bring to a boil in a large pot. • Add the pasta and
cook until al dente, 3–5 minutes (depending on the
size of the pasta). • Sprinkle with the cheese and
serve hot.

*■ ■ ■ This beef stock recipe will make about 3 quarts
(3 liters) of stock, which is far more than you will need
for four to six people. Keep the leftover stock in the
refrigerator for 2–3 days, or freeze it for later use.*

You could also use: ditalini, anelli, rotelline, quadrucci

**Beef Stock**
1 large onion, quartered
4 whole cloves
1 large carrot, halved
1 leek
2 stalks celery, including leaves
  Small bunch fresh parsley
2 bay leaves
2 cloves garlic, peeled
2 very ripe tomatoes
1 tablespoon salt
3 pounds (1.5 kg) boiling beef
2 pounds (1 kg) beef bones
  About 5 quarts (5 liters) cold water

**Soup**
8 ounces (250 g) stelline
3/4 cup 120 g freshly grated Parmesan cheese

Serves: 4
Preparation: 15 minutes
Cooking: 12 minutes
  + 3 hours for the stock
Level: 1

# MINESTRONE WITH PASTA

Heat the oil in a large, heavy saucepan over medium-high heat. Add the onion, celery, and garlic and sauté until softened, about 5 minutes. • Add the carrot and potato, and sauté until they begin to color, 3–4 minutes. • Add the tomatoes, tomato paste, and beans and stir to combine. Pour in the stock and bring to a boil. • Add the pasta, zucchini, and cabbage, decrease the heat to medium-low, and gently simmer until the pasta and vegetables are cooked, 15–20 minutes. • Stir in the parsley. Season with salt and pepper. • Serve hot sprinkled with the Parmesan.

50

2 tablespoons extra-virgin olive oil

1 red onion, diced

2 stalks celery, diced

2 cloves garlic, finely chopped

1 large carrot, diced

2 medium potatoes, peeled and diced

1 (14-ounce/400-g) can tomatoes, with juice

2 tablespoons tomato paste (concentrate)

1 (14-ounce/400-g) can borlotti or red kidney beans, drained

5 cups (1.25 liters) beef stock (see page 48)

1 cup (150 g) farfalline

2 medium zucchini (courgettes), diced

¼ Savoy or green cabbage, coarsely chopped

¼ cup finely chopped fresh flat-leaf parsley

Salt and freshly ground black pepper

⅓ cup (50 g) freshly grated Parmesan cheese

Serves: 4–6
Preparation: 20 minutes
Cooking 25–30 minutes
Level: 1

You could also use: ditalini, anellini, rotelline, coralline

# TUSCAN PASTA & GARBANZO BEAN SOUP

52

Put the garbanzo beans in a large bowl of cold water with the baking soda. Leave to soak overnight, about 12 hours. • Drain, transfer to a colander, and rinse thoroughly under cold running water. • Place in a saucepan and cover with cold water. Add 2 garlic cloves and a sprig of rosemary. Cover, leaving a space for steam to escape, and simmer until the beans are very tender, 1–2 hours. Add 1 teaspoon of salt after the beans have been cooking for about 50 minutes. • Drain, the beans reserving the cooking water. • Purée three-quarters of the garbanzo beans in a food processor, keeping the remainder whole. • Heat 3 tablespoons of oil in a large heavy-bottomed saucepan and sauté the remaining 2 cloves of garlic and rosemary sprig for 3 minutes. • Add the tomato paste and simmer over medium heat for 2 minutes. • Add the puréed and whole garbanzo beans and the reserved cooking liquid and stock and bring to a boil. • Add the pasta and cook until al dente, 4–6 minutes (depending on the size of the pasta). • Serve hot drizzled with the remaining 3 tablespoons of oil and seasoned with plenty of black pepper.

1½ cups (300 g) dried garbanzo beans (chick peas)

1 teaspoon baking soda (bicarbonate of soda)

4 cloves garlic, bruised

2 sprigs rosemary

Salt

6 tablespoons (90 ml) extra-virgin olive oil

2 tablespoons tomato paste (concentrate)

2 cups (500 ml) beef stock (see page 48)

8 ounces (250 g) ditalini

Freshly ground black pepper

Serves: 4–6
Preparation: 20 minutes + 12 hours to soak
Cooking: 1–2 hours
Level: 2

You could also use: mezze penne, anellini, farfalline, quadrucci

# PASTA & BEAN SOUP

54

Soak the beans in cold water overnight. • Cook the beans until tender, about 1 hour. • Purée three-quarters of the beans and 1 cup (250 ml) of the cooking liquid in a food processor. • Heat the oil in a heavy-bottomed pan over medium-high heat. Add the onion and rosemary and sauté until the onion is softened, 3–4 minutes. • Add the puréed beans, tomato, and water. Season with salt and pepper and simmer over medium-low heat for 10–15 minutes. • Add the pasta and remaining whole beans, and simmer until the pasta is cooked al dente, 6–8 minutes (depending on the size of the pasta). • Serve hot.

1½ cups (300 g) dried cannellini beans or white kidney beans

¼ cup (60 ml) extra-virgin olive oil

1 onion, finely chopped

1 tablespoon fresh rosemary, finely chopped

1 ripe tomato, chopped

2 cups (500 ml) cold water + extra as required

Salt and freshly ground black pepper

8 ounces (250 g) ditalini

Serves: 4–6
Preparation: 30 minutes
  + 12 hours to soak
Cooking: 75–85 minutes
Level: 1

■ ■ ■ *If you are short of time, use two (14-ounce/400-g) cans of cannellini beans instead of the dried beans. You can skip the soaking and cooking time for the beans.*

You could also use: farfalline, mezze penne, tagliatelle secche (broken up)

# FUSILLI WITH BREAD CRUMBS & GARLIC

56

Put a large pot of salted water to boil over high heat. • Cook the pasta until al dente. • While the pasta is cooking, heat the oil in a large frying pan over medium heat. Add the garlic and sauté for 1 minute. • Add the bread crumbs and oregano and sauté until the bread crumbs have browned, about 3 minutes. Remove from the heat. • Drain the pasta and add to the pan with the sauce. • Toss over medium heat until the sauce sticks to the pasta, 1–2 minutes. • Season with salt and pepper and serve hot.

| | |
|---|---|
| 1 | pound (500 g) fusilli |
| ½ | cup (120 ml) extra-virgin olive oil |
| 4 | cloves garlic, finely chopped |
| ⅔ | cup (100 g) fine dry bread crumbs |
| 2 | tablespoons finely chopped fresh oregano or 2 teaspoons dried oregano |
| | Salt and freshly ground black pepper |

Serves: 4–6
Preparation: 15 minutes
Cooking: 15 minutes
Level: 1

You could also use: penne rigate, eliche, rigatoni, ruote

# CONCHIGLIE WITH YOGURT & HERBS

58

Put a large pot of salted water to boil over high heat. • Clean the zucchini carefully by trimming one end and detaching the flower. Tear the flower into large pieces and cut the zucchini lengthwise into thin batons. • Combine the yogurt, mixed herbs, oil, garlic, nutmeg, salt, and pepper in a bowl and mix well. • Cook the pasta in the boiling water until al dente. • Drain the pasta thoroughly and transfer to a large serving bowl. Add the zucchini and yogurt mixture and sprinkle with the Parmesan. • Toss well and serve hot.

6   small, very fresh zucchini (courgettes), with flowers, if possible

1   cup (250 ml) thick, creamy Greek-style yogurt

6   tablespoons finely chopped mixed fresh herbs, such as mint, marjoram, thyme, parsley, chives, etc.

2   tablespoons extra-virgin olive oil

2   cloves garlic, finely chopped

   Pinch of freshly ground nutmeg

   Salt and freshly ground black pepper

1   pound (500 g) conchiglie

½   cup (75 g) freshly grated Parmesan cheese

Serves: 4–6
Preparation: 15 minutes
Cooking: 10–15 minutes
Level: 1

You could also use: rigatoni, farfalle, ruote, cavatappi

# PENNE WITH PISTACHIO PESTO

Put a large pot of salted water to boil over high heat. • Heat 2 tablespoons of oil in a large frying pan over medium heat. Sauté the onion until softened, 3–4 minutes. Remove from the heat and let cool. • Process the onion, pistachios, garlic, remaining 2 tablespoons of oil, and pecorino in a food processor until smooth. Season with salt and white pepper. • Cook the pasta in the boiling water until al dente. • Add 1 tablespoon of cooking water to the pesto to make it creamy. • Drain the pasta and toss with the pesto, adding more cooking water if needed. • Garnish each serving with a sprinkling of finely chopped pistachios.

| | |
|---|---|
| 4 | tablespoons (60 ml) extra-virgin olive oil |
| 1 | large white onion, finely chopped |
| 1 | cup (150 g) peeled pistachios |
| 1 | clove garlic, finely chopped |
| ½ | cup (75 g) freshly grated pecorino cheese |
| | Salt and freshly ground white pepper |
| 1 | pound (500 g) penne |
| | Finely chopped pistachios, to garnish |

Serves: 4–6
Preparation: 15 minutes
Cooking: 15–20 minutes
Level: 1

■ ■ ■ *Some people dust this dish with 1–2 tablespoons of unsweetened cocoa powder. It's an unusual touch, but fun to try.*

You could also use: farfalle, eliche

# PENNE WITH RAW ARTICHOKES

62

Put a large pot of salted water to boil over high heat. • Trim the artichoke stems, cut off the top third of the leaves, and discard the tough outer leaves by pulling them down and snapping them off at the base. Cut in half lengthwise and scrape any fuzzy choke away with a knife. Cut into very thin slices. Place in a large serving bowl. • Whisk the oil and lemon juice in a small bowl and season with salt and pepper. Drizzle this mixture over the artichokes. • Cook the pasta in the boiling water until al dente. • Drain well and place in the bowl with the sauce. Toss well, sprinkle with the Parmesan, and serve hot.

| | |
|---|---|
| **6** | **fresh artichokes** |
| **½** | **cup (120 ml) extra-virgin olive oil** |
| | **Freshly squeezed juice of 1 large lemon** |
| | **Salt and freshly ground black pepper** |
| **1** | **pound (500 g) penne** |
| **4** | **ounces (120 g) Parmesan cheese, shaved** |

Serves: 4–6
Preparation: 20 minutes
Cooking: 10–15 minutes
Level: 1

You could also use: farfalle, fusilli, rigatoni

# PASTA WITH PECORINO & LEMON

Put a large pot of salted water to boil over high heat. • Melt the butter in a large frying pan over high heat. • Mix in the lemon juice, saffron, and pecorino. Remove from the heat and set aside. • Cook the pasta in the boiling water until al dente. • Drain and add to the sauce. • Serve hot.

**64**

½ cup (120 g) butter, cut up

Freshly squeezed juice of 2 lemons

4 threads saffron, crumbled

2 cups (250 g) freshly grated pecorino cheese

1 pound (500 g) small maccheroni

Serves: 4–6
Preparation: 15 minutes
Cooking: 12 minutes
Level: 1

You could also use: farfalline, conchiglini

# RIGATONI WITH ONION SAUCE

Melt the butter in a large, heavy-bottomed saucepan over low heat. Add the onions and simmer until caramelized, 20–30 minutes. • Put a large pot of salted water to boil over high heat. • Increase the heat under the saucepan with the onions, pour in the wine, and simmer until it evaporates, 2–3 minutes. • Cook the pasta in the boiling water until al dente. • Drain and add to the pan with the sauce. • Season with salt and pepper. Sprinkle with the pecorino, toss well, and serve hot.

$2/3$ cup (150 g) butter or diced pork lard

3 large white onions, finely chopped

$1/4$ cup (60 ml) dry white wine

1 pound (500 g) rigatoni

Salt and freshly ground black pepper

6 tablespoons freshly grated pecorino cheese

Serves: 4–6
Preparation: 15 minutes
Cooking: 30–40 minutes
Level: 2

You could also use: penne rigate, sedani, tortiglioni

# PENNE WITH CAULIFLOWER

Put a large pot of salted water to boil over high heat. • Heat the oil in a large frying pan over medium heat. Add the garlic and sauté until pale gold, 3–4 minutes. • Divide the cauliflower into florets. Cook in the boiling water until just tender, about 5 minutes. • Remove with a slotted spoon and add to the pan with the garlic. Simmer over low heat. • Bring the water back to a boil. Add the pasta and cook until al dente. • Drain the pasta and add to the pan with the cauliflower. • Stir in the parsley. Season with black pepper, toss well, and serve hot sprinkled with the Parmesan.

¼ cup (60 ml) extra-virgin olive oil

2 cloves garlic, finely chopped

1 large head cauliflower

1 pound (500 g) penne rigate

2 tablespoons finely chopped fresh parsley

Salt and freshly ground black pepper

Freshly grated Parmesan cheese to serve

Serves: 4–6
Preparation: 15 minutes
Cooking: 20–25 minutes
Level: 1

You could also use: conchiglie, farfalle, cavatappi

# FARFALLE WITH VEGGIE SAUCE

Put a large pot of salted water to boil over high heat. • Heat the oil in a large frying pan over medium heat. Add the onions, celery, carrots, peas, and zucchini. Season with salt and pepper. Sauté until the vegetables are softened, about 5 minutes. • Add the tomatoes and mix well. Cover and simmer over low heat until the tomatoes have reduced, about 20 minutes. • Meanwhile, cook the pasta in the boiling water until al dente. • Drain and add to the frying pan. Toss over high heat for 1 minute. • Sprinkle with the Parmesan and serve hot.

¼ cup (60 ml) extra-virgin olive oil

2 large onions, finely sliced

6 celery stalks, finely chopped

2 medium carrots, finely chopped

1 cup (150 g) frozen peas

2 medium zucchini (courgettes), cut into small pieces

Salt and freshly ground black pepper

1 (14-ounce/400-g) can tomatoes, with juice

1 pound (500 g) whole-wheat (wholemeal) farfalle

½ cup (60 g) freshly grated Parmesan cheese

Serves: 4–6
Preparation: 15 minutes
Cooking: 25–30 minutes
Level: 1

You could also use: plain farfalle, fusilli, conchiglie, ruote

# DITALINI WITH EGGPLANT SAUCE & PINE NUTS

72

Put the eggplant in a colander. Sprinkle with coarse sea salt and let drain for 1 hour. Shake off excess salt. • Put a large pot of salted water to boil over high heat. • Heat the frying oil in a large frying pan over medium-high heat. • Fry the eggplant in batches until golden brown, 3–4 minutes. Scoop out with a slotted spoon and drain on paper towels. • Broil (grill) the bell peppers until the skins are blackened. Put in a plastic bag for 10 minutes. Discard the skins and seeds and cut the flesh into small squares. • Heat the extra-virgin oil in a small saucepan over low heat. Add the onion and garlic with a pinch of salt and sweat for 15 minutes. • Toast the pine nuts in a frying pan over medium heat until golden, 2–3 minutes. • Cook the pasta in the boiling water until al dente. • Drain and transfer to a large serving bowl. Toss with the eggplant, bell peppers, onion, pine nuts, capers, olives, basil, parsley, and oregano. • Serve hot.

| | |
|---|---|
| 2 | eggplants (aubergine), with skin, very thinly sliced |
| | Coarse sea salt |
| 2 | cups (500 ml) olive oil, for frying |
| 2 | yellow bell peppers (capsicums) |
| 3 | tablespoons extra-virgin olive oil |
| 1 | onion, finely chopped |
| 2 | cloves garlic, minced |
| | Salt |
| 4 | tablespoons pine nuts |
| 1 | pound (500 g) ditalini |
| 2 | tablespoons salt-cured capers, rinsed |
| 1 | cup (100 g) green olives, pitted and coarsely chopped |
| 1 | small bunch fresh basil, torn |
| 2 | tablespoons finely chopped fresh parsley |
| 1 | tablespoon finely chopped fresh oregano |

Serves: 4–6
Preparation: 30 minutes
  + 1 hour to drain
Cooking: 45 minutes
Level: 2

You could also use: farfalline, sedanini, mezze penne

# FUSILLI WITH PESTO, CREAM & TOMATOES

Put a large pot of salted water to boil over high heat. • Mix the pesto and tomato sauce in a large bowl. Stir in the cream until well blended. • Cook the pasta in the boiling water until al dente. • Drain the pasta into a large bowl. Add the sauce and toss well. • Garnish with the basil and serve hot.

74

| | |
|---|---|
| 1 | recipe homemade (see page 80) or storebought pesto |
| 2 | cups (500 ml) homemade (see page 86) or storebought tomato pasta sauce |
| ¼ | cup (60 ml) heavy (double) cream |
| 1 | pound (500 g) fusilli |
| | Fresh basil leaves to garnish |

Serves: 4–6
Preparation: 10 minutes
Cooking: 15 minutes
Level: 1

You could also use: farfalle, eliche, penne, spaghetti

# FUSILLI WITH MUSHROOMS

Put a large pot of salted water to boil over high heat. • Heat 2 tablespoons of the oil in a large frying pan over medium heat. Add 3 cloves of garlic and sauté until pale gold, 2–3 minutes. • Add the mushrooms and half the parsley, season with salt and pepper, and simmer until the mushrooms are tender and their juices have reduced, 10–15 minutes. • Cook the pasta in the boiling water until al dente. Drain well and add to the pan with the sauce. • Sprinkle with the remaining garlic and parsley and drizzle with the remaining 2 tablespoons of oil. • Toss for 1 minute over high heat then serve hot.

4 tablespoons (60 ml) extra-virgin olive oil

4 cloves garlic, finely chopped

1½ pounds (750 g) white mushrooms, trimmed and thickly sliced

5 tablespoons finely chopped fresh parsley

Salt and freshly ground black pepper

1 pound (500 g) fusilli

Serves: 4–6
Preparation: 15 minutes
Cooking: 20–25 minutes
Level: 1

You could also use: tortiglioni, farfalle, sedani, maccheroni

# PENNE WITH BELL PEPPERS, EGGPLANT & ZUCCHINI

78

Put a large pot of salted water to boil over high heat. • Turn on the broiler (grill) and broil the bell peppers, turning them often, until the skins are blackened. Wrap in a brown paper bag or foil for 10 minutes. Take out of the bag or foil and peel off the skins. • Heat a grill pan. Cook the eggplant and zucchini in batches until tender, 5–8 minutes each batch. • Chop all the vegetables coarsely with a large knife. • Cook the pasta in the boiling water until al dente. • Drain and place in a large serving bowl. • Add the vegetables, basil, mint, garlic, and ginger. Season with salt and pepper and drizzle with the oil. • Toss gently and serve hot.

| | |
|---|---|
| 1 | large red bell peppers (capsicum), seeded, cored, and quartered |
| 1 | large eggplant (aubergine), with skin, thinly sliced |
| 2 | zucchini (courgettes) thinly sliced lengthwise |
| 1 | pound (500 g) penne |
| 1 | tablespoon corsely chopped fresh basil |
| 1 | tablespoon finely chopped fresh mint |
| 1 | clove garlic, finely chopped |
| ½ | teaspoon finely grated ginger |
| | Salt and freshly ground black pepper |
| ⅓ | cup (90 ml) extra-virgin olive oil |

Serves: 4–6
Preparation: 30 minutes
Cooking: 30 minutes
Level: 2

You could also use: whole-wheat penne, festonati, conchiglie

# RUOTE WITH PESTO & CHERRY TOMATOES

Put a large pot of salted water to boil over high heat.

**Pesto:** Toast the pine nuts in a large frying pan over medium heat until lightly browned, about 3 minutes. Set aside. • Toast the almonds in a large frying pan over medium heat until lightly browned, about 3 minutes. • Chop the garlic and basil in a food processor until smooth. Add the almonds and pecorino and blend until smooth. Season with salt and pepper. • Gradually add the oil, blending continuously, until the pesto is thick and smooth. • Cook the pasta in the boiling water until al dente. Drain well and place in a large bowl. • Add the pesto, tomatoes, and pine nuts to the bowl and toss well. • Garnish with basil and serve hot.

**Pesto**

| | |
|---|---|
| ⅓ | cup (50 g) pine nuts |
| ½ | cup (75 g) blanched almonds |
| 4 | cloves garlic |
| 1 | bunch basil + extra leaves, to garnish |
| ⅓ | cup (50 g) freshly grated pecorino cheese |
| | Salt and freshly ground black pepper |
| ½ | cup (120 ml) extra-virgin olive oil |
| 1 | pound (500 g) ruote |
| 1 | pound (500 g) cherry tomatoes, halved |

Serves: 4–6
Preparation: 15 minutes
Cooking: 20 minutes
Level: 1

You could also use: conchiglie, fusilli, cavatappi, penne

# PENNE WITH ASPARAGUS & EGG

Put a large pot of salted water to boil over high heat. • Cook the asparagus in the boiling water until just tender, 3–5 minutes. Remove with a slotted spoon and return the water to a boil. • Heat the oil in a large frying pan over medium heat. Add the garlic and sauté until pale gold, 3–4 minutes. • Add the tomatoes and simmer until the tomatoes have broken down, about 15 minutes. • Season with salt and pepper. • Mix the egg yolks and pecorino in a large bowl. Season with pepper. • Cook the pasta in the boiling water until al dente. • Drain and transfer to the bowl with the eggs. Toss well and transfer to the frying pan with the asparagus and tomato sauce. • Toss well and serve hot.

| | |
|---|---|
| 1 | pound (500 g) asparagus, trimmed and cut into 1-inch (2.5-cm) lengths |
| 1/3 | cup (90 ml) extra-virgin olive oil |
| 2 | cloves garlic, finely chopped |
| 3 | tomatoes, peeled and coarsely chopped |
| | Salt and freshly ground white pepper |
| 2 | large egg yolks |
| 5 | tablespoons freshly grated pecorino cheese |
| 1 | pound (500 g) penne rigate |

Serves: 4–6
Preparation: 20 minutes
Cooking: 20 minutes
Level: 2

■ ■ ■ *The best season to make this dish is spring, when wild asparagus is available. It is also good with farmed asparagus, which have especially meaty tips.*

 You could also use: farfalle, rigatoni

# SPICY SPIRALI WITH EGGPLANT

84

Put a large pot of salted water to boil over high heat. • Heat the oil in a large frying pan over medium heat. Add the garlic and sauté until softened, 3–4 minutes. • Add the eggplant and chile and simmer for 10 minutes, stirring often. Season with salt and pepper. • Toast the pine nuts in a small saucepan over medium heat, 3–4 minutes. • Cook the pasta in the boiling water until al dente. • Drain thoroughly and place in the pan with the eggplant. Add the capers, oregano, and pine nuts. Toss well and serve hot.

⅓ cup (90 ml) extra-virgin olive oil

2 cloves garlic, finely chopped

1 large eggplant (aubergine), cut into small cubes

1 fresh chile, seeded and finely chopped

Salt and freshly ground black pepper

4 tablespoons pine nuts

1 pound (500 g) eliche

2 tablespoons brine-cured capers

2 tablespoons finely chopped fresh oregano

Serves: 4–6
Preparation: 15 minutes
Cooking: 20–25 minutes
Level: 1

You could also use: fusili, penne, farfalle, rigatoni

# PENNE WITH NEAPOLITAN TOMATO SAUCE

**86**

Put a large pot of salted water to boil over high heat.

**Tomato Sauce:** Heat 4 tablespoons (60 g) of butter and oil in a large saucepan over medium heat. Add the onion and sauté until softened, 3–4 minutes. • Add the tomatoes and chopped basil and simmer until the tomatoes have broken down, about 10 minutes. • Season with salt and pepper and add the remaining 2 tablespoons butter. • Remove from heat and mix until the butter has melted. • Cook the pasta in the boiling water until al dente. • Drain and transfer to the pan with the tomato sauce. Sprinkle with the cheese, garnish with basil, and serve hot.

**Tomato Sauce**

6    tablespoons (90 g) butter, cut up

2    tablespoons extra-virgin olive oil

1    red onion, finely chopped

2    pounds (1 kg) plum tomatoes, preferably San Marzano tomatoes, peeled, seeded, and finely chopped

1    tablespoon coarsely chopped fresh basil + extra leaves to garnish

     Salt and freshly ground black pepper

1    pound (500 g) penne

3/4    cup (90 g) freshly grated caciocavallo or provolone cheese

■ ■ ■ *San Marzano tomatoes are elongated and fleshy with few seeds and a strong sweet flavor. They are ideal for pasta sauces. They are named for a small town near Naples where they thrive in the rich volcanic soils. Buy them in cans if you can't get them fresh.*

Serves: 4–6
Preparation: 20 minutes
Cooking: 20 minutes
Level: 1

You could also use: farfalle, rigatoni, fusilli

# PENNE WITH SUN-DRIED TOMATO PESTO

Put a large pot of salted water to boil over high heat. • Soak the sun-dried tomatoes in the hot water and vinegar in a large bowl until softened, about 10 minutes. Drain well. • Process the soaked tomatoes, almonds, garlic, basil, oil, and oregano until smooth. Season with salt and pepper, taking care not to over-season as sun-dried tomatoes are quite flavorful. • Cook the pasta in the boiling water until al dente. • Add 1 tablespoon cooking water to the pesto to make it creamy. • Drain the pasta. Serve the pasta hot with the pesto.

88

1½ cups (150 g) sun-dried tomatoes

¾ cup (120 ml) hot water

3 tablespoons red wine vinegar

½ cup (50 g) peeled almonds

2 cloves garlic

Leaves from 2 bunches fresh basil

⅓ cup (90 ml) extra-virgin olive oil

½ teaspoon dried oregano

Salt and freshly ground black pepper

1 pound (500 g) penne lisce

Serves: 4–6
Preparation: 15 minutes
  + 10 minutes to soak
Cooking: 20 minutes
Level: 1

You could also use: spinach penne, whole-wheat penne, fusilli

# PENNE WITH SUN-DRIED TOMATOES & GREEN BEANS

Put a large pot of salted water to boil over high heat. • Heat the oil in a large frying pan over medium heat. Add the garlic and sun-dried tomatoes and sauté until the garlic is pale gold, about 3 minutes • Add the canned tomatoes and simmer until the sauce is reduced, about 10 minutes. • Cook the pasta in the boiling water for 5 minutes. Add the green beans and cook until the pasta is al dente and the beans are tender. • Drain well and add to the frying pan with the sauce. Season with salt and pepper. Toss gently over high heat for 1 minute. • Serve hot.

¼ cup (60 ml) extra-virgin olive oil

3 cloves garlic, thinly sliced

1 cup (100 g) sun-dried tomatoes, soaked in warm water for 15 minutes, drained and coarsely chopped

1 (14-ounce/400-g) can tomatoes, with juice

1 pound (500 g) penne

12 ounces (350 g) green beans, cut in short lengths

Salt and freshly ground black pepper

Serves: 4–6
Preparation: 15 minutes
Cooking: 20 minutes
Level: 1

You could also use: rigatoni, farfalle, conchiglie

# SPICY FUSILLI WITH SWISS CHARD & PINE NUTS

92

Put a large pot of salted water to boil over high heat. • Cook the Swiss chard in the boiling water until just tender, 2–3 minutes. Scoop out with a slotted spoon, drain well, and place in a bowl of cold water. Drain again, squeezing to remove excess moisture. • Return the water to a boil. • Melt the butter in a large frying pan over medium heat. Add the garlic and sauté until pale golden brown, 3–4 minutes. • Add the pine nuts and bread crumbs and sauté until golden brown and crisp, about 5 minutes. • Add the Swiss chard and golden raisins. Mix well and sauté for 2 minutes. Season with salt. • Cook the pasta in the boiling water until al dente. • Drain well and add to the pan with the Swiss chard mixture. Add the chile and toss over high heat for 2 minutes. • Serve hot

1½ pounds (750 g) Swiss chard (silver beet), shredded

¼ cup (60 g) butter

2 cloves garlic, finely sliced

⅓ cup (60 g) pine nuts

1½ cups (100 g) fresh bread crumbs

¼ cup (45 g) golden raisins (sultanas)

Salt

1 pound (500 g) whole-wheat (wholemeal) or plain fusilli

1 small fresh red chile, seeded and sliced

Serves: 4–6
Preparation: 15 minutes
Cooking: 20 minutes
Level: 1

You could also use: cavatappi, festonati, rigatoni, penne rigate

# PENNE WITH CHERRY TOMATOES & MOZZARELLA

Put a large pot of salted water to boil over high heat. • Cook the pasta in the boiling water until al dente. • Put the cherry tomatoes, mozzarella, basil, mint, garlic, and oil in a large serving bowl. • Drain the pasta and add to the bowl. Season with salt and pepper and toss well. • Serve hot.

94

| | |
|---|---|
| 1 | pound (500 g) penne |
| 2 | pounds (1 kg) cherry tomatoes, halved |
| 8 | ounces (250 g) fresh mozzarella cheese, drained and cut into small cubes |
| 2 | tablespoons coarsely chopped fresh basil |
| 1 | tablespoon finely chopped fresh mint |
| 1 | clove garlic, finely chopped |
| 1/3 | cup (90 ml) extra-virgin olive oil |
| | Salt and freshly ground black pepper |

Serves: 4–6
Preparation: 15 minutes
Cooking: 15 minutes
Level: 1

You could also use: farfalle, rigatoni, conchiglie

# FARFALLE WITH RADICCHIO & GOAT CHEESE

96

Put a large pot of salted water to boil over high heat. • Cook the pasta in the boiling water until al dente. • Heat 3 tablespoons of the oil in a large frying pan over medium heat. Add the onion and sauté until softened, 3–4 minutes. • Add the radicchio and season with salt and pepper. Sauté for a few minutes, then add the beer. When the beer has evaporated, add the goat cheese and stir well, softening the mixture with the milk. • Drain the pasta well and add to the pan with the sauce. Toss for 1–2 minutes over medium heat. • Drizzle with the remaining 1 tablespoon of oil and serve hot.

| | |
|---|---|
| 1 | pound (500 g) farfalle |
| 4 | tablespoons (60 ml) extra-virgin olive oil |
| 1 | large red onion, thinly sliced |
| 2 | heads red radicchio, cut into strips |
| | Salt and freshly ground black pepper |
| ¼ | cup (60 ml) beer |
| 1 | cup (250 g) chèvre or other soft fresh goat cheese |
| 2 | tablespoons milk |

Serves: 4–6
Preparation: 15 minutes
Cooking: 20 minutes
Level: 1

You could also use: penne, ruote, rigatoni

# FUSILLI WITH GORGONZOLA

Put a large pot of salted water to boil over high heat. • Heat the butter and Gorgonzola with the cream in a double boiler over barely simmering water until the cheese has melted. Season lightly salt and a generous grinding of white pepper. • Cook the peas in a small pan of lightly salted water until tender, 5 minutes. Drain well. • Cook the pasta in the boiling water until al dente. • Drain and place in a heated serving bowl. Add the peas and cheese mixture and toss well. Top with the extra Gorgonzola and serve hot.

| | |
|---|---|
| 1 | tablespoon butter |
| 12 | ounces (350 g) creamy Gorgonzola cheese, crumbled + extra to garnish |
| 2/3 | cup (150 ml) heavy (double) cream |
| | Salt and freshly ground white pepper |
| 2 | cups (300 g) frozen peas |
| 1 | pound (500 g) fusilli |

Serves: 4–6
Preparation: 10 minutes
Cooking: 25 minutes
Level: 1

You could also use: penne, farfalle, conchiglie

# PENNE WITH TOMATOES & GOAT CHEESE

Put a large pot of salted water to boil over high heat. • Cook the pasta in the boiling water until al dente. • Heat the oil in a large frying pan over medium heat. Add the garlic and sauté until pale gold, 3–4 minutes. • Add the cherry tomatoes, olives, and capers. Season with salt and pepper. Cook over high heat for 5 minutes, stirring frequently. • Drain the pasta, reserving 2 tablespoons of the cooking water. • Mix the goat cheese with the reserved cooking water in a small bowl. • Add the pasta to the pan with the tomatoes, stir in the goat cheese, and basil, and toss gently. • Serve hot.

| | |
|---|---|
| 1 | pound (500 g) penne |
| 1/4 | cup (60 ml) extra-virgin olive oil |
| 1 | clove garlic, finely chopped |
| 1½ | pounds (750 g) cherry tomatoes, halved |
| 12 | black olives, pitted |
| 1 | tablespoon salt-cured capers, rinsed |
| | Salt and freshly ground black pepper |
| 1 | cup (250 g) chèvre or other soft fresh goat cheese |
| 16 | leaves fresh basil, torn |

Serves: 4–6
Preparation: 20 minutes
Cooking: 15–20 minutes
Level: 2

■ ■ ■ *Capers are the salted or pickled buds of a Mediterranean bush of the same name. They are widely used in many Mediterranean cuisines, especially that of southern Italy.*

You could also use: farfalle, conchiglie, festonati, rigatoni

# FARFALLE WITH GREEN BEANS & PESTO

102

**Pasta:** Put a large pot of salted water to boil over high heat. • Add the pasta and cook for 5 minutes. • Add the green beans and peas and cook until the pasta is al dente.
**Pesto:** Chop the basil, pine nuts, garlic, oil, and salt in a food processor until smooth. Stir in the cheese. • Drain the pasta and vegetables and toss gently with the pesto. Stir in the kidney beans and walnuts. Drizzle with the oil and garnish with the basil leaves. • Serve hot.

■■■ *Pesto is made from basil, garlic, pine nuts, Parmesan, salt, and extra-virgin olive oil. It is quick and simple to prepare and delicious with pasta and fish. It comes from Liguria, the region in Italy that stretches along the northwestern coast to Provence, in France. The same sauce exists in Provence, where it is known as* pistou.

**Pasta**

1    pound (500 g) farfalle

5    ounces (150 g) green beans, cut into short lengths

1    cup (150 g) fresh or frozen peas

1    cup (200 g) canned red kidney beans, drained and rinsed

½    cup (50 g) coarsely chopped walnuts

¼    cup (60 ml) extra-virgin olive oil

     Basil leaves, to garnish

**Pesto**

1    large bunch fresh basil

2    tablespoons pine nuts

2    cloves garlic

½    cup (120 ml) extra-virgin olive oil

     Salt

4    tablespoons freshly grated Parmesan cheese

Serves: 4–6
Preparation: 10 minutes
Cooking: 15 minutes
Level: 2

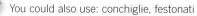

You could also use: conchiglie, festonati

# SICILIAN MACARONI

Put a large pot of salted water to boil over high heat. • Chop the anchovies finely with the capers. • Pit the olives and crush them slightly. • Sauté the garlic in the oil in a large frying pan over medium heat until pale gold, about 3 minutes. • Discard the garlic and add the eggplant to the oil. Sauté for 15 minutes. • Add the tomatoes and bell peppers and season with salt and pepper. Simmer until the bell peppers are tender, 15 minutes. • Add the olives, capers and anchovies, and basil. • Cook the pasta in the boiling water until al dente. • Drain and add to the pan with the sauce. Sprinkle with the pecorino and serve hot.

104

2   salt-cured anchovies, rinsed

2   tablespoons salt-cured capers, rinsed

⅓   cup (40 g) green olives

2   cloves garlic, lightly crushed but whole

⅓   cup (90 ml) extra-virgin olive oil

2   eggplants (aubergines), cut into cubes

1½  pounds (750 g) peeled tomatoes, finely chopped

2   yellow bell peppers (capsicums), seeded and cut into thin strips

    Salt and freshly ground black pepper

    Leaves from 1 bunch fresh basil, torn

1   pound (500 g) smooth or ridged macaroni

½   cup (60 g) freshly grated peppered pecorino cheese

Serves: 4–6
Preparation: 15 minutes
Cooking: 35–40 minutes
Level: 1

You could also use: pennette, farfalline

# CAVATAPPI WITH ROASTED VEGETABLES

Preheat the oven to 400°F (200°C/gas 6). • Arrange the tomatoes, eggplant, zucchini, bell pepper, and onions in a single layer in a roasting pan. Season with salt and pepper and drizzle with 2 tablespoons of the oil. • Roast until the vegetables are tender and lightly browned, about 40 minutes. • Mix the remaining 3 tablespoons of oil, garlic, and basil in a small bowl. • Put a large pot of salted water to boil over high heat. • Cook the pasta in the boiling water until al dente. • Drain and transfer to a heated serving dish. • Toss with the basil and oil mixture and roasted vegetables. • Serve hot, passing the Parmesan separately.

| | |
|---|---|
| 5 | firm-ripe tomatoes, halved or quartered |
| 1 | small eggplant (aubergine), thickly sliced |
| 1 | zucchini (courgette), thickly sliced |
| 1 | red or yellow bell pepper (capsicum), seeded and cut into quarters |
| 2 | onions, thickly sliced |
| | Salt and freshly ground black pepper |
| 5 | tablespoons (75 ml) extra-virgin olive oil |
| 2 | cloves garlic, finely chopped |
| 2 | tablespoons coarsely chopped fresh basil |
| 1 | pound (500 g) cavatappi |
| ¼ | cup (30 g) freshly grated Parmesan cheese |

Serves: 4–6
Preparation: 20 minutes
Cooking: 55 minutes
Level: 2

You could also use: penne, farfalle, conchiglie, rigatoni

# FESTONATI WITH SAUSAGE & BROCCOLI SAUCE

108

Put a large pot of salted water to boil over high heat. • Cook the broccoli florets, stems, and leaves in the boiling water for 2–3 minutes. Scoop out with a slotted spoon and set aside. Return the water to a boil. • Heat the oil in a large frying pan over medium heat. Add the garlic and parsley and sauté until the garlic is pale gold, 3–4 minutes. • Add the sausages and tomato paste. Cook over medium heat for 5 minutes. • Add the broccoli, season with salt and pepper, and simmer for 10–15 minutes. • Cook the pasta in the boiling water until al dente. • Drain well and add to the pan with the sauce. Toss well. • Top each portion with flakes of cheese and serve hot.

1   pound (500 g) broccoli, divided into florets, stem cut into small cubes, and leaves chopped

3   tablespoons extra-virgin olive oil

3   cloves garlic, finely chopped

2   tablespoons finely chopped fresh parsley

1   pound (500 g) Italian pork sausages, skinned and crumbled

3   tablespoons tomato paste (concentrate)

    Salt and freshly ground black pepper

1   pound (500 g) festonati

2   ounces (60 g) aged pecorino or Parmesan cheese, in flakes

Serves: 4–6
Preparation: 30 minutes
Cooking: 40 minutes
Level: 1

You could also use: conchiglie, farfalle, rigatoni, penne rigate

# PENNE WITH TUNA & CHERRY TOMATOES

Put a large pot of salted water to boil over high heat. • Cook the pasta in the boiling water until al dente. • Sauté the garlic and parsley in the oil over medium-low heat for 2 minutes. • Add the cherry tomatoes, season with salt, and simmer until heated through, 4–5 minutes. • Add the tuna, stir well, and turn off the heat immediately. • Drain the pasta well and place in a heated serving dish. Toss gently with the sauce, garnish with the basil, and serve hot.

| | |
|---|---|
| 1 | pound (500 g) penne |
| 2 | cloves garlic, finely chopped |
| 3 | tablespoons finely chopped parsley |
| ½ | cup (120 ml) extra-virgin olive oil |
| 24 | cherry tomatoes, halved |
| | Salt |
| 12 | ounces (350 g) canned tuna, drained and flaked |
| | Fresh basil, to garnish |

Serves: 4–6
Preparation: 10 minutes
Cooking: 15 minutes
Level: 1

You could also use: farfalle, sedani, ruote, spaghetti

# FARFALLE WITH CRAB STICKS

112

Put a large pot of salted water to boil over high heat. • Roughly chop the crab sticks. • Heat the oil into a large frying pan over medium heat. Add the garlic and parsley and sauté for 1 minute. • Add the crab sticks and orange zest. Mix well and simmer for 1 minute. Pour in the cognac and cook until it has evaporated. • Add the orange juice. Season with salt and a generous grinding of pepper. Simmer until the liquid has evaporated. • After about 10 minutes add the cream and simmer for 2–3 minutes. • Cook the pasta in the boiling water until al dente. • Drain and transfer to the pan with the sauce. Toss gently for 1–2 minutes. • Serve hot seasoned with plenty of freshly ground black pepper.

16 crab sticks, fresh or frozen, thawed if frozen

⅓ cup (90 ml) extra-virgin olive oil

2 cloves garlic, finely chopped

2 tablespoons finely chopped fresh parsley

1 tablespoon organic orange zest, cut in julienne strips

½ cup (120 ml) cognac

½ cup (120 ml) freshly squeezed orange juice

Salt and freshly ground black pepper

½ cup (120 ml) heavy (double) cream

1 pound (500 g) farfalle

Serves: 4–6
Preparation: 15 minutes
Cooking: 25 minutes
Level: 1

You could also use: penne rigate, rigatoni

# RUOTE WITH SHRIMP & ZUCCHINI

114

Put a large pot of salted water to boil over high heat. • Heat the butter in a large frying pan over medium heat. Add the onion and sauté until softened, 3–4 minutes. • Cook the pasta in the boiling water until al dente. • Add the zucchini to the onions and season with salt and pepper. Cover and simmer over low heat for 10 minutes, stirring often. • Add the shrimp and cook for 5 minutes. • Mix in the cream and cook until heated through. • Drain the pasta and add to the pan with the sauce. Sprinkle with the parsley and toss well. • Serve hot.

¼ cup (60 g) butter
1 onion, finely chopped
1 pound (500 g) farfalle
4 medium zucchini (courgettes), thinly sliced
    Salt and freshly ground black pepper
14 ounces (400 g) shrimp (prawns), shelled, heads removed, and deveined
½ cup (120 ml) heavy (double) cream
2 tablespoons finely chopped parsley

Serves: 4–6
Preparation: 20 minutes
Cooking: 30 minutes
Level: 1

You could also use: penne rigate, farfalle, conchiglie,

# FUSILLI WITH FISHCAKES

**Fishcakes:** Put the bread in the bowl of a food processor. Drizzle with the milk and blend for a few seconds. • Add the fish and blend for a few seconds more. Add the egg, Parmesan, and parsley. Season with salt and pepper. Blend until smooth. • Shape the mixture into marble-sized balls. Put the flour in a small bowl. Roll the balls in the flour, shaking off the excess. • Heat $1/3$ cup (90 ml) of oil in a large frying pan over medium heat. Fry the fishcakes until lightly browned, 4–5 minutes. Drain well on paper towels.

**Pasta:** Put a large pot of salted water to boil over high heat. • Cook the pasta in the boiling water until al dente. • Drain and drizzle with the oil. • Place in a large heated serving bowl and add the fishcakes and chile. Toss gently. Sprinkle with the dill and serve hot.

116

**Fishcakes**

1   large bread roll

3   tablespoons milk

14   ounces (400 g) white fish fillets (hake, cod, whiting, dogfish, rockfish, ocean perch, red snapper), boned and skin removed

1   large egg

3   tablespoons freshly grated Parmesan cheese

1   tablespoon finely chopped fresh parsley

Salt and freshly ground black pepper

3   tablespoons all-purpose (plain) flour

$1/3$   cup (90 ml) extra-virgin olive oil

**Pasta**

1   pound (500 g) fusilli

2   tablespoons extra-virgin olive oil

1   fresh red chile, seeded and finely chopped

2   tablespoons finely chopped fresh dill

Serves: 4–6
Preparation: 20 minutes
Cooking: 20–25 minutes
Level: 2

■ ■ ■ *If liked, add 12–16 halved raw cherry tomatoes along with the chile and fishcakes at the end.*

You could also use: penne, sedani, conchiglie

# PENNE WITH SWORDFISH & SALMON

Put a large pot of salted water to boil over high heat. • Cook the pasta in the boiling water until al dente. • Heat the oil in a large frying pan over medium heat. Add the garlic and onion and sauté until softened, 3–4 minutes. • Add the swordfish and salmon. Sauté for 3 minutes. Add the wine and simmer until it evaporates. Remove the fish with a slotted spoon and set aside. • Add the tomatoes to the pan and simmer over medium-low heat for 5 minutes. • Return the fish to the pan. Add the parsley and season with salt. • Drain the pasta and add to the sauce. Toss gently over high heat for 1 minute. • Serve hot.

| | |
|---|---|
| 1 | pound (500 g) penne |
| ¼ | cup (60 ml) extra-virgin olive oil |
| 1 | clove garlic, finely chopped |
| 1 | small onion, finely chopped |
| 5 | ounces (150 g) swordfish, cut into bite-size chunks |
| 5 | ounces (150 g) salmon, cut into bite-size chunks |
| ⅓ | cup (90 ml) dry white wine |
| 20 | cherry tomatoes, halved |
| 2 | tablespoons finely chopped fresh parsley |
| | Salt |

Serves: 4–6
Preparation: 15 minutes
Cooking: 15 minutes
Level: 1

■ ■ ■ *The swordfish and salmon in this dish not only provide lots of flavor, they are also rich in protein and essential omega-3 fatty acids.*

You could also use: rigatoni, conchiglie, fusilli, farfalle

# PENNE WITH SMOKED CHICKEN & PEAS

Put a large pot of salted water to boil over high heat. • Cook the penne in the boiling water until al dente. • Warm the crème fraîche and chicken in a large frying pan over low heat for 3–4 minutes. • Add the peas and simmer until tender, 3–5 minutes. • Drain the penne and add to the pan with the sauce. Season with salt and pepper. • Toss well and serve hot.

**120**

1   **pound (500 g) penne**

1   **cup (250 ml) crème fraîche**

12  **ounces (350 g) cooked smoked chicken breast, coarsely shredded**

1   **cup (150 g) frozen peas**

**Salt and freshly ground black pepper**

Serves: 4–6
Preparation: 10 minutes
Cooking: 15 minutes
Level: 1

You could also use: farfalle, conchiglie, eliche

# PENNE WITH PANCETTA & BELL PEPPERS

Heat the oil in a large frying pan over medium heat. Add the pancetta and sauté until lightly browned, 3–4 minutes. • Add the onion, garlic, parsley, basil, and bell peppers. Sauté until the bell peppers and onions are softened, about 10 minutes. • Stir in the tomatoes, chile, and oregano, and season with salt. Mix well, cover, and simmer over low heat until the tomatoes have broken down, about 25 minutes. • Put a large pot of salted water to boil over high heat. • Cook the pasta in the boiling water until al dente. • Add the capers and olives to the sauce. Mix well and cook for 2 minutes. • Drain the pasta and add to the frying pan. Toss over high heat for 1 minute. • Sprinkle with the cheese and serve hot.

122

| | |
|---|---|
| 1/3 | cup (90 ml) extra-virgin olive oil |
| 1 | cup (100 g) chopped pancetta (or bacon) |
| 1 | large onion, finely chopped |
| 1 | clove garlic, finely chopped |
| 2 | tablespoons finely chopped fresh parsley |
| 1 | tablespoon coarsely chopped fresh basil |
| 2 | red bell peppers (capsicums), seeded and finely sliced |
| 2 | yellow bell peppers (capsicums), seeded and finely sliced |
| 1 | (14-ounce/400-g) can tomatoes, with juice |
| 1 | red chile pepper, seeded and chopped |
| 1 | teaspoon dried oregano |
| | Salt |
| 2 | tablespoons salt-cured capers, rinsed |
| 1/2 | cup (50 g) green olives, pitted and coarsely chopped |
| 1 | pound (500 g) penne |
| 1/4 | cup (30 g) coarsely grated pecorino or Parmesan cheese |

Serves: 4–6
Preparation: 15 minutes
Cooking: 40 minutes
Level: 1

You could also use: farfalle, ruote, rigatoni, ruote

# CAVATELLI WITH PANCETTA & SUN-DRIED TOMATOES

124

**Tomato Sauce:** Heat the oil in a large frying pan over medium heat. Add the onion and sauté until lightly browned, about 5 minutes. • Add the tomatoes and basil and season with salt. Simmer for 15–20 minutes over low heat.

**Pasta:** Put a large pot of salted water to boil over high heat. • Cook the pasta in the boiling water until al dente. • Meanwhile, sauté the garlic and pancetta in the oil in a large frying pan over medium heat until the garlic turns pale gold, 3–4 minutes. • Drain the pasta and add to the pan with the pancetta. • Stir in the tomato sauce, sun-dried tomatoes, and arugula. Season with salt and pepper. • Serve hot, topped with shavings of Parmesan cheese.

**Tomato Sauce**

3 tablespoons extra-virgin olive oil

1 onion, finely chopped

2 pounds (1 kg) tomatoes, peeled, or 2 (14-ounce/400-g) cans tomatoes, with juice

1 tablespoon coarsely chopped fresh basil

Salt

**Pasta**

1 pound (500 g) cavatelli

2 cloves garlic, finely chopped

3/4 cup (100 g) diced pancetta

1 tablespoon extra-virgin olive oil

1 cup (180 g) sun-dried tomatoes, chopped

1 bunch arugula (rocket)

Salt and freshly ground black pepper

Parmesan cheese, in shavings, to serve

Serves: 4–6
Preparation: 15 minutes
Cooking: 30 minutes
Level: 1

You could also use: maccheroni, rigatoni, penne rigate

# PENNE WITH MEAT SAUCE

126

Heat the oil in a large frying pan over medium heat. Add the onion, celery, carrot, garlic, rosemary, and 1 tablespoon of parsley and sauté until softened, about 5 minutes. • Season with salt and pepper. • Add the beef and sauté until browned, about 5 minutes. • Pour in the wine and let it evaporate. • Stir in the tomatoes and simmer over low heat for at least 2 hours, adding stock as the sauce begins to thicken and stick to the bottom of the pan. • Remove the rosemary. • Just before the sauce is ready, cook the pasta in a large pot of salted, boiling water until al dente. • Drain well and toss with the meat sauce. • Serve hot sprinkled with the remaining parsley and cheese.

| | |
|---|---|
| ⅓ | cup (90 ml) extra-virgin olive oil |
| 1 | onion, finely chopped |
| 1 | stalk celery, finely chopped |
| 1 | carrot, finely chopped |
| 1 | clove garlic, finely chopped |
| 1 | sprig fresh rosemary |
| 2 | tablespoons finely chopped parsley |
| | Salt and freshly ground black pepper |
| 1½ | pounds (750 g) ground (minced) beef |
| ½ | cup (120 ml) dry red wine |
| 4 | large firm-ripe tomatoes, peeled and coarsely chopped |
| 2 | cups (500 ml) beef stock (see page 48) |
| 1 | pound (500 g) penne |
| | Freshly grated Parmesan cheese to serve |

■ ■ ■ *This is a very good, basic meat sauce. You can serve it with all kinds of pasta, including long, short, fresh, and filled. The important thing is to simmer the sauce for at least two hours; the longer the better.*

Serves: 4–6
Preparation: 40 minutes
Cooking: 2 hours
Level: 1

You could also use: farfalle, fusilli, rigatoni, spaghetti, tagliatelle, ravioli

# MALLOREDDUS WITH SAUSAGE SAUCE

Heat the oil in a large frying pan over medium heat. Add the sausages, onion, garlic, and torn basil and sauté until the onion turns pale gold, 4–5 minutes. • Add the tomatoes and season with salt and pepper. Simmer until the sauce thickens and reduces, 25–30 minutes. • Put a large pot of salted water to boil over high heat. • Cook the pasta in the boiling water until al dente. • Drain well and add to the pan with the sauce. Sprinkle with the pecorino and toss gently. • Garnish with the extra basil and serve hot.

¼   cup (60 ml) extra-virgin olive oil

14  ounces (400 g) Italian pork sausages, skinned and crumbled

1   large onion, finely chopped

3   cloves garlic, finely chopped

1   tablespoon coarsely chopped fresh basil + extra to garnish

1½  pounds (750 g) fresh tomatoes, peeled and chopped

Salt and freshly ground black pepper

1   pound (500 g) malloreddus

⅓   cup (45 g) freshly grated pecorino cheese

Serves: 4–6
Preparation: 15 minutes
Cooking: 45 minutes
Level: 1

You could also use: penne, fusilli, farfalle, spaghetti

# PENNE WITH PEAS & SAUSAGE

Put a large pot of salted water to boil over high heat. • Heat the butter in a medium saucepan over a medium heat. Add the onion and sauté until softened, 3–4 minutes. • Stir in the tomatoes and sausage. Pour in the cream and simmer over low heat for 15 minutes. • Heat the oil in a medium saucepan over low heat. Add the garlic and sage and sauté until the garlic is pale gold, 3–4 minutes. • Stir in the peas, sugar, and water. Simmer until the peas are tender, about 10 minutes. Season with salt and pepper and add the parsley. • Cook the pasta in the boiling water until al dente. • Drain the pasta and add to the pan. Toss well. • Sprinkle with the Parmesan and serve hot.

| | |
|---|---|
| 2 | tablespoons butter |
| 1 | onion, finely chopped |
| 2 | medium tomatoes, peeled and chopped |
| 1 | pound (500 g) Italian sausage, crumbled |
| ½ | cup (120 ml) heavy (double) cream |
| 2 | tablespoons extra-virgin olive oil |
| 1 | clove garlic, finely chopped |
| 2 | tablespoons finely chopped fresh sage |
| 2 | cups (300 g) frozen peas |
| | Pinch of sugar |
| 1 | cup (250 ml) hot water, + more as needed |
| | Salt and freshly ground black pepper |
| 2 | tablespoons finely chopped fresh parsley |
| 1 | pound (500 g) penne |
| ½ | cup (60 g) freshly grated Parmesan cheese |

Serves: 4–6
Preparation: 15 minutes
Cooking: 20–30 minutes
Level: 1

You could also use: fusilli, farfalle, rigatoni

# PENNE WITH HAM & PISTACHIOS

132

Put a large pot of salted water to boil over high heat. • Heat the oil in a large frying pan over medium heat. Add the white part of the scallions. Sauté until softened, 2–3 minutes. • Add the wine and let evaporate for 3 minutes. • Add the zucchini and season with salt. Mix well and sauté until the zucchini are tender, about 5 minutes. • Add the ham, pistachios, and half the green part of the scallions. Mix well and sauté for 1 minute. Season with pepper. • Cook the pasta in the boiling water until al dente. Drain well and add to the pan with the sauce. Toss over high heat for 1 minute. • Add the butter and Parmesan and toss well. • Sprinkle with the remaining scallions and serve hot.

1/4 cup (60 ml) extra-virgin olive oil

8 scallions (spring onions), white and green parts sliced separately

1/3 cup (90 ml) dry white wine

8 small zucchini (courgettes), cut into small cubes

Salt

8 ounces (250 g) smoked ham, cut into small cubes

2/3 cup (100 g) blanched pistachios, coarsely chopped

Freshly ground black pepper

1 pound (500 g) penne

2 tablespoons butter

1/2 cup (60 g) freshly grated Parmesan cheese

Serves: 4–6
Preparation: 15 minutes
Cooking: 20 minutes
Level: 1

You could also use: conchiglie, farfalle, rigatoni

# MACCHERONI WITH SMOKED HAM

134

Put a large pot of salted water to boil over high heat. • Place the oil in a large frying pan over medium heat. Add the shallots and sauté until softened, 3–4 minutes. • Stir in the tomatoes, fennel seeds, and basil. Simmer until the tomatoes begin to break down, about 10 minutes. • Add the smoked ham and simmer for 5 minutes. Season with salt and pepper. • Cook the pasta in the boiling water until al dente. Drain and add to the sauce. • Toss over high heat for 1 minute. Sprinkle with the Parmesan and garnish with the extra basil. Serve hot.

¼ cup (60 ml) extra-virgin olive oil

2 shallots, finely chopped

2 pounds (1 kg) ripe tomatoes, peeled and chopped

2 teaspoons fennel seeds

1 tablespoon torn basil + extra to garnish

1 cup (120 g) diced smoked ham or bacon

Salt and freshly ground black pepper

1 pound (500 g) maccheroni (macaroni)

6 tablespoons freshly grated Parmesan cheese

Serves: 4–6
Preparation: 10 minutes
Cooking: 20 minutes
Level: 1

■ ■ ■ *In Italy, this recipe is made using speck, a type of smoked ham with a salty flavor from Tyrol, in the north, near Austria.*

You could also use: fusilli, farfalle, rigatoni

# PENNE WITH CREAMY BACON SAUCE

Put a large pot of salted water to boil over high heat. • Cook the penne in the boiling water until al dente. • Dry-fry the bacon in a large frying pan over medium heat until crisp, about 3 minutes. • Add the cream, garlic, and Parmesan and cook over low heat for 4 minutes. • Drain the penne and add to the pan with the sauce. • Toss well and serve hot.

| | |
|---|---|
| 1 | pound (500 g) penne |
| 8 | slices bacon, rinds removed and thinly sliced |
| 1¼ | cups (300 ml) heavy (double) cream |
| 3 | cloves garlic, finely chopped |
| ½ | cup (60 g) freshly grated Parmesan cheese |

Serves: 4–6
Preparation: 10 minutes
Cooking: 20 minutes
Level: 1

You could also use: fusilli, sedani, maccheroni

# GARGANELLI WITH CREAMY SAUSAGE SAUCE

138

Put a large pot of salted water to boil over high heat. • Heat the butter in a large frying pan over medium heat. Add the onion and sauté until softened, 3–4 minutes. • Add the sausages and sauté over high heat until browned all over, about 3 minutes. • Pour in the cream and simmer over very low heat for about 10 minutes. Season with nutmeg, salt, and pepper. • Cook the pasta in the boiling water until al dente. Drain and add to the sauce. • Sprinkle with the Parmesan and parsley and toss gently. Serve hot.

| | |
|---|---|
| 1 | tablespoon butter |
| 1 | onion, finely chopped |
| 1 | pound (500 g) Italian pork sausage, skinned and crumbled |
| ³/4 | cup (180 ml) light (single) cream |
| ¹/4 | teaspoon freshly grated nutmeg |
| | Salt and freshly ground black pepper |
| 1 | pound (500 g) garganelli or penne |
| ¹/2 | cup (60 g) freshly grated Parmesan cheese |
| 2 | tablespoons finely chopped fresh parsley |

Serves: 4–6
Preparation: 15 minutes
Cooking: 15 minutes
Level: 1

■ ■ ■ *Garganelli are a short pasta from the Emilia-Romagna region of Italy. They are traditionally served with thick, meaty sauces like this one.*

You could also use: penne, fusilli, cavatappi, festonati

# SEDANI WITH MEATBALLS

140

Put a large pot of salted water to boil over high heat. • Pour the milk into a small bowl and add the bread. • Put the beef, prosciutto, parsley, and garlic in a food processor and chop until smooth. Transfer to a bowl and add the well-squeezed bread, egg yolk, lemon zest, and nutmeg. Season with salt and pepper and mix well. • Put the flour ina small bowl. Shape the mixture into balls about the size of a marble and roll in the flour. Set aside. • Heat the oil in a large frying pan and sauté the onion until translucent, 3–4 minutes. • Add the tomatoes and oregano and simmer over low heat for 10–15 minutes. Season with salt and pepper. • Cook the meatballs in a medium pan of simmering water for 3 minutes. Scoop out with a slotted spoon and drain on a clean cloth. • Cook the pasta in the boiling water until al dente. • Drain and add to the pan with the tomato sauce. Add the meatballs and toss gently over medium heat for 1–2 minutes. • Sprinkle with the Parmesan and serve hot.

| | |
|---|---|
| ⅓ | cup (90 ml) milk |
| 2 | thick slices day-old bread, crusts removed, crumbled |
| 1 | pound (500 g) ground (minced) beef |
| 4 | ounces (120 g) prosciutto |
| | Small bunch fresh parsley |
| 1 | clove garlic, peeled |
| 1 | large egg yolk |
| | Finely grated zest of 1 organic lemon |
| | Pinch of nutmeg |
| | Salt and freshly ground black pepper |
| ½ | cup (75 g) all-purpose (plain) flour + extra, to dust |
| 5 | tablespoons (75 ml) extra-virgin olive oil |
| 1 | small onion, finely chopped |
| 2 | pounds (1 kg) tomatoes, peeled and chopped |
| 1 | teaspoon dried oregano |
| 1 | pound (500 g) sedani |
| ½ | cup (60 g) freshly grated Parmesan cheese |

Serves: 4–6
Preparation: 20 minutes
Cooking: 20 minutes
Level: 2

You could also use: penne, rigatoni, farfalle, ruote

# LONG PASTA

# ANGEL HAIR WITH CHILE, LEMON & BASIL

Put a large pot of salted water to boil over high heat. • Cook the pasta in the boiling water until al dente. • Combine the lemon juice, oil, chiles, and Parmesan in a medium bowl. Stir until well combined. • Drain the pasta and return to the pan. • Add the lemon mixture, basil, and lemon zest. Season with salt and pepper. • Toss over low heat until well combined. • Serve hot.

**144**

| | |
|---|---|
| 1 | **pound (500 g) angel hair pasta** |
| ½ | **cup (125 ml) freshly squeezed lemon juice** |
| ⅓ | **cup (90 ml) extra-virgin olive oil** |
| 2 | **fresh red chiles, seeded and thinly sliced** |
| ¾ | **cup (90 g) freshly grated Parmesan cheese** |
| ½ | **cup (25 g) fresh basil leaves** |
| 2 | **teaspoons finely grated organic lemon zest** |
| | **Salt and freshly ground black pepper** |

Serves: 4–6
Preparation: 10 minutes
Cooking: 3–5 minutes
Level: 1

■ ■ ■ *Angel hair pasta is a type of thin spaghetti. It is also known as vermicelli in English.*

You could also use: spaghettini, spaghetti, linguine

# LINGUINE WITH PARSLEY & CREAM

Put a large pot of salted water to boil over high heat. • Cook the pasta in the boiling water until al dente. • Melt the butter in a large frying pan over low heat. Add the cream and cheese and simmer over low heat for 4 minutes. Stir in the parsley. Season with salt and pepper. • Drain the pasta and add to the pan with the sauce. Toss well and serve hot.

1   **pound (500 g) linguine**

⅓   **cup (90 g) butter**

1¼  **cups (300 ml) light (single) cream**

½   **cup (60 g) freshly grated Parmesan cheese**

3   **tablespoons finely chopped fresh parsley**

**Salt and freshly ground black pepper**

Serves: 4–6
Preparation: 10 minutes
Cooking: 10–15 minutes
Level: 1

You could also use: angel hair pasta, spaghettini, spaghetti. tagliatelle

# SPAGHETTI WITH BURNT BUTTER & PINE NUTS

148

Put a large pot of salted water to boil over high heat. • Cook the pasta in the boiling water until al dente. • Heat the butter in a large frying pan over medium-low high heat until the foam turns slightly brown and subsides. Set aside. • Toast the pine nuts in a heavy saucepan over medium heat, 3–4 minutes, shaking the pan often. • Drain the pasta and place in a large bowl. Drizzle with the butter. Add the pine nuts and parsley and season generously with pepper. Top with the Parmesan and toss well. • Serve hot.

| | |
|---|---|
| 1 | pound (500 g) spaghetti |
| ½ | cup (125 g) best quality salted butter |
| ½ | cup (75 g) pine nuts |
| 2 | tablespoons finely chopped fresh parsley |
| | Freshly ground black pepper |
| | Freshly grated Parmesan cheese |

Serves: 4–6
Preparation: 10 minutes
Cooking: 10–15 minutes
Level: 1

You could also use: spaghettini, whole-wheat spaghetti, tagliatelle

# LINGUINE WITH ALMOND PESTO

Put a large pot of salted water to boil over high heat. • Chop the almonds, garlic, and basil finely in a food processor. • Add the tomato paste, Parmesan, and oil, and mix well. • Cook the pasta in the boiling water until al dente. • While the pasta is cooking, dilute the sauce with 1–2 tablespoons of cooking water. Season with salt. • Drain the pasta and serve hot with the almond pesto.

**150**

| | |
|---|---|
| 8 | ounces (250 g) blanched almonds |
| 3 | cloves garlic |
| | Leaves from 1 small bunch basil |
| 2 | tablespoons tomato paste (concentrate) |
| 3/4 | cup (90 g) freshly grated Parmesan cheese |
| 1/3 | cup (90 ml) extra-virgin olive oil |
| 1 | pound (500 g) linguine |
| | Salt |

Serves: 4–6
Preparation: 20 minutes
Cooking: 15 minutes
Level: 1

You could also use: spaghetti, penne, fusilli

# LINGUINE WITH PECORINO & BLACK PEPPER

152

Put a large pot of salted water to boil over high heat. • Cook the pasta in the boiling water until al dente. • Mix the pecorino and pepper in a large bowl. Stir in the oil. • Drain the pasta, reserving 2 tablespoons of cooking water, and add to the bowl with the pecorino. Add the cooking water and extra black pepper to taste. • Serve hot.

1   pound (500 g) spaghetti

1¼ cups (150 g) freshly grated aged pecorino cheese

1   teaspoon freshly ground black pepper

½   cup (120 ml) extra-virgin olive oil

Serves: 4–6
Preparation: 5 minutes
Cooking: 10–15 minutes
Level: 1

You could also use: angel hair pasta, spaghettini, spaghetti, penne rigate

# SPAGHETTI WITH CHILE, OIL & GARLIC

154

Put a large pot of salted water to boil over high heat. • Cook the pasta in the boiling water until al dente. • Heat 2 tablespoons of oil in a large frying pan over medium heat. Add the garlic and chiles and sauté until pale gold, 2–3 minutes. • Drain the pasta and add to the pan. Add the remaining 6 tablespoons (90 ml) of oil and the bread crumbs. Season with salt and pepper. • Toss gently and serve hot.

| 1 | pound (500 g) spaghetti |
|---|---|
| 8 | tablespoons (120 ml) extra-virgin olive oil |
| 5 | cloves garlic, lightly crushed but whole |
| 4 | dried chiles, crumbled or 1 teaspoon dried red pepper flakes |
| ½ | cup (75 g) fine dry bread crumbs |
| | Salt and freshly ground black pepper |

Serves: 4–6
Preparation: 10 minutes
Cooking: 10–15 minutes
Level: 1

You could also use: angel hair pasta, spaghettini, linguine

# HOT & SPICY SPAGHETTI

Put a large pot of salted water to boil over high heat. • Cook the pasta in the boiling water until al dente. • Warm the oil in a small frying pan over low heat and add the chiles and garlic. Leave to infuse (not sizzle) over low heat; turn off the heat if the garlic takes on color. • When the spaghetti is cooked, drain well then add to the pan with the oil. Add the parsley and season with pepper. • Sprinkle with the Parmesan and toss well. • Serve hot with extra Parmesan and extra oil, if liked.

156

| 1 | pound (500 g) spaghetti |
| 1/2 | cup (120 ml) extra-virgin olive oil + extra to drizzle (optional) |
| 2 | fresh red chiles, seeded and thinly sliced |
| 4 | cloves garlic, thinly sliced |
| 2 | tablespoons finely chopped fresh parsley |
| | Freshly ground black pepper |
| 1/2 | cup (60 g) coarsely grated Parmesan cheese + extra to serve |

Serves: 4–6
Preparation: 10 minutes
Cooking: 10–15 minutes
Level: 1

You could also use: angel hair, spaghettini, linguine, bucatini

# SPAGHETTI WITH BLACK OLIVES & HERBS

**158**

Put a large pot of salted water to boil over high heat. • Cook the pasta in the boiling water until al dente. • Chop the basil coarsely, reserving 16 large leaves. Mix the chopped basil, rosemary, parsley, and bread crumbs in a bowl. • Heat 3 tablespoons of oil in a large frying pan over medium heat. Add the scallions, garlic, capers, and olives and sauté for 3 minutes. Add the chopped herb mixture and sauté for 2 more minutes. • Sauté the reserved basil leaves in 3 tablespoons of oil in a small frying pan over medium heat for a few seconds, until wilted. Drain on paper towels. • Drain the pasta and add to the pan with the scallions and herbs. Sauté for 1 minute over medium heat. Season with pepper. Drizzle with the remaining oil and top with the basil. • Serve hot.

| | |
|---|---|
| 1 | **pound (500 g) spaghetti** |
| 1 | **large bunch fresh basil** |
| 1 | **tablespoon finely chopped fresh rosemary** |
| 2 | **tablespoons finely chopped fresh parsley** |
| 4 | **tablespoons fine dry bread crumbs** |
| 8 | **tablespoons (120 ml) extra-virgin olive oil** |
| 2 | **scallions (spring onions), finely sliced** |
| 1 | **clove garlic, finely chopped** |
| 1 | **tablespoon salt-cured capers, rinsed** |
| 1 | **cup (100 g) black olives, pitted and chopped** |
| | **Freshly ground black pepper** |

Serves: 4–6
Preparation: 15 minutes
Cooking: 10–15 minutes
Level: 1

You could also use: angel hair pasta, spaghettini, linguine

# SPAGHETTI WITH ANCHOVIES, PINE NUTS, & RAISINS

160

Put a large pot of salted water to boil over high heat. • Heat the oil in a large frying pan over medium heat. Add the garlic and sauté until softened, 3–4 minutes. • Add the pine nuts and raisins and toast until the pine nuts are golden, about 2 minutes. • Stir in the tomato paste mixture. Add the anchovies and stir until they dissolve, about 5 minutes. Remove from the heat. • Cook the pasta in the boiling water until al dente. • Drain well and add to the sauce, adding some of the cooking water if needed. • Sprinkle with the parsley and serve hot.

⅓  **cup (90 ml) extra-virgin olive oil**

1  **clove garlic, finely chopped**

2  **tablespoons pine nuts**

2  **tablespoons golden raisins (sultanas)**

5  **tablespoons tomato paste (concentrate) dissolved in ¼ cup (60 ml) lukewarm water**

8  **salt-cured anchovy fillets**

1  **pound (500 g) spaghetti**

1  **teaspoon finely chopped fresh parsley**

Serves: 4–6
Preparation: 15 minutes
Cooking: 15–20 minutes
Level: 1

You could also use: spaghettini, linguine, bucatini

# SPICY SPAGHETTI WITH PINE NUTS & RAISINS

162

Put a large pot of salted water to boil over high heat. • Cook the pasta in the boiling water until al dente. • Heat the oil in a large frying pan over medium heat. Add the garlic and chile and sauté until the garlic turns pale gold, 2–3 minutes. • Add the pine nuts and golden raisins. Season with salt and pepper. Sauté for 1 minute more. • Drain the pasta and add to the pan with the sauce. Add the parsley and toss over high heat. • Serve hot.

| | |
|---|---|
| 1 | pound (500 g) spaghetti |
| ⅓ | cup (90 ml) extra-virgin olive oil |
| 2 | cloves garlic, finely chopped |
| 1 | fresh red chile, seeded and finely chopped |
| ½ | cup (90 g) pine nuts |
| ½ | cup (90 g) golden raisins (sultanas) |
| | Salt and freshly ground black pepper |
| 4 | tablespoons finely chopped fresh parsley |

Serves: 4–6
Preparation: 10 minutes
Cooking: 10–15 minutes
Level: 1

You could also use: spaghettini, linguine, penne rigate, farfalle

# LINGUINE WITH FRESH TOMATO & LEMON SAUCE

Put a large pot of salted water to boil over high heat. • Blanch the tomatoes in boiling water for 2 minutes. Drain and peel them. Chop coarsely. • Cook the pasta in the boiling water until al dente. • Drain well and transfer to a large serving dish. • Add the tomatoes, basil, oil, lemon juice, and garlic. Season with salt and pepper. Toss well. • Garnish with extra whole basil leaves and serve hot.

| | |
|---|---|
| 2 | pounds (1 kg) ripe tomatoes |
| 1 | pound (500 g) linguine |
| 4 | tablespoons finely chopped fresh basil + extra leaves to garnish |
| 1/3 | cup (90 ml) extra-virgin olive oil |
| | Freshly squeezed juice of 1 lemon |
| 2 | cloves garlic, finely chopped |
| | Salt and freshly ground black pepper |

Serves: 4–6
Preparation: 10 minutes
Cooking: 10–15 minutes
Level: 1

You could also use: penne, tagliatelle, spaghettini, spaghetti

# SPAGHETTI WITH TOMATO & BASIL

166

Put a large pot of salted water to boil over high heat. • Heat the oil in a large frying pan to very hot. Add the chiles and 1 tomato and fry for 2–3 minutes. • Add all the tomatoes one by one, frying each one and pushing it to the edge of the pan, until all the tomatoes are in the pan and fried. Season with salt and pepper and remove the chiles. • Cook the pasta in the boiling water until al dente. • Drain the pasta and add to the pan with the tomatoes. Add the basil and pecorino, toss well, and serve hot.

½  cup (120 ml) extra-virgin olive oil

2  large fresh red chiles, whole

2  pounds (1 kg) San Marzano tomatoes, peeled, seeded, and cut in half lengthwise

Salt and freshly ground black pepper

1  pound (500 g) spaghetti

Fresh basil, torn

1  cup (120 g) freshly grated aged pecorino cheese

Serves: 4–6
Preparation: 15 minutes
Cooking: 20–25 minutes
Level: 2

■ ■ ■ *You will need meaty tomatoes with plenty of flesh and not too many seeds or liquid for this dish. We suggest you use San Marzanos but any meaty and flavorful variety will work just as well.*

You could also use: linguine, bucatini, penne, farfalle

# LINGUINE WITH ARUGULA PESTO

Put a large pot of salted water to boil over high heat. • Cook the pasta in the boiling water until al dente. • Chop the garlic, pine nuts, salt, arugula, and 1/4 cup (60 ml) of oil in a food processor until smooth. Stir in the Parmesan and a little more of the oil. Mix well. • Drain the pasta, reserving 2 tablespoons of the cooking water. • Place the pasta in a large bowl and add the pesto, reserved cooking water, and remaining 1/4 cup (60 ml) of oil. • Toss well and serve hot.

1   pound (500 g) linguine
2   cloves garlic
1/4   cup (45 g) pine nuts
    Salt
4   cups (200 g) fresh arugula (rocket)
1/2   cup (120 ml) extra-virgin olive oil
1/2   cup (60 g) freshly grated Parmesan cheese

Serves: 4–6
Preparation: 15 minutes
Cooking: 10–15 minutes
Level: 1

You could also use: angel hair, spaghettini, spaghetti, penne lisce

# SPAGHETTI WITH CAVOLO NERO PESTO

170

Put a large pot of salted water to boil over high heat. • Cook the cavolo nero in the boiling water for 10 minutes. Drain well, reserving the water. Return the water to a boil. • Process the cavolo nero, garlic, pecorino, and oil in a food processor until puréed. Season with salt and pepper. • Cook the pasta in the boiling water used to cook the cavolo nero until al dente. • Drain well. Serve the pasta hot with the pesto and extra cheese on hand to sprinkle.

1   pound (500 g) cavolo nero (Tuscan kale), tough stalks removed

2   cloves garlic, peeled

½   cup (60 g) freshly grated pecorino cheese + extra to serve

⅔   cup (150 ml) extra-virgin olive oil

    Salt and freshly ground black pepper

1   pound (500 g) spaghetti

Serves: 4–6
Preparation: 20 minutes
Cooking: 15–20 minutes
Level: 1

■ ■ ■ *Cavolo nero, also know as Tuscan kale, dinosaur kale, laciniato kale, or black cabbage, is a variety of kale. The leaves have a strong, pleasantly bitter flavor. It is now widely grown outside of Italy, but if you can't find it substitute with the same weight of Swiss chard (silverbeet) or spinach.*

You could also use: spaghetti, penne

# LINGUINE WITH CHILE PESTO

Put a large pot of salted water to boil over high heat. • Cook the pasta in the boiling water until al dente. • Combine the basil, chiles, garlic, and salt in a food processor and blend for 5 seconds. Add the pine nuts, both cheeses, and half the oil and blend for 5 more seconds. Scrap down the sides, add the remaining oil, and blend until a smooth pesto is formed. • Drain the pasta, toss with the pesto, and serve hot.

172

| | |
|---|---|
| 1 | pound (500 g) linguine |
| 2 | cups (100 g) fresh basil leaves |
| 1–2 | fresh red chiles, seeded and coarsely chopped |
| 2 | cloves garlic, coarsely chopped |
| 1/2 | teaspoon salt |
| 2/3 | cup (120 g) pine nuts, lightly toasted |
| 1/3 | cup (50 g) freshly grated Parmesan cheese |
| 1/3 | cup (50 g) freshly grated pecorino cheese |
| 1/3 | cup (90 ml) extra-virgin olive oil |

Serves: 4–6
Preparation: 10 minutes
Cooking: 10–15 minutes
Level: 1

You could also use: angel hair pasta, spaghettini, spaghetti, fusilli, cavatappi

# SPAGHETTI WITH GREEN OLIVE PESTO & FRIED TOMATOES

174

Put several layers of paper towels on a large plate and put the slices of tomatoes on top. Set aside in the refrigerator, changing the paper a couple of times, to drain as much as possible. • Put a large pot of salted water to boil over high heat. • Chop the parsley, olives, and pine nuts in a food processor until smooth. Add the Parmesan. Gradually stir in the extra-virgin olive oil. • Heat the frying oil in a large frying pan until very hot. • Dip the tomato slices in the flour until well coated. • Fry in small batches until crisp. Drain on paper towels. Sprinkle lightly with salt. • Cook the pasta in the boiling water until al dente. • Drain well, transfer to a serving bowl. and toss with the olive pesto. Top with the fried tomatoes. • Serve hot.

| 1 | pound (500 g) meaty tomatoes, such as San Marzano, peeled and thinly sliced |
| 1 | small bunch fresh parsley |
| 1 | cup (100 g) green olives, pitted |
| 6 | tablespoons pine nuts |
| 6 | tablespoons freshly grated Parmesan cheese |
| 1/3 | cup (90 ml) extra-virgin olive oil |
| 1/2 | cup (120 ml) vegetable oil, for frying |
| 1/2 | cup (75 g) all-purpose (plain) flour |
| | Salt |
| 1 | pound (500 g) spaghetti |

Serves: 4–6
Preparation: 45 minutes
Cooking: 20–30 minutes
Level: 2

■ ■ ■ *Choose a meaty type of tomato with few seeds for this dish.*

You could also use: spaghettini, linguine, bucatini

# LINGUINE WITH CHERRY TOMATOES & PESTO

Preheat the oven to 350°F (180°C/gas 4). • Place the cherry tomatoes on a baking sheet, sliced side up, and drizzle with 2 tablespoons of oil. Lightly dust with salt and white pepper. • Bake for 15 minutes. • Put a large pot of salted water to boil over high heat. • Combine the basil, Parmesan, garlic, almonds, and remaining 4 tablespoons (60 ml) of oil in a food processor and process until smooth. Season with salt and white pepper. • Cook the pasta in the boiling water until al dente. • Drain well and place in a heated serving dish. • Add the pesto and baked tomatoes and toss gently. • Serve hot.

1½ **pounds (750 g) cherry tomatoes, halved**

6 **tablespoons (90 ml) extra-virgin olive oil**

**Salt and freshly ground white pepper**

2 **cups (100 g) fresh basil**

½ **cup (60 g) freshly grated Parmesan cheese**

2 **cloves garlic, peeled**

⅓ **cup (45 g) blanched almonds**

1 **pound (500 g) linguine**

Serves: 4–6
Preparation: 25 minutes
Cooking: 20–30 minutes
Level: 1

You could also use: farfalle, spaghetti

# LINGUINE WITH WALNUTS & GORGONZOLA

Put a large pot of salted water to boil over high heat. • Cook the pasta in the boiling water until al dente. • While the pasta is cooking, heat the apple cider vinegar and walnuts in a medium saucepan. • Drain the pasta well and return to the pan. • Pour the apple cider mixture over the linguine and add the spinach and cheese. Season with white pepper. • Toss well and serve hot.

178

| | |
|---|---|
| 1 | pound (500 g) linguine |
| 1/3 | cup (90 ml) apple cider vinegar |
| 1 | cup (120 g) walnuts, toasted |
| 12 | ounces (350 g) baby spinach leaves, tough stems removed |
| 8 | ounces (250 g) Gorgonzola cheese, crumbled |
| | Freshly ground white pepper |

Serves: 4–6
Preparation: 20 minutes
Cooking: 10–15 minutes
Level: 1

You could also use: spaghetti, penne, farfalle

# SPAGHETTI ALL'ARRABBIATA

180

Put a large pot of salted water to boil over high heat. • Heat the oil in a large frying pan over medium heat. Add the pancetta and sauté until crisp and lightly browned, 3–4 minutes. • Scoop out the pancetta with a slotted spoon and set aside. • In the same oil, sauté the chiles and garlic until the garlic is pale gold, 2–3 minutes. • Stir in the tomatoes and season with salt. Add the chopped parsley and simmer until the tomatoes have broken down, 10–15 minutes. • Add the pancetta and simmer for 3 minutes. • Cook the pasta in the boiling water until al dente. • Drain and add to the sauce. Sprinkle with the pecorino, toss well, and serve hot garnished with the extra parsley.

⅓ cup (90 ml) extra-virgin olive oil

5 ounces (150 g) pancetta (or bacon), cut into small strips

2 fresh red chiles, seeded and thinly sliced

3 cloves garlic, finely chopped

2 (14-ounce/400-g) cans tomatoes, with juice

Salt

1 tablespoon finely chopped fresh parsley + extra to garnish

1 pound (500 g) penne

½ cup (60 g) freshly grated pecorino cheese

Serves: 4–6
Preparation: 15 minutes
Cooking: 25–35 minutes
Level: 1

■ ■ ■ *Arrabbiata, which means "angry," in Italian, is a common pasta sauce in central Italy. The heat, or "anger," in the dish is provided by the chiles.*

You could also use: spaghettini, linguine, bucatini, penne

# SPAGHETTI WITH TOMATOES & CHEESE

Put a large pot of salted water to boil over high heat. • Heat the oil in a large frying pan over medium heat. Add the onion and sauté until softened, 3–4 minutes. • Add the tomatoes and season with salt and pepper. Simmer for 15 minutes, then add the basil. • Cook the pasta in the boiling water until al dente. • Drain well and add to the sauce. Toss over high heat for 1 minute. • Remove from the heat and add both cheeses. Toss well. • Garnish with the extra basil and serve hot.

1/3 cup (90 ml) extra-virgin olive oil

1 small onion, finely chopped

2 (14-ounce/400-g) cans tomatoes, with juice

Salt and freshly ground black pepper

1 tablespoon coarsely chopped fresh basil, torn + extra to garnish

1 pound (500 g) spaghetti

3 ounces (90 g) mozzarella cheese, cut in cubes

3/4 cup (90 g) freshly grated caciocavallo or Parmesan cheese

Serves: 4–6
Preparation: 15–20 minutes
Cooking: 15–20 minutes
Level: 1

You could also use: spaghettini, linguine, penne, farfalle, rigatoni

# SPAGHETTI WITH TOMATO & VEGGIE SAUCE

184

Heat the oil in a large frying pan over medium heat. Add the onion, carrot, and celery and season with salt and pepper. Cover and sweat over low heat for 10 minutes. • Add the garlic and mint and sauté over medium heat for 3 minutes. • Stir in the tomatoes and simmer for 30 minutes. Season with salt. • Put a large pot of salted water to boil over high heat. • Cook the pasta in the boiling water until al dente. • Drain well and add to the sauce. Toss well. • Sprinkle with the pecorino and serve hot.

⅓ cup (90 ml) extra-virgin olive oil

1 large onion, finely chopped

1 carrot, finely chopped

1 stalk celery, chopped

Salt and freshly ground black pepper

2 cloves garlic, sliced

1 tablespoon finely chopped fresh mint

2 pounds (1 kg) tomatoes, peeled and chopped

1 pound (500 g) spaghetti

6 tablespoons freshly grated pecorino cheese

Serves: 4–6
Preparation: 20 minutes
Cooking: 40–45 minutes
Level: 1

You could also use: linguine, bucatini, fusilli, farfalle, penne rigate

# LINGUINE WITH FLOWERING BROCCOLI

186

Put a large pot of salted water to boil over high heat. • Cook the flowering broccoli in the water for 2 minutes. • Remove with a slotted spoon and drain well. Return the water to a boil. Cook the pasta in the boiling water until al dente. • Heat the oil in a large frying pan over medium-high heat. Add the broccoli and simmer over low heat for 5 minutes. • Add the chiles, garlic, and sesame seeds and simmer until the pasta is cooked. • Drain the pasta and add to the pan. Add the parsley and lime juice and toss well. • Serve hot.

1 pound (500 g) flowering broccoli, trimmed and halved lengthways

1 pound (500 g) linguine

1/4 cup (60 ml) extra-virgin olive oil

3 fresh red chiles, seeded and thinly sliced lengthwise

4 cloves garlic, thinly sliced

4 tablespoons sesame seeds

2 tablespoons finely chopped fresh parsley

Freshly squeezed juice of 2 limes

Serves: 4–6
Preparation: 20 minutes
Cooking: 20–25 minutes
Level: 2

You could also use: spaghetti, conchiglie, rigatoni

# BUCATINI WITH SWEET & SOUR CAULIFLOWER

Put a large pot of salted water to boil over high heat. • Cook the cauliflower in the boiling water until almost tender, 3–5 minutes. Scoop out with a slotted spoon and set aside. • Return the water back to a boil. Cook the pasta in the boiling cauliflower water until al dente. • Heat the oil in a large frying pan over medium heat. Add the onion and sauté until softened, 3–4 minutes. • Add the anchovies, golden raisins, pine nuts, and saffron mixture. Stir for 2–3 minutes, then add the cauliflower. Simmer over low heat until the pasta is cooked. • Drain the pasta and add to the cauliflower mixture. Toss gently and season with black pepper and pecorino. • Serve hot.

| | |
|---|---|
| 1 | medium cauliflower, broken into florets |
| | Salt and freshly ground black pepper |
| 1 | pound (500 g) bucatini |
| 1/3 | cup (90 ml) extra-virgin olive oil |
| 1 | onion, thinly sliced |
| 4 | salt-cured anchovy fillets |
| 4 | tablespoons golden raisins (sultanas) |
| 4 | tablespoons pine nuts |
| 1/4 | teaspoon saffron, dissolved in 3 tablespoons hot water |
| 6 | tablespoons freshly grated pecorino cheese |

Serves: 4–6
Preparation: 15 minutes
Cooking: 15–20 minutes
Level: 1

You could also use: spaghetti, bucatini, maccheroni, conchiglie

# SPAGHETTI WITH TOMATO SAUCE & EGGPLANT

190

**Eggplant:** Put the eggplant slices in a colander and sprinkle with the coarse sea salt. Let drain for 1 hour. Shake off excess salt. • Heat the oil in a large, deep frying pan until very hot. • Fry the eggplant in small batches until golden brown, 5–7 minutes per batch. Drain on paper towels.

**Tomato Sauce:** Combine the tomatoes, onion, garlic, basil, oil, sugar, and salt in a medium-low saucepan. Cover and simmer over medium heat until the tomatoes have broken down, about 15 minutes. • Uncover and simmer over very low heat until the sauce has thickened, 15–20 minutes. • Put a large pot of salted water to boil over high heat. • Transfer the tomato sauce to a food processor and process until smooth. • Cook the pasta in the boiling water until al dente. • Drain well and add to the sauce. Toss well. • Place the fried eggplant on a large heated serving dish and top with the spaghetti. Sprinkle with Parmesan and serve hot.

**Eggplant**

1 pound (500 g) eggplant (aubergine), with skin, thinly sliced

Coarse sea salt

1 cup (250 ml) olive oil, for frying

**Tomato Sauce**

2 pounds (1 kg) tomatoes, peeled and coarsely chopped

1 red onion, chopped

2 cloves garlic, finely chopped

Leaves from 1 small bunch fresh basil, torn

2 tablespoons extra-virgin olive oil

1/8 teaspoon sugar

Salt

1 pound (500 g) spaghetti

1 cup (120 g) freshly grated Parmesan cheese

Serves: 4–6
Preparation: 30 minutes
  + 1 hour to drain
Cooking: 1 hour
Level: 2

You could also use: spaghettini, linguine, bucatini

# LINGUINE WITH SPICY TOMATOES & OLIVE SAUCE

192

Put a large pot of salted water to boil over high heat. • Heat the oil in a large frying pan over medium heat. Add the garlic and sauté until pale gold, 2–3 minutes. • Add the tomatoes and season with salt and pepper. Simmer for 10 minutes, then stir in the capers and olives. Simmer until reduced, 10–15 minutes. • Cook the pasta in the boiling water until al dente. • Drain and add to the pan with the sauce. Toss over high heat for 1 minute. • Sprinkle with parsley and paprika, toss well, and serve hot.

⅓ cup (90 ml) extra-virgin olive oil

4 cloves garlic, finely chopped

2 pounds (1 kg) ripe tomatoes, peeled and coarsely chopped

Salt and freshly ground black pepper

2 tablespoons brine-cured capers, drained

1½ cups (150 g) pitted black olives, coarsely chopped

1 pound (500 g) linguine

3 tablespoons finely chopped fresh parsley

½ teaspoon hot paprika

Serves: 4–6
Preparation: 15 minutes
Cooking: 15–20 minutes
Level: 1

You could also use: spaghettini, spaghetti, bucatini, penne

# SPAGHETTI WITH CHAMPIGNONS

194

Put a large pot of salted water to boil over high heat. • Heat 4 tablespoons (60 ml) of oil in a large frying pan over medium heat. Add the garlic and sauté until pale gold, 2–3 minutes. • Add the mushrooms and sauté until tender, 7–10 minutes. Season with salt and pepper. • Heat the remaining 2 tablespoons of oil in a small frying pan over medium heat. Add the pancetta and sauté until lightly browned and crisp, 3–4 minutes. Add the pancetta to the frying pan with the mushrooms. Mix well and simmer over low heat for 2 minutes. • Cook the pasta in the boiling water until al dente. • Drain the pasta and add to the pan with the mushrooms. Toss well, add the parsley, and season with pepper. • Sprinkle with the cheese and serve hot.

6   tablespoons (90 ml) extra-virgin olive oil

2   cloves garlic, finely chopped

1½  pounds (750 g) button mushrooms, sliced

    Salt and freshly ground black pepper

8   ounces (250 g) pancetta, cut into small pieces

1   pound (500 g) spaghetti

2   tablespoons finely chopped fresh parsley

1   cup (120 g) freshly grated pecorino or Parmesan cheese

Serves: 4–6
Preparation: 15 minutes
Cooking: 15–20 minutes
Level: 1

You could also use: linguine, penne, fusilli, rigatoni

# LINGUINE WITH MIXED MUSHROOM SAUCE

196

Slice any large mushrooms into small pieces. • Heat the oil in a frying pan over low heat. Add the onion, cover, and sweat for 20 minutes. • Season with salt and add the garlic and chile. • Put a large pot of salted water to boil over high heat. • Increase the heat under the frying pan and pour in the wine. Add the mushrooms and simmer over high heat until the wine has evaporated. • Stir in the tomatoes, basil, and parsley, and simmer on medium-low until the mushrooms are tender, about 10 minutes. Season with salt. • Cook the pasta in the boiling water until al dente. • Drain and add to the sauce. Toss well and serve hot.

1½ pounds (750 g) mixed mushrooms (porcini, white button mushrooms, chanterelle, enoki)

¼ cup (60 ml) extra-virgin olive oil

1 small onion, finely chopped

Salt

2 cloves garlic, finely chopped

1 dried chile, crumbled

¼ cup (60 ml) dry white wine

20 cherry tomatoes, quartered

2 tablespoons coarsely chopped fresh basil

1 tablespoon finely chopped fresh parsley

1 pound (500 g) linguine

Serves: 4–6
Preparation: 20 minutes
Cooking: 20–30 minutes
Level: 1

You could also use: spaghetti, penne rigate, rigatoni sedani

# SPAGHETTI WITH PESTO, POTATOES & BEANS

198

**Pesto:** Combine the basil, garlic, and pine nuts in a food processor and process until finely chopped, gradually adding the oil as you chop. • Transfer to a small bowl. Stir in the cheese, and season with salt and pepper.

**Pasta:** Put a large pot of salted water to boil over high heat. • Cook the green beans in the boiling water until just tender, 4–5 minutes. Scoop out with a slotted spoon and set aside. • Return the water to a boil. Cook the pasta in the boiling water for 5 minutes. Add the potatoes and cook until the pasta is al dente and the potatoes are tender, 7–8 minutes more. • Drain well. Put the pasta and potatoes in a heated serving bowl. • Pour the pesto into the pasta and potatoes, add the green beans, and toss well. • Season with pepper. Serve hot.

**Pesto**

- **1** large bunch fresh basil leaves
- **2** cloves garlic, peeled
- **2** tablespoons pine nuts
- **½** cup (120 ml) extra-virgin olive oil
- **4** tablespoons freshly grated pecorino cheese
- Salt and freshly ground black pepper

**Pasta**

- **12** ounces (350 g) green beans, cut into short lengths
- **1** pound (500 g) spaghetti
- **8** new potatoes, cut into small cubes
- Freshly ground black pepper

Serves: 4–6
Preparation: 20 minutes
Cooking: 20–25 minutes
Level: 1

■ ■ ■ *This dish comes from Genova, the capital city of Liguria, in northwestern Italy. Genova is the hometown of pesto.*

You could also use: whole-wheat spaghetti, linguine

# SPAGHETTI WITH SCALLIONS & TOMATOES

**200**

Heat 6 tablespoons (90 ml) oil in a large frying pan over low heat. Add the scallions, garlic, and bouquet garni and sweat, uncovered, stirring frequently, until soft and reduced to less than a quarter of their original volume, about 20 minutes. • Put a large pot of salted water to boil over high heat. • Discard the bouquet garni from the frying pan. Add the tomatoes and chiles to the pan. Season with salt and simmer, stirring occasionally. • Cook the pasta in the boiling water until al dente. • Drain well and add to the pan with the scallions. Toss gently. Drizzle with the remaining 1 tablespoon of oil and garnish with the basil. • Serve hot.

| | |
|---|---|
| 7 | **tablespoons (100 ml) extra-virgin olive oil** |
| 1 | **pound (500 g) scallions (spring onions), sliced** |
| 3 | **cloves garlic, finely chopped** |
| 1 | **bouquet garni** |
| 8 | **ounces (250 g) ripe tomatoes, peeled and chopped** |
| 2 | **fresh red chiles, thinly sliced** |
| | **Salt** |
| 1 | **pound (500 g) spaghetti** |
| | **Fresh basil leaves** |

Serves: 4–6
Preparation: 30 minutes
Cooking: 35–40 minutes
Level: 1

You could also use: linguine, bucatini, ziti, rigatoni

# WHOLE-WHEAT SPAGHETTI WITH CARAMELIZED ONIONS

Place the onions in a heavy-bottomed pan with the oil over low heat. Season with a little salt (use less than you normally would because the very slow cooking enhances the taste of the salt). Add a grinding of black pepper and cover. • Simmer very gently over very low heat for about 1 hour. The onions must not burn, but should slowly melt. Stir frequently, adding stock as required to keep the sauce moist. When cooked, the sauce should be creamy and golden. • Put a large pot of salted water to boil over high heat. • Cook the pasta in the boiling water until al dente. • Drain well and place in a serving bowl. Add the onion sauce and parsley. Toss gently and serve hot.

6 **large white onions, very thinly sliced**

1/3 **cup (90 ml) extra-virgin olive oil**

**Salt and freshly ground black pepper**

1 **cup (250 ml) beef stock (see page 48)**

1 **pound (500 g) whole-wheat (wholemeal) spaghetti**

**Finely chopped parsely, to garnish**

Serves: 4–6
Preparation: 25 minutes
Cooking: 1 1/4 hours
Level: 1

You could also use: spaghetti, linguine, penne, fusilli

# SPAGHETTI WITH SPICY CHERRY TOMATO SAUCE

204

Put a large pot of salted water to boil over high heat. • Place the tomatoes in a bowl with the garlic, pepper flakes, and basil. • Heat the oil in a large frying pan over high heat and add the tomato mixture. Cook for 5–6 minutes, stirring at frequent intervals. Season with salt and pepper. • Cook the pasta in the boiling water until very al dente. • Drain and add to the pan. Toss over high heat until the sauce is absorbed by the pasta as it finishes cooking. • Serve hot.

| | |
|---|---|
| 2 | pounds (1 kg) cherry tomatoes, halved |
| 2 | cloves garlic, thinly sliced |
| ½ | teaspoon dried red pepper flakes or 1 small dried chile, crumbled |
| | Fresh basil leaves, torn |
| ½ | cup (120 ml) extra-virgin olive oil |
| | Salt and freshly ground black pepper |
| 1 | pound (500 g) spaghetti |

Serves: 4–6
Preparation: 15 minutes
Cooking: 15 minutes
Level: 1

You could also use: spaghettini, penne rigate, cavatappi

# SPAGHETTI WITH BELL PEPPER SAUCE

Put a large pot of salted water to boil over high heat. • Heat the oil in a large frying pan over medium heat. Add the onions and sauté until softened, 3–4 minutes. • Stir in the tomatoes and simmer until they begin to break down, about 10 minutes. Add the bell peppers and anchovies. Simmer for 5 minutes. Season with salt. • Cook the pasta in the boiling water until al dente. • Drain the pasta and add to the sauce. Toss well and serve hot.

⅓ cup (90 ml) extra-virgin olive oil

3 medium onions, thinly sliced

4 large ripe tomatoes, peeled and chopped

12 ounces (350 g) canned or bottled bell peppers (capsicums), drained

4 salt-cured anchovy fillets, finely chopped

Salt

1 pound (500 g) spaghetti

Serves: 4–6
Preparation: 15 minutes
Cooking: 10–15 minutes
Level: 1

You could also use: linguine, bucatini. penne, fusilli

# SPAGHETTI WITH BLUE CHEESE & BROCCOLI

208

Put a large pot of salted water to boil over high heat. • Cook the broccoli in the boiling water until just tender, about 5 minutes. Drain, reserving the cooking water. • Bring the water back to a boil and cook the pasta until al dente. • Heat the oil in a large frying pan over medium heat. Add the garlic and sauté until pale gold, 2–3 minutes. • Add the broccoli to the pan and mix gently. • Drain the pasta and place in a heated serving bowl. Top with the broccoli mixture, Gorgonzola, and Parmesan. Season with cracked pepper. • Toss gently and serve hot.

1   pound (500 g) broccoli, broken into florets
1   pound (500 g) spaghetti
¼   cup (60 ml) extra-virgin olive oil
2   cloves garlic, finely chopped
8   ounces (250 g) Gorgonzola cheese, cubed
½   cup (75 g) freshly grated Parmesan cheese
    Cracked pepper

Serves: 4–6
Preparation: 15 minutes
Cooking: 15–20 minutes
Level: 1

You could also use: whole-wheat spaghetti, linguine, rigatoni, conchiglie

# SPAGHETTI WITH SPICY SICILIAN SAUCE

Put a large pot of salted water to boil over high heat. • Heat the oil in a large frying pan over medium heat. Add the garlic, onion, and chile and sauté until softened, 3–4 minutes. • Add the anchovies and stir until they dissolve into the oil. Add the tomatoes, olives, and capers and simmer over low heat for 15–20 minutes. • Cook the pasta in the boiling water until al dente. • Drain and add to the pan with the sauce. Toss over high heat for 1–2 minutes. • Serve hot.

$\frac{1}{3}$ cup (90 g) extra-virgin olive oil

2 cloves garlic, finely chopped

1 large onion, finely chopped

1 fresh red chile, seeded and thinly sliced

6 salt-cured anchovy fillets

$1\frac{1}{2}$ pounds (750 g) ripe tomatoes, peeled and chopped

1 cup (100 g) black olives, pitted

2 tablespoons salt-cured capers, rinsed

1 pound (500 g) whole-wheat (wholemeal) spaghetti

Serves: 4–6
Preparation: 15 minutes
Cooking: 20–25 minutes
Level: 1

You could also use: bucatini, maccheroni

# LINGUINE WITH SPICY CLAM SAUCE

212

Soak the clams in cold water for 1 hour. • Put a large pot of salted water to boil over high heat. • Place the clams in a large pan over medium heat with a little water. Cook until they open, 5–10 minutes. Discard any clams that do not open. Remove from the heat and discard most of the clam shells. Leave a few mollusks in their shells to garnish. • Heat the oil in a large frying pan over medium heat. Add the garlic and chile and sauté until softened, 3–4 minutes. • Add the tomatoes and wine, season with salt, and simmer until the tomatoes begin to break down, about 15 minutes. Add the clams and stir well. • Meanwhile, cook the pasta in the boiling water until al dente. • Drain and add to the pan with the clams. Toss over high heat for 1–2 minutes. • Sprinkle with the parsley and serve hot.

| | |
|---|---|
| 2 | pounds (1 kg) clams, in shell |
| 1/3 | cup (90 ml) extra-virgin olive oil |
| 4 | cloves garlic, finely chopped |
| 1 | fresh red chile, seeded and thinly sliced |
| 6 | large tomatoes, sliced |
| 1/3 | cup (90 ml) dry white wine |
| | Salt |
| 1 | pound (500 g) linguine |
| 2 | tablespoons finely chopped fresh parsley, to garnish |

Serves: 4–6
Preparation: 20 minutes
+ 1 hour to soak
Cooking: 30 minutes
Level: 1

■ ■ ■ *You can vary the sauce by replacing the clams with mussels or using one pound (500 g) each of mussels and clams. The method is the same.*

You could also use: angel hair pasta, spaghettini, spaghetti

# SPAGHETTI WITH SCAMPI & OLIVE PESTO

214

Put a large pot of salted water to boil over high heat. • Place the pine nuts in a large frying pan over medium-high heat and toast until golden brown, 2–3 minutes. • Chop almost all the olives (reserve a few whole to garnish), 4 tablespoons of pine nuts, the parsley, and 5 tablespoons of oil in a food processor until smooth. Season with salt and pepper. • Heat the remaining 3 tablespoons of oil in a large frying pan over high heat. Add the scampi and garlic and sauté until cooked, 3–5 minutes. • Cook the pasta in the boiling water until al dente. • Drain well and add to the pan with the scampi. Add the pesto, reserved olives, and remaining 2 tablespoons of pine nuts and toss gently. • Serve hot.

| | |
|---|---|
| 6 | tablespoons pine nuts |
| 1 | cup (100 g) pitted black olives |
| | Large bunch fresh parsley |
| 8 | tablespoons (120 ml) extra-virgin olive oil |
| | Salt and freshly ground black pepper |
| 12 | scampi, shelled, deveined, and coarsely chopped |
| 1 | clove garlic, finely chopped |
| 1 | pound (500 g) spaghetti |

Serves: 4–6
Preparation: 25 minutes
Cooking: 15–20 minutes
Level: 2

You could also use: spaghettini, linguine

# SPAGHETTI WITH TUNA, TOMATOES & CILANTRO

216

Put a large pot of salted water to boil over high heat. • Cook the pasta in the boiling water until al dente. • Heat the oil in a large frying pan over medium heat. Add the garlic, sugar, cilantro, and chile and sauté until the garlic is pale gold, 2–3 minutes. • Add the tomatoes, season with salt and pepper, and simmer for 5 minutes. Add the tuna, stir well, then turn off the heat. • Drain the pasta and transfer to a heated serving dish. • Toss gently with the sauce and serve hot.

| | |
|---|---|
| 1 | pound (500 g) spaghetti |
| 3 | tablespoons extra-virgin olive oil |
| 3 | cloves garlic, finely chopped |
| ½ | teaspoon sugar |
| 2 | tablespoons finely chopped fresh cilantro (coriander) |
| 1 | small dried chile, crumbled |
| 1 | pound (500 g) cherry tomatoes, halved |
| | Salt and freshly ground black pepper |
| 1 | (14-ounce/400-g) can tuna, drained and crumbled |

Serves: 4–6
Preparation: 20 minutes
Cooking: 15–20 minutes
Level: 1

You could also use: spaghettini, linguine, bucatini

# SPAGHETTI WITH TUNA & CAPERS

218

Put a large pot of salted water to boil over high heat. • Rinse the capers under cold running water and cover with fresh water in a small saucepan. Place over medium heat. Bring to a boil, drain the capers, rinse them again, and pat dry on paper towels. • Chop the tuna, capers, mint, oil, and red pepper flakes, if using. • Transfer to a large bowl and mix in the oil. • Cook the pasta in the boiling water until al dente. • Drain the pasta, reserving 2–3 tablespoons of cooking water, and add to the bowl with the tuna sauce. Toss gently, adding the cooking water if needed. • Serve immediately.

1   cup (100 g) salt-cured capers

12  ounces (350 g) tuna packed in oil, drained

Leaves from 1 bunch fresh mint

5   tablespoons (75 ml) extra-virgin olive oil

¼   teaspoon red pepper flakes (optional)

1   pound (500 g) spaghetti

Serves: 4–6
Preparation: 10 minutes
Cooking: 15 minutes
Level: 1

You could also use: spaghettini, linguine, penne, farfalle

# LINGUINE WITH SALMON, CILANTRO & LIME

220

Put a large pot of salted water to boil over high heat. • Cook the pasta in the boiling water until al dente. • Heat the oil in a large frying pan over high heat. Sauté the garlic, chile, and cilantro until the garlic is pale gold, 2–3 minutes. Add the salmon and sauté until tender, 2–3 minutes. • Drain the pasta and add to the pan. Add the lime juice and zest and season with salt and pepper. • Toss gently and serve hot.

1   pound (500 g) linguine

¼   cup (60 ml) extra-virgin olive oil

2   cloves garlic, finely chopped

1   fresh red chile, seeded and finely chopped

1   tablespoon finely chopped fresh cilantro (coriander)

14   ounces (400 g) fresh salmon fillets, cut in thin strips

    Freshly squeezed juice and finely grated zest of 1 lime

    Salt and freshly ground black pepper

Serves: 4–6
Preparation: 15 minutes
Cooking: 10–15 minutes
Level: 1

You could also use: spaghettini, spaghetti, tagliatelle

# SPAGHETTI WITH FRESH TUNA & THYME

222

Put a large pot of salted water to boil over high heat. • Toss the tuna in the flour, shaking to remove any excess. • Heat the oil in a large frying pan over medium heat. Add the garlic, olives, chiles, and half the thyme. Sauté until the garlic is pale gold, 2–3 minutes. • Season with salt and pepper. Add the tuna and zucchini. Sauté gently over medium heat until the tuna is cooked through, 5–6 minutes. Drizzle with the wine and simmer until it evaporates. • Cook the pasta in the boiling water until al dente. • Drain the pasta and add to the tuna sauce. Toss well. • Sprinkle with the remaining thyme and serve hot.

| | |
|---|---|
| 14 | ounces (400 g) tuna steak, cut into small pieces |
| 1/3 | cup (50 g) all-purpose (plain) flour |
| 1/4 | cup (60 ml) extra-virgin olive oil |
| 1 | clove garlic, finely chopped |
| 20 | black olives, pitted and finely chopped |
| 2 | fresh red or green chiles, seeded and finely chopped |
| 1 | tablespoon fresh thyme leaves |
| | Salt and freshly ground black pepper |
| 4 | zucchini (courgettes), cut into small cubes |
| 1/2 | cup (120 ml) dry white wine |
| 1 | pound (500 g) spaghetti |

Serves: 4–6
Preparation: 15 minutes
Cooking: 15–20 minutes
Level: 2

You could also use: linguine, bucatini, conchiglie giganti

# SPAGHETTI WITH FISH SAUCE

224

Put a large pot of salted water to boil over high heat. • Place the fish in a pot with a little water and the rosemary and bring to a boil. Simmer over low heat until tender, 3–5 minutes. Take the fish out and crumble the cooked meat. Strain the liquid and reserve. Discard the rosemary. • Heat the oil in a large frying pan over medium heat. Add the onion and garlic and sauté until pale gold, 3–3 minutes. • Add the fish meat and 1 cup (250 ml) of the reserved stock. Season with salt and pepper and simmer over low heat until reduced, about 10 minutes. • Cook the pasta in the boiling water until al dente. • Drain well, toss with the fish sauce, and serve hot.

1½ pounds (750 g) assorted fresh fish fillets, such as hake, sea bass, sea bream, and red snapper

2 tablespoons fresh rosemary leaves

½ cup (120 ml) extra-virgin olive oil

1 onion, finely chopped

1 clove garlic, finely chopped

Salt and freshly ground black pepper

1 pound (500 g) spaghetti

Serves: 4–6
Preparation: 15 minutes
Cooking: 20 minutes
Level: 2

You could also use: spaghettini, linguine, penne

# SPAGHETTI WITH SMOKED SALMON, ARUGULA & CAPERS

Put a large pot of salted water to boil over high heat. • Heat 2 tablespoons of the oil in a small frying pan over medium heat. Add the bread crumbs and sauté until golden, 3–5 minutes. Set aside. • Cook the pasta in the boiling water until al dente. • Heat the remaining 6 tablespoons (90 ml) of oil in a small pan over low heat. Add the garlic and chiles. Warm gently to flavor the oil without letting the garlic color. • Drain the pasta and place in a heated serving bowl. • Add the lemon zest and capers to the oil and pour over the pasta. Toss well, add the arugula and salmon and toss again. • Top with the bread crumbs and serve hot with the tomatoes.

| | |
|---|---|
| 8 | tablespoons (120 ml) extra-virgin olive oil |
| 2 | ounces (60 g) fresh white bread crumbs |
| 1 | pound (500 g) spaghetti |
| 2 | cloves garlic, finely chopped |
| 2 | small dried chiles, crumbled |
| | Finely grated zest of 1 organic lemon |
| 4 | tablespoons brine-cured capers, drained |
| | Handful of fresh arugula (rocket) leaves |
| 8 | ounces (250 g) smoked salmon, flaked |
| 2 | sliced tomatoes, to serve |

Serves: 4–6
Preparation: 20 minutes
Cooking: 20 minutes
Level: 2

You could also use: spaghettini, linguine, bucatini

# CHILE & SHRIMP LINGUINE

Put a large pot of salted water to boil over high heat. • Cook the pasta in the boiling water until al dente. Add the sugar snap peas for the last minute or so of cooking time. • While the pasta is cooking, combine the oil, garlic, and chiles in a small bowl. Season with salt and pepper. • Heat the oil mixture in a large frying pan over medium heat without letting the garlic color. Add the shrimp and sauté over high heat until they turn pink, 2–3 minutes. • Add the tomatoes and sauté until they just start to soften, 2–3 minutes. • Drain the pasta and sugar snaps and add to the pan. Toss well. Add the basil, toss well, and serve hot.

| | |
|---|---|
| 1 | pound (500 g) linguine |
| 14 | ounces (400 g) sugar snap peas, trimmed |
| 1/3 | cup (90 ml) extra-virgin olive oil |
| 4 | large garlic cloves, finely chopped |
| 2 | fresh red chiles, seeded and finely chopped |
| | Salt and freshly ground black pepper |
| 24 | jumbo shrimp (king prawns), peeled |
| 24 | cherry tomatoes, halved |
| | Handful of fresh basil leaves |

Serves: 4–6
Preparation: 15 minutes
Cooking: 15 minutes
Level: 1

You could also use: spaghettini, spaghetti, ruote

# SPAGHETTI WITH PANCETTA & CROUTONS

230

Put a large pot of salted water to boil over high heat. • Heat the pancetta and garlic in a large non-stick frying pan over medium heat and sauté until crisp, about 5 minutes. Scoop the pancetta out of the pan and keep warm. • Place the bread in the pan with 2 tablespoons of oil and sauté until golden brown, about 5 minutes. • Cook the pasta in the boiling water until al dente. • Drain the pasta and add to the pan with the bread. Add the pancetta, parsley, remaining 2 tablespoons of oil, and pecorino. Season with salt and pepper. • Toss well and serve hot.

| | |
|---|---|
| 6 | ounces (180 g) pancetta, cut in thin strips |
| 2 | cloves garlic, finely chopped |
| 5 | ounces (150 g) day-old bread, cut in cubes |
| 4 | tablespoons (60 ml) extra-virgin olive oil |
| 1 | pound (500 g) spaghetti |
| 2 | tablespoons finely chopped fresh parsley |
| | Salt and freshly ground black pepper |
| 1 | cup (120 g) freshly grated pecorino cheese |

Serves: 4–6
Preparation: 20 minutes
Cooking: 15–20 minutes
Level: 1

You could also use: linguine, bucatini, penne rigate, farfalle

# BUCATINI ALLA CARBONARA

232

Put a large pot of salted water to boil over high heat. • Cook the pasta in the boiling water until al dente. • While the pasta is cooking, sauté the onion in the oil in a small saucepan over medium heat until lightly browned, 2–3 minutes. • Add the bacon and sauté until crisp, about 5 minutes. Remove from the heat and set aside. • Beat the eggs and cream in a large bowl. Season with salt and pepper and sprinkle with the Parmesan. • Drain the pasta and add to the bacon. Return to high heat, add the egg mixture, and toss the briefly so that the eggs cook lightly but are still creamy. • Serve hot with extra black pepper.

| | |
|---|---|
| 1 | pound (500 g) bucatini |
| 1 | onion, finely chopped |
| ¼ | cup (60 ml) extra-virgin olive oil |
| 1⅓ | cups (150 g) diced bacon |
| 6 | large eggs |
| ⅓ | cup (90 ml) heavy (double) cream |
| | Salt and freshly ground black pepper |
| ¾ | cup (100 g) freshly grated Parmesan cheese |

Serves: 4–6
Preparation: 15 minutes
Cooking: 15–20 minutes
Level: 2

■ ■ ■ *La carbonara is a classic Roman sauce. The trick is to toss the pasta very quickly with the egg until it is just cooked and serve as quickly as possible.*

You could also use: spaghetti, linguine

# SPAGHETTI WITH PANCETTA

Put a large pot of salted water to boil over high heat. • Heat the oil in a saucepan over medium heat. Add the pancetta and sauté until crisp, 3–5 minutes. Remove and set aside. • Sauté the onion in the oil remaining from the pancetta in the same saucepan until softened, 3–4 minutes. • Add the tomatoes and simmer over medium heat until they reduce, 10–15 minutes. • Add the pancetta and marjoram. Season with salt and pepper. • Cook the pasta in the boiling water until al dente. • Drain the pasta and transfer to a heated serving dish. Toss with the sauce, sprinkle with the pecorino, and serve hot.

¼ cup (60 ml) extra-virgin olive oil

1½ cups (180 g) pancetta, cut into small cubes

1 large onion, finely chopped

1½ pounds (750 g) tomatoes, peeled, seeded, and coarsely chopped

1 small bunch marjoram, finely chopped

Salt and freshly ground black pepper

1 pound (500 g) spaghetti

½ cup (60 g) freshly grated pecorino cheese

Serves: 4–6
Preparation: 20 minutes
Cooking: 20–30 minutes
Level: 1

234

You could also use: angel hair pasta, spaghettini, spaghetti, bucatini

# SPAGHETTI WITH MEAT SAUCE

236

Heat the oil in a large frying pan over medium heat. Add the onion, celery, carrot, garlic, rosemary, and 2 tablespoons of parsley and sauté until softened, about 5 minutes. • Add the beef. Season with salt and pepper. Sauté until browned, about 5 minutes. • Pour in the wine and let it evaporate. Stir in the tomatoes and simmer over low heat for at least 2 hours, adding stock as the sauce begins to reduce. Remove the rosemary. • About 20 minutes before the sauce is ready, put a large pot of salted water to boil over high heat. • Cook the pasta in the boiling water until al dente. • Drain the pasta and toss with the sauce. • Serve hot with the remaining 1 tablespoon of parsley.

¼ cup (60 ml) extra-virgin olive oil

1 onion, finely chopped

1 stalk celery, finely chopped

1 carrot, finely chopped

2 cloves garlic, finely chopped

1 sprig fresh rosemary

3 tablespoons finely chopped fresh parsley

1½ pounds (750 g) ground (minced) beef

Salt and freshly ground black pepper

½ cup (120 ml) dry red wine

4 large ripe tomatoes, peeled and coarsely chopped

1–2 cups (250–500 ml) beef stock (see page 48)

1 pound (500 g) spaghetti

Serves: 4–6
Preparation: 20 minutes
Cooking: 2¹/₂ hours
Level: 1

You could also use: spaghettini, linguine, bucatini, penne, fusilli, tagliatelle

# SPAGHETTI WITH BOLOGNESE MEAT SAUCE

238

Melt the butter in a large frying pan over medium heat. Add the pancetta, onion, celery, and carrot and sauté until softened, 3–4 minutes. • Add the beef, pork, and sausage and sauté until browned, 5–10 minutes. • Add the clove, cinnamon, and pepper. Stir in the tomatoes and simmer over medium heat for 15 minutes. • Add the milk and season with salt. Turn the heat down to low and simmer for at least 2 hours, stirring often. • About 20 minutes before the sauce is ready, put a large pot of salted water to boil over high heat. • Cook the pasta in the boiling water until al dente. • Drain the pasta and serve hot with the sauce and Parmesan.

¼ cup (60 g) butter

½ cup (60 g) pancetta, diced

1 medium onion, finely chopped

1 stalk celery, finely chopped

1 small carrot, finely chopped

8 ounces (250 g) ground (minced) beef

2 ounces (60 g) ground (minced) pork

2 ounces (60 g) Italian pork sausage, crumbled

⅛ teaspoon ground cloves

¼ teaspoon ground cinnamon

¼ teaspoon freshly ground black pepper

1 (14-ounce/400-g) can tomatoes, with juice

1 cup (250 ml) milk

Salt

1 pound (500 g) spaghetti

½ cup (60 g) coarsely grated Parmesan cheese

Serves: 4–6
Preparation: 30 minutes
Cooking: 2¹/₂ hours
Level: 1

You could also use: tagliatelle, lasagna, pappardelle, linguine, penne, fusilli

# FRESH
# PASTA

## ■ PREPARING FRESH PASTA DOUGH

Plain fresh pasta is made of a simple mixture of flour and eggs. For four people, you will need: $2^2/_3$ cups (400 g) of all-purpose (plain) flour and four very fresh large eggs.

**1.** SIFT the flour onto a clean work surface and shape into a mound. Make a hollow in the center.

**2.** USE a fork to beat the eggs lightly in a small bowl. Pour the beaten eggs into the center of the mound of flour.

**3.** USE the fork to incorporate the eggs into the flour. Take care not to break the wall of flour or the eggs will run.

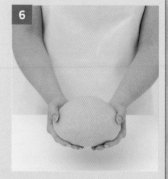

**4.** WHEN almost all the flour has been absorbed, use your hands and a pasta scraper to gather the dough up into a ball.

**5.** KNEAD by pushing down and forward on the pasta with the heel of your palm. Fold in half, give a quarter-turn, and repeat.

**6.** AFTER 10–15 minutes, it will be smooth and silky, with tiny air bubbles on the surface. Let rest for 30 minutes.

Fresh ribbon pasta types are named according to their width. The narrowest ribbons, taglierini or tagliolini, are about $1/4$ inch (5–6 mm) wide. Tagliatelle (also known as fettuccine) are normally about $1/2$ inch (1 cm) wide, while pappardelle can be up to 1 inch (2.5 cm) wide.

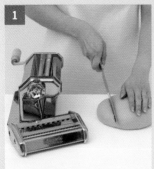

**1.** DIVIDE the dough into six pieces (for 14 ounces or 400 g of pasta, enough for four people).

**2.** ROLL a piece of dough at the thickest setting. Continue rolling, reducing the thickness one notch at a time.

**3.** THE SHEETS should be evenly shaped. Long sheets are hard to manage; keep at about 12–14 inches (30–35 cm).

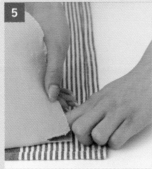

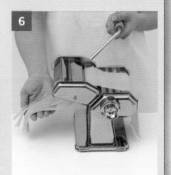

**4.** DUST the sheets with semolina and cover with a clean dry cloth. Let dry a little before you begin to cut them.

**5.** TEST to see if ready to cut: insert your index finger into a fold of pasta and pull slightly. If it tears, it is ready.

**6.** SET the machine to the width required and run each sheet through. Gather the pasta up and shape into "nests."

## ■ ROLLING FRESH PASTA DOUGH BY HAND

Pasta machines are ideal for novice pasta makers, but as you gain in experience you may wish to try rolling the pasta by hand. When properly done, hand-rolled pasta is the best. Rolling by hand requires lots of energy and a large, flat work surface. You will need a very long, thin rolling pin made especially for pasta.

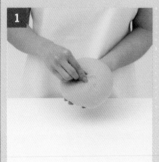

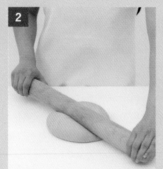

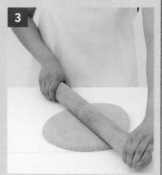

**1.** UNWRAP the pasta and use your fingertips to pull up a "button" on the top. This will keep the center as thick as the edges when you roll.

**2.** PUT the ball of pasta on a large clean work surface. Place the rolling pin on top and begin rolling from the center.

**3.** KEEP ROLLING the pasta by exerting an even pressure along the length of the pin. Give the pasta a quarter-turn from time to time.

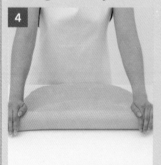

**4.** WRAP around the rolling pin and roll back and forward, running your hands along the pin.

**5.** DUST with semolina or coarsely ground cornmeal and cover with a clean cloth and let dry before you begin to cut it.

**6.** TO TEST to see if the pasta is ready to cut, tear it gently. If it stretches, it is not ready; if it tears, it is ready to cut.

## CUTTING FRESH PASTA DOUGH BY HAND

Cutting ribbon pasta by hand gives it a special "homemade look." Always remember to let the pasta dry a little in a floured cloth before cutting.

**1. PREPARE THE SHEETS** Cut into rectangles measuring about 5 x 6 inches (13 x 15 cm).

**2. RIBBON PASTA** Put the pasta sheets on a work surface dusted with semolina or coarsely ground cornmeal and fold into flat rolls.

**3. TO CUT** Use a sharp knife to cut the ribbon pasta to the desired width. The narrowest ribbons, taglierini or tagliolini, are about $1/4$ inch (5 mm) wide. Tagliatelle (also known as fettuccine) are normally about $1/2$ inch (1 cm) wide, while pappardelle can be up to 1 inch (2.5 cm) in width.

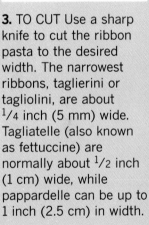

**4. TO UNFOLD** Grasp the ends of the pasta and lift up. Shape into "nests" or lie in flat strips on a floured cloth.

**5. PAPPARDELLE** Finished pappardelle can be quite wide.

# TAGLIOLINI WITH MASCARPONE & EGGS

246

If using homemade pasta, prepare it first. • Put a large pot of salted water to boil over high heat. • Whisk the mascarpone and egg yolks in a large bowl until smooth and creamy • Season with a little salt and the nutmeg. • Cook the tagliolini in the boiling water until al dente, 2–3 minutes. • Pour a little of the pasta water into a large serving dish to warm it, then pour off the water. • Drain the pasta, reserving 1–2 tablespoons of the cooking liquid, and transfer to the serving dish. • Add the mascarpone mixture to the tagliolini, diluting with the cooking water. • Toss gently and serve hot sprinkled with the cheese.

1   recipe homemade tagliolini (see pages 242–5) or 14 ounces (400 g) fresh storebought tagliolini

1   cup (250 g) mascarpone cheese, at room temperature

4   very fresh large egg yolks

    Salt

¼   teaspoon freshly grated nutmeg

½   cup (60 g) freshly grated Parmesan cheese

Serves: 4
Preparation: 10 minutes
    + time to make the pasta
Cooking: 2–3 minutes
Level: 2

You could also use: tagliatelle, spaghetti, linguine, bucatini

# PICI WITH GARLIC SAUCE

248

**Pici:** Mound the flour and salt up on a clean work surface and make a well in the center. Add enough lukewarm water to make a firm dough. Knead until smooth and elastic, 15–20 minutes. Set aside for 30 minutes. • Break off pieces of dough and roll them into thick spaghetti about 8 inches (20 cm) long. Cover with a cloth and leave to dry for at least 1 hour.

**Garlic Sauce:** Pour the oil into a large frying pan over medium heat. Add the garlic and sauté until pale gold, 3–4 minutes. • Add the tomatoes and red pepper flakes and season with salt. Partially cover the pan and simmer over low heat until the garlic has almost dissolved into the sauce, about 45 minutes. Season with salt. • Put a large pot of salted water to boil over high heat. • Cook the pasta in the boiling water until al dente, 3–4 minutes. • Drain well and place in a heated serving bowl. Add the sauce, tossing gently. • Serve hot.

**Pici**

2⅓ cups (350 g) all-purpose (plain) flour

¼ teaspoon salt

Lukewarm water

**Garlic Sauce**

5 tablespoons (75 ml) extra-virgin olive oil

10 cloves garlic, lightly crushed, but whole

2 pounds (1 kg) tomatoes, peeled and finely chopped

½ teaspoon dried red pepper flakes

Salt

Serves: 4
Preparation: 45 minutes
    + 1 hour to dry
Cooking: 1 hour
Level: 3

■ ■ ■ *Pici are a type of thick, homemade spaghetti. They come from southern Tuscany.*

You could also use: tagliatelle, spaghetti, linguine, bucatini, penne

# TAGLIATELLE WITH EGG & MOZZARELLA CHEESE

250

If using homemade pasta, prepare it first. • Put a large pot of salted water to boil over high heat. • Whisk the egg yolks in a small bowl. Add the anchovies and mozzarella and mix well. • Cook the pasta in the boiling water until al dente, about 3–4 minutes. • While the pasta is cooking, melt the butter in a large frying pan. • Drain the pasta, reserving 4 tablespoons of cooking liquid, and add to the pan with the butter. Add the cooking water and the egg mixture and toss gently until the sauce is creamy (the egg should not cook into hard pieces). • Season with pepper and sprinkle with the Parmesan. • Serve hot.

1 recipe homemade tagliatelle (see pages 242–5) or 14 ounces (400 g) fresh storebought tagliatelle

3 large egg yolks

6 salt-cured anchovy fillets

5 ounces (150 g) mozzarella cheese, cut in ½-inch (1-cm) cubes

5 tablespoons (75 g) butter

Salt and freshly ground white pepper

4 tablespoons freshly grated Parmesan cheese

Serves: 4
Preparation: 15 minutes + time to make the pasta
Cooking: 3–4 minutes
Level: 2

You could also use: pappardelle, spaghetti, linguine, bucatini

# CHESTNUT TAGLIATELLE WITH RICOTTA CHEESE

252

**Chestnut Tagliatelle:** Sift both flours and the salt into a mound on a clean work surface. • Whisk the eggs and water in a small bowl. • Make a well in the flour mixture and pour in the egg mixture. Use a fork to gradually incorporate the egg mixture into the flour to make a smooth dough. • Knead the chestnut pasta dough and cut into tagliatelle following the instructions for fresh pasta on pages 242–5.

**Sauce:** Bring 2 cups (500 ml) of milk to a boil in a small saucepan over medium heat. Add the chestnuts and simmer until tender, 45–60 minutes. Drain and chop coarsely in a food processor.
• Combine the remaining 4 cups (1 liter) of milk and enough water to fill a large pan over high heat. Season with salt, cover, and bring to a boil. • Heat the ricotta and cream in a large frying pan over low heat. Season with salt, pepper, and nutmeg and keep warm. • Cook the pasta in the pan of boiling milk and water until al dente, 2–3 minutes. • Drain and add to the pan with the ricotta. Toss gently with most *of the Parmesan and the chestnuts. • Serve hot sprinkled with the remaining Parmesan.

**Chestnut Tagliatelle**

2   cups (300 g) all-purpose (plain) flour

²/₃  cup (100 g) chestnut flour

¹/₄  teaspoon salt

2   large fresh eggs

¹/₄  cup (60 ml) water

**Sauce**

6   cups (1.5 liters) milk

    Salt and freshly ground white pepper

16  dried chestnuts

12  ounces (350 g) fresh ricotta cheese, strained

¹/₂  cup (120 ml) heavy (double) cream

    Freshly grated nutmeg

1¹/₄ cups (150 g) freshly grated Parmesan cheese

Serves: 4
Preparation: 30 minutes
  + time to make the pasta
Cooking: 55–70 minutes
Level: 3

You could also use: tagliatelle, spinach tagliatelle

# TAGLIATELLE WITH ROASTED TOMATO SAUCE

254

If using homemade pasta, prepare it first. • Preheat the oven to 400°F (200°C/gas 6). • Put a large pot of salted water to boil over high heat. • Place the tomatoes in a baking dish. Season with salt and pepper and drizzle with 3 tablespoons of the oil. • Bake until softened and just beginning to brown, 15–20 minutes. • Cook the pasta in the salted boiling water until al dente, 3–4 minutes. • Drain well and place in a heated serving dish. • Tip the tomatoes into the dish over the pasta. Add the garlic, remaining 3 tablespoons of oil, and basil. • Toss gently, garnish with the whole basil leaves, and serve hot.

| | |
|---|---|
| 1 | recipe homemade tagliatelle (see pages 242–5) or 14 ounces (400 g) fresh storebought tagliatelle |
| 2 | pounds (1 kg) cherry tomatoes |
| | Salt and freshly ground black pepper |
| 6 | tablespoons (90 ml) extra-virgin olive oil |
| 2 | cloves garlic, finely chopped |
| 1 | tablespoon finely chopped basil + extra leaves to garnish |

Serves: 4
Preparation: 15 minutes
   + time to prepare the
   pasta
Cooking: 20–25 minutes
Level: 2

You could also use: tagliolini, spaghetti, linguine, penne, fusilli

# TAGLIATELLE WITH FRESH TOMATO & ANCHOVY SAUCE

256

If using homemade pasta, prepare it first. • Put a large pot of salted water to boil over high heat.
• Heat the oil in a small saucepan over medium heat and add the anchovies. Mash with a fork until dissolved in the oil. Remove from the heat.
• Combine the cherry tomatoes in a bowl with the garlic, basil, and chile. • Cook the pasta in the boiling water until al dente, 3–4 minutes. • Drain well and transfer to a serving bowl. Add the tomato mixture and mozzarella, then pour the anchovy-flavored oil over the top. Season with pepper.
• Toss gently and serve hot.

1   recipe homemade tagliatelle (see pages 242–5) or 14 ounces (400 g) fresh storebought tagliatelle

1/4   cup (60 ml) extra-virgin olive oil

6   salt-cured anchovy fillets

24   cherry tomatoes, halved

2   cloves garlic, finely chopped

2   tablespoons finely chopped fresh basil

1   red or green chile, seeded and finley chopped

8   ounces (250 g) mozzarella cheese, cut in small cubes

Freshly ground black pepper

Serves: 4
Preparation: 20 minutes + time to make the pasta
Cooking: 5–7 minutes
Level: 2

You could also use: fresh farfalle, spaghetti, linguine, rigatoni

# WHOLE-WHEAT TAGLIATELLE WITH ARUGULA & SUN-DRIED TOMATOES

**Whole-Wheat Tagliatelle:** Sift both flours into a mound on a clean work surface. • Whisk the eggs in a small bowl. • Make a well in the flour mixture and pour in the egg mixture. Use a fork to gradually incorporate the egg mixture into the flour to make a smooth dough. • Knead the whole-wheat pasta dough and cut into tagliatelle following the instructions for fresh pasta on pages 242–5.

**Arugula & Sun-Dried Tomato Sauce:** Put a large pot of salted water to boil over high heat. • Put the sun-dried tomatoes in a large bowl with the hot water. Soak until softened, 10 minutes. Drain well and coarsely chop. • Mix the arugula, tomatoes, garlic, basil, olives, oil, salt, and pepper in a bowl. • Cook the pasta in the boiling water until al dente, 3–4 minutes. • Drain the pasta and transfer to a heated serving bowl. • Add the arugula mixture, toss gently, and serve hot.

**Whole-Wheat Tagliatelle**

1⅓ cups (200 g) whole-wheat (wholemeal) flour

1⅓ cups (200 g) all-purpose (plain) flour

4 large fresh eggs

**Arugula & Sun-Dried Tomato Sauce**

12 sun-dried tomatoes

1 cup (250 ml) hot water

2 cup (100 g) arugula (rocket), coarsely chopped

2 cloves garlic, finely chopped

20 leaves fresh basil, torn

1 cup (100 g) black olives, pitted (stoned) and lightly crushed

4 tablespoons (60 ml) extra-virgin olive oil

Salt and freshly ground black pepper

Serves: 4
Preparation: 15 minutes
+ 10 minutes to stand +
time to make the pasta
Cooking: 3–4 minutes
Level: 2

You could also use: spinach tagliatelle, tagliatelle, spaghetti, fusilli, penne

# TAGLIATELLE WITH ASPARAGUS & EGG

260

If using homemade pasta, prepare it first. • Put a large pot of salted water to boil over high heat. • Separate the lower part of the asparagus stalks from the tender tips and cut the stalks into thick rounds. • Heat the oil in a large frying pan over medium-high heat and sauté the pancetta, until golden, about 5 minutes. • Add the asparagus stalks and sauté for 3–4 minutes. • Season with salt and pepper and pour in half the stock. Simmer over low heat for 5 minutes. • Add the asparagus tips and simmer until tender, 3–4 minutes. • Cook the pasta in the boiling water until al dente, 3–4 minutes. • Drain well and add to the pan with the asparagus. Increase the heat and add the egg yolks and remaining stock, gently tossing all the time so that no lumps form. • Sprinkle with the Parmesan and mint and season with white pepper. • Serve immediately.

1   recipe homemade tagliatelle (see pages 242–5) or 14 ounces (400 g) fresh storebought tagliatelle

1   pound (500 g) tender asparagus stalks

3   tablespoons extra-virgin olive oil

8   ounces (250 g) pancetta, thickly sliced, then cut in thin strips

    Salt and freshly ground white pepper

3/4 cup (180 ml) beef stock (see page 48)

3   large egg yolks

1   cup (125 g) freshly grated Parmesan cheese

1   tablespoon fresh mint to garnish

Serves: 4
Preparation: 20 minutes + time to make the pasta
Cooking: 20–25 minutes
Level: 2

You could also use: pappadelle, stracci, bucatini

# TAGLIATELLE WITH HAM & CURRY

262

If using homemade pasta, prepare it first. • Put a large pot of salted water to boil over high heat. • Melt the butter in a large frying pan over low heat. Add the onion and a pinch of salt. Cover and simmer until caramelized, about 20 minutes. • Add the garlic and ham and sauté over medium heat until the garlic is pale gold. • Add the curry powder and stir for 2 minutes. • Stir in the almonds and simmer for 2 minutes. • Pour in the cream. Bring to a boil, season with salt, and turn off the heat. • Meanwhile, cook the pasta in the boiling water until al dente, 3–4 minutes. • Drain the pasta and add to the pan with the sauce. Toss gently for 1 minute. • Serve immediately.

| | |
|---|---|
| 1 | recipe homemade tagliatelle (see pages 242–5) or 14 ounces (400 g) fresh storebought tagliatelle |
| 2 | tablespoons butter |
| 2 | medium onions, finely chopped |
| | Salt |
| 1 | clove garlic, finely chopped |
| 1 | cup (120 g) ham, cut in small cubes |
| 1–2 | tablespoons hot curry powder |
| 15 | almonds, peeled and coarsely chopped |
| 3/4 | cup (180 ml) heavy (double) cream |

Serves: 4
Preparation: 30 minutes + time to make the pasta
Cooking: 35 minutes
Level: 2

■ ■ ■ *If you like spicy food, add more curry powder or some crumbled dried chiles to the sauce.*

You could also use: fresh farfalle, spaghetti, linguine, penne

# TAGLIATELLE WITH SALAMI

If using homemade pasta, prepare it first. • Heat the oil in a large frying pan over medium heat. Add the onion and sauté until softened, 3–4 minutes. • Add the salami and sauté over high heat for 30 seconds. • Pour in the wine and cook until evaporated. • Stir in the tomatoes. Season with salt, partially cover, and simmer over low heat for 20 minutes. • Put a large pot of salted water to boil over high heat. • Cook the pasta in the boiling water until al dente, 3–4 minutes. • Add the provolone to the salami mixture in the pan so that it melts slightly. • Drain the pasta and add to the pan with the salami. Toss gently for 1 minute, then turn off the heat. Sprinkle with the parsley and Parmesan. • Serve hot.

1    recipe homemade tagliatelle (see pages 242–5) or 14 ounces (400 g) fresh storebought tagliatelle

1/4  cup (60 ml) extra-virgin olive oil

1    large onion, thinly sliced

5    ounces (150 g) salami, thickly sliced and cut in strips

1/4  cup (60 ml) dry white wine

1    pound (500 g) tomatoes, peeled and chopped

     Salt

4    ounces (120 g) provolone cheese, cut in strips

1    tablespoon finely chopped fresh parsley

4    tablespoons freshly grated Parmesan cheese

Serves: 4
Preparation: 30 minutes
+ time to make the pasta
Cooking: 35–40 minutes
Level: 2

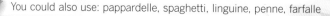

You could also use: pappardelle, spaghetti, linguine, penne, farfalle

# TAGLIATELLE WITH SHRIMP & GARLIC SAUCE

If using homemade pasta, prepare it first. • Put a large pot of salted water to boil over high heat. • Place the garlic in a small saucepan with 1/4 cup (60 ml) of milk. Bring to a boil and then strain, discarding the milk. Repeat twice more with the remaining milk and the same garlic. Discard the milk. Set aside in a small bowl. • Place the garlic in a food processor with 5 tablespoons (75 ml) of oil and chop until smooth. • Place the water in a small saucepan over low heat. Add the anchovies and stir until dissolved. Add the 2 tablespoons of oil, and chop in a food processor until smooth. • Heat the remaining 1 tablespoon of oil in a large frying pan over high heat. Add the shrimp and sauté until pink and cooked, 2–3 minutes. Season with salt and keep warm. • Cook the pasta in the boiling water until al dente, 3–4 minutes. • Drain the pasta and add to the pan with the shrimp. Add the garlic sauce. Toss gently. • Transfer to four serving bowls. Spoon the anchovy sauce over the top and garnish with the parsley and basil. • Serve immediately.

| | |
|---|---|
| 1 | recipe homemade tagliatelle (see pages 242–5) or 14 ounces (400 g) fresh storebought tagliatelle |
| 8 | ounces (250 g) garlic, peeled |
| 3/4 | cup (200 ml) milk |
| 8 | tablespoons (120 ml) extra-virgin olive oil |
| 1 | tablespooon water |
| 12 | salt-cured anchovy fillets |
| 8 | ounces (250 g) small shrimp (prawns), peeled and deveined |
| 1 | tablespoon finely chopped fresh parsley |
| | Fresh basil leaves, torn |
| | Salt |

Serves: 4
Preparation: 45 minutes
  + time to make the pasta
Cooking: 20–30 minutes
Level: 2

You could also use: maltagliati, stracci, linguine, farfalle

# TAGLIATELLE
# WITH MUSSELS

If using homemade pasta, prepare it first. • Soak the mussels in a large bowl of warm salted water for 1 hour. Scrub well, removing any beards. • Pour $^1/_2$ cup (120 ml) of the wine into a large saucepan and add the mussels. Cover and cook over high heat, shaking the pot occasionally, until they open up, 5–10 minutes. Discard any that do not open. • Let the mussels cool a little then remove from the shells. • Heat the oil in a large frying pan over medium heat. Add the garlic, chile, and parsley and sauté until softened, 2–3 minutes. • Pour in the remaining $^1/_4$ cup (60 ml) of wine, and simmer until it evaporates. • Stir in the tomatoes and simmer over medium heat until the tomatoes have broken down, about 20 minutes. • Season with salt and add the shelled mussels. • Cook the pasta in the boiling water until al dente, 3–4 minutes. • Drain and transfer to a serving dish. Add the mussel sauce and toss well. • Serve hot.

1   recipe homemade tagliatelle (see pages 242–5) or 14 ounces (400 g) fresh storebought tagliatelle

4   pounds (2 kg) mussels, in shell

$^3/_4$   cup (180 ml) dry white wine

$^1/_4$   cup (60 ml) extra-virgin olive oil

2   cloves garlic, finely chopped

1   fresh red chile, seeded and finely chopped

1   tablespoon finely chopped fresh parsley

3   pounds (1.5 kg) tomatoes, peeled and coarsely chopped

Salt

Serves: 4
Preparation: 30 minutes + 1 hour to soak the mussels + time for the pasta
Cooking: 35–40 minutes
Level: 3

You could also use: maltagliati, linguine, conchiglie, rigatoni

# TAGLIATELLE WITH SCAMPI

If using homemade pasta, prepare it first. • Peel the scampi and devein them. Remove the heads (and reserve them). Cut the meat in small cubes. • Place the heads in a large saucepan with plenty of cold water, season with salt, and bring to a boil. Simmer, uncovered, over medium heat for 30 minutes. Strain, discarding the heads and reserve the stock to cook the pasta. • Melt 2 tablespoons of butter in a large frying pan over medium heat. Add the garlic and scampi and sauté for 2–3 minutes. • Pour in the wine and cook until evaporated. • Add the cream and tarragon and cook for 2 minutes. Discard the garlic. • Meanwhile, cook the pasta in the boiling stock until al dente, 3–4 minutes. • Drain well and add to the pan with the scampi. Add the remaining 2 tablespoons of butter and 4 tablespoons (60 ml) of the stock in which the pasta was cooked. Toss gently for 1 minute, then turn off heat. Sprinkle with the parsley. • Serve hot.

1   recipe homemade tagliatelle (see pages 242–5) or 14 ounces (400 g) fresh storebought tagliatelle

2   pounds (1 kg) scampi (Dublin Bay prawns)

Salt and freshly ground white pepper

4   tablespoons (60 g) butter

1   clove garlic, whole but crushed with the blade of a knife

¼   cup (60 ml) dry white wine

½   cup (120 ml) heavy (double) cream

1   tablespoon finely chopped fresh tarragon

1   tablespoon finely chopped fresh parsley

Serves 4
Preparation: 1 hour + time to make the pasta
Cooking: 50 minutes
Level: 2

You could also use: pappardelle, fresh farfalle, rigatoni

# TAGLIATELLE WITH DUCK & VEGETABLES

272

If using homemade pasta, prepare it first. • Put a large pot of salted water to boil over high heat. • Bring a small pan of salted water to a boil and blanch the carrots for 2 minutes. Drain and cool in a bowl of cold water and ice. Separately blanch and cool the leek, celery, and onions in the same way. • Heat the oil in a large frying pan over medium heat and sauté the shallot and ginger until softened, 3–4 minutes. Add half the sherry and simmer until evaporated. • Add the mushrooms and sauté until softened, about 5 minutes. Stir in the blanched vegetables. Cook for 3 minutes more, then stir in the Swiss chard and half the stock. Cook over high heat for 2 minutes. • Lightly flour the pieces of duck. • Melt the butter in a large frying pan over high heat and sauté the duck for 1 minute. Season with salt and pepper. Pour in the remaining 1/4 cup (60 ml) of sherry and cook until evaporated. • Add the duck to the vegetables. • Stir the cornstarch into the remaining stock in a small bowl and pour into the pan. Bring the sauce to a boil, then turn off the heat.• Meanwhile, cook the pasta in the boiling water until al dente, about 4–5 minutes. • Drain well and add to the pan with the sauce. Toss gently for 1 minute, adding a little cooking water if needed. Sprinkle with the parsley. • Serve hot.

| | |
|---|---|
| 1 | recipe homemade tagliatelle (see pages 242–5) or 14 ounces (400 g) fresh storebought tagliatelle |
| 2 | carrots, cut in julienne strips (matchsticks) |
| 1 | leek, cut in julienne strips (matchsticks) |
| 2 | stalks celery, cut in julienne strips (matchsticks) |
| 2 | baby onions, sliced |
| 4 | tablespoons (60 ml) extra-virgin olive oil |
| 1 | shallot, finely chopped |
| 1 | tablespoon finely chopped fresh ginger |
| 1/2 | cup (125 ml) sherry |
| 6 | champignons, sliced |
| 1 | bunch Swiss chard, sliced |
| 2 | cups (500 ml) chicken or vegetable stock |
| 1 | boneless, skinless duck breast, cut in thin strips |
| 2 | tablespoons all-purpose (plain) flour |
| 1 | tablespoon cornstarch (cornflour) |
| 3 | tablespoons butter |
| | Salt and freshly ground black pepper |
| 2 | tablespoons finely chopped fresh parsley |

Serves: 4–6
Preparation: 1 hour + time
  to make the pasta
Cooking: 45 minutes
Level: 3

You could also use: maltagliati, fresh farfalle

# SICILIAN PAPPARDELLE

274

If using homemade pasta, prepare it first. • Heat the oil in a large frying pan over medium heat. Add the pork and beef and sauté until browned, 5–8 minutes. • Add the tomato paste and wine. Simmer for 4–5 minutes, then add the tomatoes and season with salt and pepper. Partially cover the pan and simmer over low heat for 40 minutes. • Put a large pot of salted water over high heat to boil. Cook the pappardelle in the boiling water until al dente, 3–5 minutes. • While the pasta is cooking, use a fork to break the ricotta salata into small, crumbly pieces. • When the pasta is nearly done, mix the fresh ricotta with 2 tablespoons of the cooking water in a large, heated serving dish. • Drain the pasta and toss carefully with the fresh ricotta and meat sauce. • Sprinkle with the ricotta salata and pecorino, toss gently, and serve hot.

1 recipe homemade papparelle (see pages 242–5) or 14 ounces (400 g) fresh storebought pappardelle

¼ cup (60 ml) extra-virgin olive oil

8 ounces (250 g) ground (minced) pork

8 ounces (250 g) ground (minced) beef

2 tablespoons tomato paste (concentrate)

½ cup (125 ml) dry white or dry red wine

1 (14-ounce/400-g) can tomatoes, with juice

Salt and freshly ground black pepper

3 ounces (90 g) ricotta salata cheese

8 ounces (250 g) fresh ricotta cheese, drained

½ cup (60 g) freshly grated pecorino cheese

Serves: 4
Preparation: 10 minutes
+ time to make pasta
Cooking: 1 hour
Level: 2

You could also use: tagliatelle, rigatoni, farfalle

# SPINACH TAGLIATELLE WITH CHERRY TOMATOES & MOZZARELLA

276

**Spinach Tagliatelle: Step 1:** Sift the flour onto a clean work surface and shape into a mound. Make a well in the center of the mound. • **Step 2:** Use a fork to beat the eggs and spinach purée in a small bowl. Pour into the well in the flour. • **Step 3:** Use the fork to incorporate the spinach mixture into the flour. When all the flour has been absorbed, gather into a ball with your hands. • **Step 4:** Knead the spinach pasta dough until smooth and silky, 10–15 minutes. • **Step 5:** Wrap in plastic wrap (cling film) and let rest at room temperature for 30 minutes. • **Step 6:** Roll the pasta into sheets with a pasta machine or by hand. Cut into tagliatelle following the instructions on pages 244-245.
**Sauce:** Bring a large pan of salted water to a boil over high heat. • Heat the oil in a small saucepan and add the anchovies. Mash with a fork until dissolved in the oil. Remove from the heat. • Combine in a bowl with the garlic, parsley, and basil. • Cook the pasta in the boiling water until al dente, 3–4 minutes. • Drain and transfer to a serving bowl. Add the tomato mixture and bocconcini, then pour the flavored oil over the top. Season with salt and pepper. • Toss gently and serve hot.

■ ■ ■ *For spinach, Swiss chard, bell pepper, carrot, or beet pasta, cook the vegetable in lightly salted water until just tender then chop in a food processor until smooth. For tomato pasta use ready-made tomato paste (concentrate).*

**Spinach Tagliatelle**

2⅓ cups (350 g) all-purpose (plain) flour
3 large fresh eggs
½ cup (50 g) spinach purée

**Sauce**

¼ cup (60 ml) extra-virgin olive oil
20 cherry tomatoes, halved
1 clove garlic, finely chopped
1 tablespoon finely chopped fresh parsley
1 tablespoon finely chopped fresh basil
8 ounces (250 g) bocconcini (mozzarella cheese balls)
Salt and freshly ground black pepper

Serves: 4
Preparation: 25 minute + time to make pasta
Cooking: 5 minutes
Level: 1

## ■ PREPARING COLORED & AROMATIC FRESH PASTA

Colored fresh pasta can be made by adding purées of spinach, Swiss chard, tomato, bell pepper (capsicum), carrot, beet (beetroot), or herbs. You can also make striking black pasta using squid's ink. Remember that the coloring agent will add extra flavor; be sure that your sauce does not clash with or override this flavor.

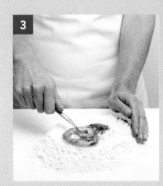

**1.** SIFT the flour onto a clean work surface and shape into a mound. Make a well in the center of the mound.

**2.** USE a fork to beat the eggs and spinach purée in a small bowl. Pour into the well in the flour.

**3.** USE the fork to incorporate the spinach mixture into the flour. When all the flour has been absorbed, gather into a ball with your hands.

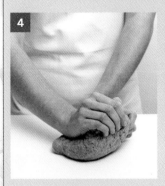

**4.** KNEAD the spinach pasta dough until smooth and silky, 10–15 minutes.

**5.** WRAP in plastic wrap (cling film) and let rest at room temperature for 30 minutes.

**6.** ROLL the pasta into sheets with a pasta machine or by hand. Cut into tagliatelle.

# PAGLIA & FIENO WITH GORGONZOLA

280

Prepare the pasta. • Put a large pot of salted water to boil over high heat.

**Sauce:** Melt the butter in a medium saucepan over low heat. Add the Gorgonzola and cream. Season with salt and pepper. Cook over low heat, stirring constantly, until the cheese has melted. • Cook the pasta in the boiling water until al dente, 2–3 minutes. • Drain the pasta and transfer to a heated serving dish. Add the Gorgonzola sauce, mixing carefully with two forks. • Sprinkle with the Parmesan, garnish with parsley, and serve hot.

**Pasta**

½ recipe plain fresh tagliatelle (see pages 242–5)

½ recipe spinach tagliatelle (see pages 276–7)

**Sauce**

¼ cup (60 g) butter

8 ounces (250 g) Gorgonzola cheese, cut into small cubes

⅔ cup (150 ml) heavy (double) cream

Salt and freshly ground white pepper

4 tablespoons freshly grated Parmesan cheese

Fresh parsley, to garnish

Serves: 4
Preparation: 10 minutes
+ time to prepare the pasta
Cooking: 10 minutes
Level: 2

You could also use: tagliatelle, maltagliati

# SPINACH TAGLIATELLE WITH CREAM & HAM

282

If using homemade pasta, prepare it first. • Put a large pot of salted water to boil over high heat. • Melt the butter in a large frying pan over medium heat. Add the ham and sauté until crisp, about 5 minutes. • Pour in the cream and simmer until thickened, about 5 minutes. • Season with salt, pepper, and nutmeg. • Cook the pasta in the boiling water until al dente, 3–4 minutes. • Drain and add to the pan with the sauce. Toss gently until the pasta is well flavored with the sauce. • Sprinkle with the Parmesan and serve hot.

| | |
|---|---|
| 1 | recipe homemade spinach tagliatelle (see pages 276–7) or 14 ounces (400 g) fresh storebought spinach tagliatelle |
| ¼ | cup (60 g) butter |
| 1 | cup (120 g) ham, cut into thin strips |
| ¾ | cup (200 ml) heavy (double) cream |
| | Salt and freshly ground white pepper |
| ¼ | teaspoon freshly grated nutmeg |
| ½ | cup (60 g) freshly grated Parmesan cheese |

Serves: 4
Preparation: 15 minutes
  + time to make pasta
Cooking: 15 minutes
Level: 2

You could also use: tagliatelle, pappardelle, stracci

# ROMAN FETTUCCINE

1   recipe homemade spinach tagliatelle (see pages 276–7) or 14 ounces (400 g) fresh storebought spinach tagliatelle

¼   cup (60 ml) extra-virgin olive oil

1   onion, finely chopped

1   carrot, finely chopped

1   stalk celery, finely chopped

8   ounces (250 g) lean ground (minced) beef

⅓   cup (90 ml) dry red wine

4   ounces (120 g) chicken livers, trimmed and diced

2   cups (400 g) tomato passata (purée)

½   ounce (15 g) dried porcini mushrooms, soaked in warm water for 15 minutes and finely chopped

1   bay leaf

    Salt and freshly ground black pepper

1   cup (120 g) freshly grated Parmesan cheese

1–2 tablespoons butter

284

If using homemade pasta, prepare it first. • Heat the oil in a large saucepan over medium heat. Add the onion, carrot, and celery and sauté until softened, 3–4 minutes. • Stir in the beef and sauté until browned all over, about 5 minutes. • Pour in the wine and cook until it has evaporated, 3–4 minutes. • Add the chicken livers and simmer over low heat for 15 minutes. • Add the tomatoes, mushrooms, and bay leaf and season with salt and pepper. Cover and simmer over low heat for at least 1 hour. • Put a large pot of salted water to boil over high heat. • Cook the pasta in the boiling water until al dente, 3–4 minutes. • Drain and add to the sauce. Sprinkle with the Parmesan, dot with the butter, toss well, and serve hot.

Serves: 4
Preparation: 30 minutes + time to make pasta
Cooking: 1 hour 30 minutes
Level: 2

You could also use: pappardelle, orecchiette, potato gnocchi, rigatoni

# SPICY TAGLIATELLE WITH CREAMY EGGPLANT SAUCE

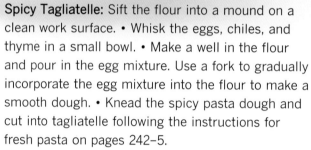

**Spicy Tagliatelle:** Sift the flour into a mound on a clean work surface. • Whisk the eggs, chiles, and thyme in a small bowl. • Make a well in the flour and pour in the egg mixture. Use a fork to gradually incorporate the egg mixture into the flour to make a smooth dough. • Knead the spicy pasta dough and cut into tagliatelle following the instructions for fresh pasta on pages 242–5.

**Creamy Eggplant Sauce:** Peel the eggplants and chop into 1 inch (2.5 cm) cubes. Boil in lightly salted water for 4 minutes. Drain, squeezing out the excess moisture. • Put a large pot of salted water to boil over high heat. • Heat the oil in a large frying pan over medium heat. Add the garlic and thyme and sauté for 2 minutes. • Add the eggplant and cook for 6–7 minutes, mashing gently with a fork. • Remove from the heat, add half the basil, and season with salt and pepper. Chop in a food processor until smooth. • Return the eggplant cream to the pan and add the tomatoes. Cook until the tomatoes have broken down and the sauce is creamy. • Cook the pasta in the boiling water until al dente, about 3–4 minutes. • Drain the pasta and add to the pan with the sauce. Add 2–3 tablespoons of cooking water, sprinkle with the cheese and remaining basil, and toss gently. • Serve hot.

**Spicy Tagliatelle**

- 2²/₃ cups (400 g) all-purpose (plain) flour
- 4 very fresh large eggs
- 2 dried chiles, crumbled
- 1 teaspoon finely chopped fresh thyme

**Creamy Eggplant Sauce**

- 3 medium eggplants (aubergines)
- 1/₃ cup (90 ml) extra-virgin olive oil
- 2 cloves garlic, finely chopped
- 1 tablespoon finely chopped fresh thyme
- 15 leaves fresh basil, torn
   Salt and freshly ground white pepper
- 3 large tomatoes, peeled, and finely chopped
- 6 tablespoons freshly grated pecorino romano cheese

Serves: 4
Preparation: 30 minutes
   + time to make the pasta
Cooking: 30 minutes
Level: 3

You could also use: tagliatelle, orecchiette

# BORAGE FETTUCCINE
# WITH BUTTER & CHEESE

**Borage Fettuccine:** Bring 1 quart (1 liter) of water to a boil in a saucepan with a generous pinch of salt and cook the borage until tender, about 20 minutes. Drain and let cool. • Chop the borage in a food processor until very fine, then strain it. Place in a clean cloth and squeeze well to eliminate excess moisture. • Beat the eggs in a bowl with a fork then mix in the borage. • Sift the flour onto a clean work surface and shape into a mound. Make a well in the center of the mound. Pour the egg mixture into the well in the flour. Use a fork to stir until the flour is incorporated. • Knead until smooth and silky, 10–15 minutes. Wrap in plastic wrap (cling film) and let rest at room temperature for 30 minutes. • Divide the dough into four pieces and roll through the pasta machine or by hand until very thin. • Cut the pasta into fettuccine about 1/2 inch (1 cm) wide. Let dry on a lightly floured cloth for 30 minutes. • Put a large pot of salted water to boil over high heat. • Cook the pasta in the boiling water until al dente, 1–2 minutes.

**Sauce:** While the pasta is cooking, melt the butter over medium heat until pale golden brown. • Drain the pasta and transfer to a heated serving dish. Drizzle with the butter, sprinkle with the Parmesan, and toss gently. • Serve hot.

**Pasta**

Salt

12 ounces (350 g) borage leaves

3 very fresh large eggs

2 cups (300 g) all-purpose (plain) flour

**Sauce**

1/2 cup (120 g) butter

1 cup (120 g) freshly grated Parmesan cheese

Serves: 4
Preparation: 1 hour
  + 1 hour to rest the
  pasta
Cooking: 25 minutes
Level: 3

You could also use: tagliatelle, spinach tagliatelle

# LEMON TAGLIATELLE WITH SUN-DRIED TOMATO SAUCE

**Lemon Tagliatelle:** Sift the flour into a mound on a clean work surface. • Whisk the eggs, lemon juice, and lemon zest in a small bowl. • Make a well in the flour and pour in the egg mixture. Use a fork to gradually incorporate the egg mixture into the flour to make a smooth dough. • Knead the lemon pasta dough and cut into tagliatelle following the instructions for fresh pasta on pages 242–5.

**Sun-Dried Tomato Sauce:** Place the sun-dried tomatoes in a small bowl with the vinegar and water. Soak for 15 minutes, stirring occasionally. • Put a large pot of salted water to boil over high heat. • Drain the tomatoes, squeezing out the moisture. Finely chop with a knife or in a food processor, leaving a few whole or coarsely chopped to garnish. • Place in a serving dish and add the lemon juice and zest and the oil. Season with salt and pepper—not too much salt, because the tomatoes will already be fairly salty. Taste first. • Cook the pasta in the boiling water until al dente, about 2–3 minutes. • Drain well and add to the serving dish with the sauce. • Toss gently and garnish with the whole or coarsely chopped tomatoes. • Serve immediately.

**Pasta**

2   cups (300 g) all-purpose (plain) flour

3   very fresh large eggs

2   tablespoons freshly squeezed lemon juice

2   tablespoons finely grated organic lemon zest

**Sun-Dried Tomato Sauce**

5   ounces (150 g) sun-dried tomatoes

2   tablespoons white wine vinegar

2–3 tablespoons water

Freshly squeezed juice and zest of ½ organic lemon (zest should be cut into a long, thin length)

4   tablespoons (60 ml) extra-virgin olive oil

Salt and freshly ground white pepper

Serves: 4
Preparation: 30 minutes + time to make the pasta
Cooking: 2–3 minutes
Level: 3

You could also use: tagliatelle, spaghetti, linguine

# BASIL TAGLIATELLE WITH VEGETABLE SAUCE

292

**Basil Tagliatelle:** Sift the flour into a mound on a clean work surface. • Whisk the eggs and basil in a small bowl. • Make a well in the flour and pour in the egg mixture. Use a fork to gradually incorporate the egg mixture into the flour to make a smooth dough. • Knead the basil pasta dough and cut into tagliatelle following the instructions for fresh pasta on pages 242–5.

**Vegetable Sauce:** Put a large pot of salted water to boil over high heat. • Heat the butter in a large frying pan over high heat. Add the zucchini, carrots, and shallots and sauté for 3 minutes. • Pour with the wine and simmer until evaporated. • Add the cream and stock. Simmer until the vegetables are tender-crunchy, and the sauce has thickened slightly, about 5 minutes. Season with salt and white pepper. • Cook the pasta in the boiling water until al dente. • Drain well and add to the pan with the sauce. • Toss gently, sprinkle with Parmesan, and serve hot.

**Basil Tagliatelle**

2⅓ cups (350 g) all-purpose (plain) flour

3   very fresh large eggs

1   cup (50 g) minced fresh basil

**Vegetable Sauce**

2   tablespoons butter

2   zucchini (courgettes), cut in julienne strips (matchsticks)

2   carrots, cut in julienne strips (matchsticks)

2   shallots, cut in julienne strips (matchsticks)

½   cup (125 ml) dry white wine

½   cup (125 ml) heavy (double) cream

½   cup (125 ml) vegetable stock

Salt and freshly ground white pepper

Freshly grated Parmesan cheese

Serves: 4
Preparation: 40 minutes
+ time to prepare the pasta
Cooking: 20 minutes
Level: 3

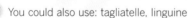

You could also use: tagliatelle, linguine

# BEET TAGLIATELLE WITH BLACK OLIVE SAUCE

294

**Beet Tagliatelle:** Sift the flour into a mound on a clean work surface. • Whisk the eggs and beets in a small bowl. • Make a well in the flour and pour in the egg mixture. Use a fork to gradually incorporate the egg mixture into the flour to make a smooth dough. • Knead the beet pasta dough and cut into tagliatelle following the instructions for fresh pasta on pages 242–5.

**Black Olive Sauce:** Put a large pot of salted water to boil over high heat. • Heat the oil and butter in a large frying pan over medium heat. Add the olives and chile. Season with salt. Sauté for 4–5 minutes. • Cook the pasta in the boiling water until al dente, 3–4 minutes. • Drain well and add to the pan with the olive sauce. Toss gently, adding 1–2 tablespoons of cooking water, if needed. • Remove from heat and sprinkle with the Parmesan. Serve hot garnished with the basil.

### Beet Tagliatelle

- 2¹⁄₃ cups (350 g) all-purpose (plain) flour
- 3 very fresh large eggs
- ¹⁄₃ cup (50 g) cooked beets (beetroot), finely chopped or mashed

### Black Olive Sauce

- 3 tablespoons extra-virgin olive oil
- 2 tablespoons butter
- 14 ounces (400 g) black olives, pitted and coarsely chopped
- 1 small fresh chile, seeded and finely chopped

  Salt

- 1 cup (125 g) freshly grated Parmesan cheese

  Fresh basil leaves

Serves: 4
Preparation: 45 minutes + time to make the pasta
Cooking: 10 minutes
Level: 3

You could also use: tagliatelle, maltagliati

# NETTLE TAGLIATELLE WITH GOAT CHEESE

296

**Nettle Tagliatelle:** Cook the nettles in a large pan of salted water for 4 minutes. Drain well, let cool, and chop finely with a knife. • Sift the flour into a mound on a clean work surface. • Whisk the eggs and half the chopped nettles in a small bowl. • Make a well in the flour and pour in the egg mixture. Use a fork to gradually incorporate the egg mixture into the flour to make a smooth dough. • Knead the nettle pasta dough and cut into tagliatelle following the instructions for fresh pasta on pages 242–5.

**Sauce:** Put a large pot of salted water to boil over high heat. • Heat the oil in a large frying pan over low heat. Add the onion and simmer for 15 minutes, adding a little water if necessary. • Add the garlic and remaining cooked nettles and season with salt and pepper. Simmer for 5 minutes. • Mash the goat cheese with the cream in a small bowl with a fork. • Cook the pasta in the boiling water until al dente, 3–4 minutes. • Drain well and add to the pan with the sauce. Toss gently for 1 minute, adding a little cooking water to make the sauce creamy, if necessary. • Spoon the goat's cheese over the top and turn off heat. • Serve hot.

**Nettle Tagliatelle**

| | |
|---|---|
| 14 | ounces (400 g) nettles |
| 3 | cups (450 g) all-purpose (plain) flour |
| 4 | very fresh large eggs |

**Sauce**

| | |
|---|---|
| 3 | tablespoons extra-virgin olive oil |
| ½ | onion, finely chopped |
| 1 | clove garlic, finely chopped |
| | Salt and freshly ground white pepper |
| 4 | ounces (125 g) fresh creamy goat cheese |
| 4 | tablespoons (60 ml) double (heavy) cream |

Serves: 4–6
Preparation: 45 minutes
+ time to make the pasta
Cooking: 20–30 minutes
Level: 3

You could also use: tagliatelle

# SPINACH TAGLIATELLE WITH SEAFOOD & EGG

298

If using homemade pasta, prepare it first. • Soak the mussels and clams in a large bowl of cold water for 1 hour. • Put a large pot of salted water to boil over high heat. • Rinse the shellfish thoroughly and scrub the beards off the mussels with a wire brush. Discard any that are open or broken. • To open the shellfish, place in a large frying pan with the wine over high heat. Cook until they have opened. Discard any that do not open. • Remove the mollusks from their shells (leave a few in the shell to garnish). • Strain the liquid remaining in the pan and reserve. • Heat the oil in the same frying pan over medium heat and sauté the garlic, shrimp tails, and parsley for 3 minutes. Turn off the heat. • Beat the egg yolks in a serving dish and season with salt and pepper. Add 2 tablespoons of the reserved cooking liquid. • Cook the pasta in the boiling water until al dente, 3–4 minutes. • Drain well and add to the pan with the seafood. Toss gently for 1–2 minutes over medium heat then transfer to the serving dish with the egg yolks. • Toss gently until the sauce is creamy. Season with a little more pepper, if liked. • Serve hot.

1 recipe homemade spinach tagliatelle (see pages 276–7) or 14 ounces (400 g) fresh storebought spinach tagliatelle

3 pounds (1.5 kg) mixed mussels and clams, in shell

½ cup (125 ml) dry white wine

4 tablespoons (60 ml) extra-virgin olive oil

3 cloves garlic, finely chopped

8 ounces (250 g) shrimp tails

2 tablespoons finely chopped fresh parsley

3 large egg yolks

Salt and freshly ground black pepper

Serves: 4
Preparation: 45 minutes + 1 hour to soak the seafood + time to prepare the pasta
Cooking: 20 minutes
Level: 3

You could also use: tagliatelle, bucatini

# SQUID INK TAGLIATELLE WITH SHRIMP

**Squid Ink Tagliatelle:** Sift the flour into a mound on a clean work surface. • Whisk the eggs and squid ink in a small bowl. • Make a well in the flour and pour in the egg mixture. Use a fork to gradually incorporate the egg mixture into the flour to make a smooth dough. • Knead the squid ink pasta dough and cut into tagliatelle following the instructions for fresh pasta on pages 242–5.

**Shrimp Sauce:** Rinse the reserved shrimp heads and place in a small saucepan with the water, onion, and parsley stalks. Bring to a boil and simmer for 20 minutes. Strain, reserving the liquid. • Put a large pot of salted water to boil over high heat. • Melt the butter in a large frying pan over high heat and sauté the garlic and shrimp for 3 minutes. Remove from the pan and set aside. • Return the pan to medium heat. Pour in the wine and 2–3 tablespoons of the reserved shrimp liquid. Simmer until reduced a little, 3–4 minutes. Add the cream and simmer for 2–3 minutes. Season with salt and pepper. • Cook the pasta in the boiling water until al dente, 2–3 minutes. • Drain the pasta and add to the pan with the sauce and shrimp. Toss gently, adding the reserved shrimp liquid. • Sprinkle with the finely chopped parsley. • Serve hot.

**Squid Ink Tagliatelle**

- 2⅓ cups (350 g) all-purpose (plain) flour
- 3 very fresh large eggs
- ¼ cup (60 ml) squid ink

**Shrimp Sauce**

- 1½ pounds (750 g) shrimp, peeled, deveined, heads removed (reserve the heads), and cut in small pieces
- 1¼ cups (300 ml) water
- 1 small onion, quartered
- Small bunch of parsley, stalks whole and leaves finely chopped
- 3 tablespoons butter
- 2 cloves garlic, finely chopped
- 1¼ cups (300 ml) dry white wine
- ¾ cup (180 ml) heavy (double) cream
- Salt and freshly ground white pepper

Serves: 4
Preparation: 40 minutes + time to prepare the pasta
Cooking: 30–35 minutes
Level: 3

You could also use: tagliatelle, spaghetti, linguine, bucatini

300

# HERB TAGLIATELLE WITH MEAT SAUCE

302

**Herb Tagliatelle:** Sift the flour into a mound on a clean work surface. • Whisk the eggs and minced herbs in a small bowl. • Make a well in the flour and pour in the egg mixture. Use a fork to gradually incorporate the egg mixture into the flour to make a smooth dough. • Knead the herb pasta dough and cut into tagliatelle following the instructions for fresh pasta on pages 242–5.

**Meat Sauce:** Heat the oil in a large frying pan over medium heat. Add the onion, celery, and carrot and sauté until softened, 3–4 minutes. • Add the beef and sauté until browned all over, about 5 minutes. • Add the mushrooms and parsley and simmer for 3 minutes. • Stir in the flour, letting it soak up the oil. • Pour in the wine and cook until evaporated. • Add the tomatoes and season with salt and pepper. Cover and simmer over low heat, stirring occasionally, until the meat is tender, at least 1 hour. Adding a little water if the sauce begins to dry out. • Put a large pot of salted water to boil over high heat. • Cook the pasta in the boiling water until al dente, 3–4 minutes. • Drain and add to the pan with the meat sauce. • Toss gently and serve hot.

**Herb Tagliatelle**

2⅓ cups (350 g) all-purpose (plain) flour

3 very fresh large eggs

2 ounces (60 g) mixed fresh herbs (parsley, thyme, basil, mint), minced

**Meat Sauce**

¼ cup (60 ml) extra-virgin olive oil

1 large onion, finely chopped

1 stalk celery, finely chopped

1 carrot, finely chopped

14 ounces (400 g) stew beef, cut into large chunks

½ ounce (15 g) dried porcini mushrooms, soaked in warm water, drained, and finely chopped

1 tablespoon finely chopped fresh parsley

1 tablespoon all-purpose/plain flour

½ cup (120 ml) dry white wine

1 pound (500 g) tomatoes, peeled and coarsely chopped

Salt and freshly ground black pepper

Serves: 4

Preparation: 1 hour + time to make the pasta

Cooking: 1–2 hours

Level: 3

You could also use: tagliatelle, pappardelle, stracci

# SAFFRON PAPPARDELLE WITH LAMB SAUCE

304

**Saffron Pappadelle:** Sift the flour into a mound on a clean work surface. • Whisk the eggs and saffron water mixture in a small bowl. • Make a well in the flour and pour in the egg mixture. Use a fork to gradually incorporate the egg mixture into the flour to make a smooth dough. • Knead the saffron pasta dough and cut into pappardelle following the instructions for fresh pasta on pages 242–5.

**Lamb Sauce:** Heat the oil and butter in a large saucepan over medium heat. Add the lamb and sauté until browned all over, 5–10 minutes. • Pour in the sherry and simmer until evaporated. • Season with salt and pepper, lower the heat, and simmer until very tender, about 2 hours. Add stock as required to keep the meat moist. • Take the lamb out of the pan and remove the meat from the bone. Cut the meat into small strips. • Add 3 tablespoons of stock to the pan with the cooking juices. Add the onion and cook for 5 minutes. • Add the lamb and cook for 3–5 minutes. • Stir in the flour and 2 cups (500 ml) of stock. Add the lettuce, marjoram, and saffron and season with salt and pepper. Cook over low heat until the lettuce has wilted and the sauce has thickened, about 5 minutes. • About 30 minutes before the sauce is ready, put a large pot of salted water to boil over high heat. add a pinch of saffron to the cooking water. • Cook the pappardelle until al dente, 3–4 minutes. Drain well and transfer to a heated serving dish. Spoon the sauce over the top and toss gently. • Serve hot.

**Saffron Pappardelle**

- 3⅓ cups (500 g) all-purpose (plain) flour
- 4 fresh large eggs + 2 fresh large egg yolks
- 1 teaspoon ground saffron, dissolved in 1 tablespoon warm water
- Pinch of ground saffron (for the cooking water)

**Lamb Sauce**

- ¼ cup (60 ml) extra-virgin olive oil
- 3 tablespoons butter
- 1 leg of lamb (about 3 pounds/1.5 kg)
- ½ cup (120 ml) sherry
- Salt and freshly ground white pepper
- 4 cups (1 liter) beef stock (see page 48)
- 1 small onion, finely chopped
- 2 tablespoons all-purpose (plain) flour
- 1 lettuce heart, cut in strips
- 1 tablespoon finely chopped fresh marjoram
- 8 threads saffron, crumbled

Serves: 6
Preparation: 40 minutes + time to make the pasta
Cooking: 2½ hours
Level: 3

# ROSEMARY TAGLIATELLE IN LAMB SAUCE

**Rosemary Tagliatelle:** Sift the flour into a mound on a clean work surface. • Whisk the eggs and minced rosemary in a small bowl. • Make a well in the flour and pour in the egg mixture. Use a fork to gradually incorporate the egg mixture into the flour to make a smooth dough. • Knead the rosemary pasta dough and cut into tagliatelle following the instructions for fresh pasta on pages 242–5.

**Lamb Sauce:** Heat the oil in a large frying pan over medium heat. Add the garlic, rosemary, and chile and sauté for 3 minutes. • Add the lamb and sauté until browned all over, 5–10 minutes. • Drizzle with the wine and cook until evaporated. • Add the tomatoes and season with salt and pepper. Cover and simmer over low heat for 30 minutes. • Put a large pot of salted water to boil over high heat.
• About 3–4 minutes before the sauce is ready, add the pasta to the pan of boiling water and cook until al dente. • Drain the pasta and transfer to the pan with the sauce. Add the parsley, toss gently, and remove from the heat. • Serve hot.

**Rosemary Tagliatelle**

2⅓ cups (350 g) all-purpose (plain) flour

3 very fresh large eggs

2 ounces (60 g) fresh rosemary, minced

**Lamb Sauce**

¼ cup (60 ml) extra-virgin olive oil

2 cloves garlic, finely chopped

1 sprig fresh rosemary

1 dried chile, crumbled

14 ounces (400 g) boned lamb, cut in small cubes

¼ cup (60 ml) dry white wine

6 large tomatoes, peeled and coarsely chopped

Salt and freshly ground black pepper

1 tablespoon finely chopped fresh parsley

Serves: 4
Preparation: 40 minutes + time to prepare the pasta
Cooking: 45–50 minutes
Level: 2

You could also use: pappardelle, fusilli

# FRESH FARFALLE WITH SALMON

308

**Fresh Farfalle: Step 1:** Prepare the pasta dough and roll out into paper thin sheets. Use a fluted pastry cutter to cut the sheets of pasta into $2^1/2$ x 1-inch (6 x 2.5-cm) rectangles. • **Step 2:** Use the tips of your index finger and thumb to pinch each rectangle together in the center. • **Step 3:** Repeat until all the rectangles have been pinched together in bows. • Dust a clean kitchen towel with semolina flour and let dry for 30 minutes before cooking. **Salmon Sauce:** Put a large pot of salted water to boil over high heat. • Cut the salmon into small cubes or strips. • Heat 2 tablespoons of oil in a large frying pan over low heat. Add the onion and a pinch of salt and sauté until softened, 7–10 minutes. • Increase the heat to medium and add the salmon, capers, and remaining oil. Season with salt, if required – the capers will still be quite salty, so taste first. Cook for 1–2 minutes only; the salmon should not be overcooked. • Cook the pasta in the boiling water until al dente, 3–4 minutes. • Drain well and add to the pan with the salmon and basil. • Toss gently and serve hot.

**Pasta**

1 recipe plain fresh pasta dough (see page 242)

**Salmon Sauce**

8 ounces (250 g) fresh salmon fillet, sliced

4 tablespoons extra-virgin olive oil

1 onion, finely chopped

Salt

2 tablespoons capers preserved in salt, rinsed, dried, and coarsely chopped

6 leaves fresh basil, torn

Serves: 4
Preparation: 40 minutes + time to make the pasta
Cooking: 15–20 minutes
Level: 3

You could also use: pappardelle, maltagliati, stracci

Farfalle means butterflies in Italian, so this pasta shape is also named for its shape. In English the shape is commonly referred to as bow ties. You can also use any of the colored or aromatic pasta doughs in this chapter to prepare this pasta.

309

**1. PREPARE** the pasta dough and roll out into paper thin sheets. Use a fluted pastry cutter to cut the sheets of pasta into 2$^1/_2$ x 1-inch (6 x 2.5-cm) rectangles.

**2. USE** the tips of your index finger and thumb to pinch each rectangle together in the center.

**3. REPEAT** until all the rectangles have been pinched together in bows. Dust a kitchen towel with semolina flour and let dry for 30 minutes.

# MALTAGLIATI WITH SAUSAGE SAUCE

**Maltagliati:** Prepare the pasta dough and cut into irregular shapes following the instructions below.
**Sausage Sauce:** Prick the sausages well with a fork and cook for 3 minutes in a pan of boiling water. Drain, peel, and chop coarsely. • Heat the oil in a large frying pan over low heat and sweat the onion with a pinch of salt for 10 minutes. • Put a large pot of salted water to boil over high heat. • Add the chopped sausage meat and sauté over high heat for 5 minutes. • Season with the cinnamon, salt, and pepper. Pour in the wine and simmer until evaporated. • Add the tomatoes and simmer for 20 minutes over low heat. • Cook the pasta in the boiling water until al dente, 2–3 minutes. • Drain well and add to the pan with the sauce. Toss gently and sprinkle with the Parmesan. • Serve hot garnished with the parsley.

**Maltagliati**

1 recipe plain fresh pasta dough (see page 242)

**Sausage Sauce**

14 ounces (400 g) fresh Italian-style sausages

2 tablespoons extra-virgin olive oil

1 onion, finely chopped

Salt and freshly ground black pepper

1 pinch ground cinnamon

½ cup (120) ml dry red wine

2 (14-ounce/400-g) cans tomatoes, with juice

4 tablespoons freshly grated Parmesan cheese

Fresh parsley to garnish

Serves: 4
Preparation: 30 minutes + time to make the pasta
Cooking: 35–40 minutes
Level: 2

---

### ■ PREPARING MALTAGLIATI

Maltagliati means "badly cut" in Italian and this accurately describes the irregularly cut shapes of this pasta.

**1.** PREPARE the pasta dough and roll out into paper thin sheets. Use a sharp knife to cut the sheets of pasta into small diamonds, rectangles, triangles, and other irregular shapes.

# MALTAGLIATI WITH BEANS

314

If using homemade pasta, prepare it first. • Put a large pot of salted water to boil over high heat. • Heat 4 tablespoons (60 ml) of oil in a large frying pan over high heat and sauté the garlic, herbs, and chile pepper for 1 minute. • Add the drained beans and cook for 5 minutes over medium heat. Add the tomatoes, season with salt, cover, and simmer for 10 minutes. • Heat the remaining oil in a small pan over high heat and sauté the prosciutto until the pieces of fat are transparent. Add to the bean sauce. • Bring the 2 cups (500 ml) of water to a boil with the vinegar and a pinch of salt and cook the onion in it for 2 minutes. Drain and set aside. • Cook the pasta in the boiling water until al dente, 2–3 minutes. • Drain well and add to the pan with the sauce. Toss gently, adding the onion and little of the cooking water if the sauce is too dry. • Serve hot.

| | |
|---|---|
| 1 | recipe homemade maltagliati (see pages 312) or 14 ounces (400 g) fresh storebought maltagliati |
| 5 | tablespoons (75 ml) extra-virgin olive oil |
| 2 | cloves garlic, finely chopped |
| 1 | tablespoon finely chopped fresh sage |
| 1 | tablespoon finely chopped fresh rosemary |
| 1 | dried chile, crumbled |
| 1 | pound (500 g) mixed cooked or canned beans (cannellini, borlotti, azuki), drained |
| 4 | medium tomatoes, peeled and chopped |
| | Salt |
| 3 | ounces (90 g) prosciutto, cut in thin strips |
| 2 | cups (500 ml) water |
| 5 | tablespoons red wine vinegar |
| 1 | large red onion, sliced |

Serves: 4
Preparation: 30 minutes + time to make the pasta
Cooking: 30 minutes
Level: 2

You could also use: tagliatelle, stracci

# MALTAGLIATI WITH ZUCCHINI & CLAMS

If using homemade pasta, prepare it first. • Soak the clams in a large bowl of water for 1 hour. • Drain the clams and rinse well in cold running water. Discard any that are open or broken. • Put a large pot of salted water to boil over high heat. • Heat half the wine in a large frying pan with half the clams. Cover and cook over medium heat until the clams are open. Check the clams often; they should not be allowed to cook for too long. Repeat with the remaining wine and clams. Discard any clams that have not opened. • Strain the cooking liquid and reserve. • Heat the oil in a large frying pan over medium heat and sauté the zucchini for 5 minutes. • Add the sugar, clams, and 3–4 tablespoons of cooking liquid. Season with salt and add the mint. Cook for 2–3 minutes, then turn off heat. • Cook the pasta in the boiling water until al dente, 3–4 minutes. • Drain the pasta and add to the pan with the clam sauce. Toss gently over medium heat, adding a little more cooking liquid, if necessary. • Garnish with the mint leaves and serve hot.

| | |
|---|---|
| 1 | recipe homemade maltagliati (see pages 284–5) or 14 ounces (400 g) fresh storebought maltagliati |
| 2 | pounds (1 kg) clams, in shell |
| ½ | cup (125 ml) dry white wine |
| 5 | tablespoons (75 ml) extra-virgin olive oil |
| 12 | ounces (350 g) zucchini (courgettes), cut in wheels |
| | Pinch of sugar |
| | Salt |
| 4 | sprigs fresh mint, finely chopped + extra leaves to garnish |

Serves 4
Preparation: 30 minutes
  + 1 hour to soak clams
  + time to prepare the
  pasta
Cooking: 20–25 minutes
Level: 2

You could also use: tagliatelle, spaghetti, linguine

# CORNMEAL SQUARES WITH BEANS & SAUSAGE SAUCE

318

**Cornmeal Squares:** Sift the cornmeal and flour into a mound on a clean work surface. • Whisk the eggs in a small bowl. • Make a well in the flour and pour in the egg mixture. Use a fork to gradually incorporate the egg mixture into the flour to make a smooth dough. • Knead the pasta dough and roll out into thin sheets following the instructions for fresh pasta on pages 242–5. • Use a fluted pastry cutter to cut into small squares. • Let dry on a lightly floured kitchen towel for 30 minutes.

**Bean & Sausage Sauce:** Put the soaked beans in a large saucepan with 2 tablespoons of oil and a sprig of rosemary. Cover with plenty of cold water and simmer until tender, 1–2 hours. Season with salt just before they are cooked. • Put a large pot of salted water to boil over high heat. • Drain the beans, discarding the rosemary and reserving the cooking water. • Chop the beans in a food processor until smooth. Add enough of the reserved cooking water to obtain a soft purée. • Prick the sausages a fork and cook in a pan of boiling water for 3 minutes. Remove the skins and break up using a fork. • Heat the remaining oil in a large frying pan over high heat and sauté the sausages for 5 minutes. • Add the chopped rosemary and drizzle with the wine. Remove from the heat. • Cook the pasta in the boiling water until al dente, 4–5 minutes. • Drain and place in a heated serving dish. • Reheat the bean purée and toss gently with the pasta and sausage. • Serve hot.

**Cornmeal Squares**

1  cup (150 g) finely ground yellow cornmeal

1⅓  cups (200 g) all-purpose (plain) flour

4  very fresh large eggs

**Bean & Sausage Sauce**

1  cup (200 g) dried cannellini beans, soaked in cold water for 12 hours

4  tablespoons (60 ml) extra-virgin olive oil

2  sprigs fresh rosemary, 1 whole and 1 with leaves finely chopped

   Salt and freshly ground black pepper

14  ounces (400 g) very fresh Italian sausages (about 4 sausages)

½  cup (125 ml) dry white wine

Serves: 4

Preparation: 2 hours + 12 hours to soak the beans + time to prepare the pasta

Cooking: 2 hours 30 minutes

Level: 3

# PASTA SQUARES WITH SQUID

320

**Pasta Squares:** Sift the semolina and all-purpose flours into a mound on a clean work surface. • Whisk the eggs in a small bowl. • Make a well in the flour mixture and pour in the egg mixture. Use a fork to gradually incorporate the egg mixture into the flour to make a smooth dough. • Knead the pasta dough and roll out into thin sheets following the instructions for fresh pasta on pages 242–5.
• Use a pastry cutter to cut into small squares.
• Let dry on a lightly floured kitchen towel for 30 minutes.

**Squid Sauce:** Put a large pot of salted water to boil over high heat. • Heat the oil in a large frying pan over high heat and sauté the squid, tomato, chervil, marjoram, and thyme for 3 minutes. • Pour in the fish stock. Season with salt and pepper and cook until the sauce has reduced by half, about 2–3 minutes. • Cook the pasta in the boiling water until al dente, 4–5 minutes. • Drain well and add to the pan with the squid sauce. Toss gently and serve immediately.

**Pasta Squares**

- 1¹/₃ cups (200 g) semolina (durum wheat) flour
- 1¹/₃ cups (200 g) all-purpose (plain) flour
- 4 very fresh large eggs

**Squid Sauce**

- ¹/₂ cup (125 ml) extra-virgin olive oil
- 14 ounces (400 g) small squid, skinned, bodies cut in thin rings (the tentacles can be frozen for use in other dishes)
- 1 large tomato, cut in small pieces
- 1 tablespoon finely chopped fresh chervil
- 1 tablespoon finely chopped fresh marjoram
- 1 tablespoon finely chopped fresh thyme
- ³/₄ cup (180 ml) boiling fish stock
- Salt and freshly ground white pepper

Serves: 4
Preparation: 2 hours + time to prepare the pasta + time to make the fish stock
Cooking: 20 minutes
Level: 3

You could also use: tagliatelle, spaghetti, linguine, penne

# PIZZOCCHERI WITH PUMPKIN & GORGONZOLA SAUCE

322

**Pizzoccheri:** Sift both flours and the salt into a clean work surface. Shape into a mound and make a well in the center. Add enough water to obtain a fairly firm dough. Knead for 20 minutes, then wrap in plastic wrap (cling film) and let rest for 30 minutes. • Roll the pasta into thin sheets. Dry the sheets of pasta on a lightly floured cloth for 30 minutes. • Cut into $1/2$ x 2-inch (1 x 5-cm) pieces.
**Pumpkin & Gorgonzola Sauce:** Preheat the oven to 400°F (200°C/gas 6). • Bake the pumpkin for about 40 minutes, until tender. Cool a little, then remove the peel and cut the flesh into small dice. • Put a large pot of salted water to boil over high heat. • Melt the butter in a casserole and sauté the pumpkin with the sugar for 2–3 minutes. Season with salt and remove from the heat. • Cook the pasta in the boiling water until al dente, 3–4 minutes. • While the pasta is cooking, melt the Gorgonzola in a heavy-bottomed pan with 1–2 tablespoons of cooking water from the pan. • Drain the pasta and add to the casserole with the sauce. Toss gently, adding the pieces of pumpkin. • Serve hot garnished with the parsley.

■ ■ ■ *Pizzoccheri are a type of short buckwheat ribbon pasta from the Valtellina, in the northern Lombardy region of Italy.*

 You could also use: tagliatelle, whole-wheat tagliatelle

**Pizzoccheri**

2    cups (300 g) buckwheat flour

1    cup (150 g) all-purpose (plain) flour

     Salt

$3/4$ cup (180 ml) water

**Pumpkin & Gorgonzola Sauce**

$1^{1}/2$ pounds (750 g) winter squash or pumpkin, cut in pieces but not peeled

3    tablespoons butter

     pinch of sugar

     Salt

5    ounces (150 g) Gorgonzola cheese

     Fresh parsely to garnish

Serves: 4
Preparation: 30 minutes + time to make the pasta
Cooking: 50 minutes
Level: 2

# STRACCI WITH ZUCCHINI FLOWERS

**Stracci:** Prepare the pasta dough and tear into irregular shapes following the instructions below.

**Zucchini Flower Sauce:** Put a large pot of salted water to boil over high heat. • Heat the oil in a large frying pan and sauté the prosciutto and zucchini for 3–5 minutes. • Pour in the cream and simmer for 3 minutes. • Add the saffron and stir well. Season with salt and turn off the heat. • Cook the pasta in the boiling water until al dente, 2–3 minutes. • Reheat the sauce and add the sliced zucchini flowers. • Drain the pasta and add to the pan with the sauce. Toss gently for 1 minute. • Serve hot, decorating each portion with a zucchini flower and a sprinkling of parsley.

**Stracci**

1 recipe plain fresh pasta dough (see page 242)

**Zucchini Flower Sauce**

1 tablespoon extra-virgin olive oil

2 ounces (60 g) prosciutto, cut in thin strips

4 small zucchini (courgettes), sliced

3/4 cup (180 ml) heavy (double) cream

1/8 teaspoon ground saffron

Salt

4 zucchini (courgette) flowers, sliced in 4 lengthwise + 4 extra to garnish

1 tablespoon finely chopped fresh parsley

Serves: 4
Preparation: 30 minutes + time to make the pasta
Cooking: 15 minutes
Level: 2

---

### ◼ PREPARING STRACCI

The word stracci means "rags" in Italian. Use your fingertips to tear this pasta into irregular shapes. It goes well with creamy sauces that are not too chunky.

**1.** PREPARE the pasta dough and roll out into paper thin sheets. Use your hands to tear the sheets of pasta into small irregular shapes.

# ORECCHIETTE WITH SPICY BROCCOLI & ANCHOVY SAUCE

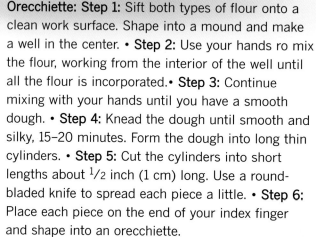

**Orecchiette: Step 1:** Sift both types of flour onto a clean work surface. Shape into a mound and make a well in the center. • **Step 2:** Use your hands ro mix the flour, working from the interior of the well until all the flour is incorporated.• **Step 3:** Continue mixing with your hands until you have a smooth dough. • **Step 4:** Knead the dough until smooth and silky, 15–20 minutes. Form the dough into long thin cylinders. • **Step 5:** Cut the cylinders into short lengths about $1/2$ inch (1 cm) long. Use a round-bladed knife to spread each piece a little. • **Step 6:** Place each piece on the end of your index finger and shape into an orecchiette.

**Spicy Broccoli & Anchovy Sauce:** Heat the oil in a large frying pan over medium heat. Add the garlic and anchovies and stir until the anchovies have dissolved into the oil. • Remove from the heat and let cool. • Bring a large pot of salted water to a boil. Add the broccoli stems and cook for 2 minutes. Add the florets and cook until just tender, 4–6 minutes. Remove with a slotted spoon and add to the pan with the garlic and anchovy oil. • Bring the water back to a boil. Add the pasta and cook until al dente, 3–5 minutes. • Drain the pasta and add to the pan with the broccoli. Season with the chiles and serve hot.

**Orecchiette**

- $1^{1}/_{3}$ **cups (200 g) semolina (durum wheat) flour**
- $1^{1}/_{3}$ **cups (200 g) all-purpose (plain) flour**

**Spicy Broccoli & Anchovy Sauce**

- $^{1}/_{4}$ **cup (60 ml) extra-virgin olive oil**
- **2 cloves garlic, finely chopped**
- **4–6 salt-cured anchovy fillets**
- **1 pound (500 g) broccoli, broken into florets, stem chopped**
- **Salt**
- **1–2 dried chiles, crumbled**

**Serves: 4**
**Preparation: 15 minutes + time to make the pasta**
**Cooking: 20–30 minutes**
**Level: 2**

You could also use: potato gnocchi, rigatoni

Orecchiette come from Puglia, the southern region occupying the heel of the boot-shaped Italian peninsula. In Italian, orecchiette means "little ears" and refers to the shape of the pasta.

**1.** SIFT both types of flour onto a clean work surface, make a well in the center, and pour in the warm water.

**2.** USE your hands to mix the flour, working from the interior of the well, until all the flour is incorporated.

**3.** CONTINUE mixing with your hands until a smooth dough forms.

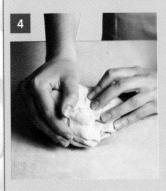  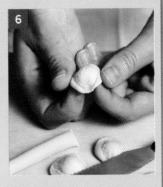

**4.** KNEAD the dough until smooth and silky, 15–20 minutes. Form the dough into long, thin cylinders.

**5.** CUT the cylinders into short lengths, about 1/2 inch (1 cm) long. Use round-bladed knife to "spread" each piece.

**6.** PLACE each piece on the end of your index finger and shape into an orecchiette.

# ORECCHIETTE WITH ARUGULA & POTATOES

330

If using homemade orecchiette, prepare them first. • Put a large pot of salted water to boil over high heat. • Cook the potatoes in the boiling water for 10 minutes. • Add 2 cloves garlic and cook for 5–10 minutes more. • Add the orecchiette and arugula and cook until the pasta is al dente. • Sauté the remaining 2 cloves garlic and chile in the oil in a large frying pan over low heat for 3–4 minutes. Season with salt. • Drain the pasta with the arugula and potatoes and transfer to the pan. • Discard the garlic, toss to mix, and serve.

1   recipe orecchiette (see pages 326–327) or 1 pound (500 g) fresh storebought orecchiette

1   pound (500 g) potatoes, peeled and cut into ¼ inch (5 mm) thick slices

4   cloves garlic, lightly crushed but whole

12   ounces (350 g) arugula (rocket) leaves

1   dried chile, crumbled

½   cup (120 ml) extra-virgin olive oil

Salt

Serves: 4
Preparation: 10 minutes + time to make the pasta
Cooking: 15–20 minutes
Level: 2

You could also use: penne, fusilli

# ORECCHIETTE WITH MEAT SAUCE

332

If using homemade orecchiette, prepare them first.
• Heat the oil in a large saucepan over medium heat. Add the onions and sauté until softened, 3–4 minutes. • Add the meat and sauté until browned all over, 5–10 minutes. • Add the tomatoes, celery, and basil. Season with salt and pepper. Cover and simmer over low heat for at least 1 hour. • Put a large pot of salted water to boil over high heat. • Cook the pasta in the boiling water until al dente, 3–4 minutes. Drain well and then add to the sauce. • Toss well over high heat for 1 minute. Sprinkle with the cheese and serve hot.

| | |
|---|---|
| 1 | recipe orecchiette (see pages 326–327) or 1 pound (500 g) fresh storebought orecchiette |
| ⅓ | cup (90 ml) extra-virgin olive oil |
| 2 | large onions, finely chopped |
| 1 | pound (500 g) lean ground (minced) beef, lamb, or pork |
| 1 | pound (500 g) tomatoes, peeled and chopped |
| 2 | stalks celery, finely chopped |
| 2 | tablespoons freshly chopped basil |
| | Salt and freshly ground black pepper |
| ½ | cup (60 g) freshly grated pecorino or Parmesan cheese |

Serves: 4–6
Preparation: 15 minutes + time to make the pasta
Cooking: 70 minutes
Level: 2

You could also use: tagliatelle, pappardelle, spaghetti, penne

# POTATO GNOCCHI WITH BUTTER & SAGE

334

**Potato Gnocchi:** Cook the potatoes whole in their skins in salted boiling water until tender, 25–30 minutes. • **Step 1:** Drain the potatoes and scrape off their skins while they are still warm. Mash until smooth in a bowl. • **Step 2:** Mix in the flour, salt, egg, and Parmesan and stir with a wooden spoon until smooth and well mixed. • **Step 3:** Shape the dough into a ball. Break off pieces and roll into cylinders just slightly thicker than your index finger. Cut into short lengths about 1 inch (2.5 cm) long. **Step 4:** If liked, you can make ridges in the gnocchi (to hold sauces better), by rolling the gnocchi one by one down the tines of a fork. • Place the gnocchi on a lightly floured clean cloth and let dry for 1–2 hours. Make sure the gnocchi are not touching each other or they may stick together. • **Step 5:** Put a large pot of salted water to boil over high heat. • Cook the gnocchi in small batches in the boiling water until they rise to the surface, 2–3 minutes each batch. Scoop out with a slotted spoon and place in a heated serving dish.

**Sauce:** Melt the butter with the sage in a small saucepan over medium heat until the butter is golden and infused with the flavor of the sage. • Drizzle over the gnocchi. Season with pepper. Sprinkle with the Parmesan and serve hot.

**Potato Gnocchi**

- **2** pounds (1 kg) baking (floury) potatoes, with peel
- **1²/₃ cups** (250 g) all-purpose (plain) flour
- **½ teaspoon** salt
- **1** large egg, lightly beaten
- **3** tablespoons freshly grated Parmesan cheese

**Sauce**

- **½ cup** (125 g) butter, melted
- **12** leaves fresh sage
- **1** cup (150 g) freshly grated Parmesan cheese

  Freshly ground black pepper

Serves: 4–6
Preparation: 1 hour
   + 1–2 hours to rest
Cooking: 45 minutes
Level: 2

You could also use: tagliatelle, fresh farfalle, stracci

## ■ PREPARING POTATO GNOCCHI

Potato gnocchi are made with varying combinations of boiled mashed potatoes, flour, and salt, often with the addition of egg. They are delicious with this simple combination of butter and fresh sage, but go well with a range of sauces.

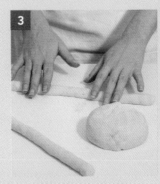

335

**1.** BOIL the potatoes. Scrape the skins off while still warm. Mash until smooth in a bowl.

**2.** MIX IN the flour, salt, egg, and Parmesan and stir with a wooden spoon until well mixed.

**3.** SHAPE the gnocchi dough into a ball. Break off pieces and roll them into cylinders just slightly thicker than your index finger. Cut into short pieces, about 1 inch (2.5 cm) long.

**4.** TO MAKE ridged gnocchi (which hold sauces better), roll the gnocchi one by one down the tines of a fork.

**5.** COOK the gnocchi in a large pot of salted boiling water until they rise to the surface, 2–3 minutes. Scoop out with a slotted spoon.

# GNOCCHI WITH FOUR-CHEESE SAUCE

338

If using homemade gnocchi, prepare them first. **Four-Cheese Sauce:** Melt the butter in a small saucepan over medium heat. Stir in the flour and nutmeg. Cook for 1–2 minutes, stirring constantly. • Remove from the heat and add the milk all at once. Stir until smooth then return to low heat and simmer, stirring constantly, until smooth and thick. • Add the four cheeses, reserving a little of the Parmesan to serve, and stir over low heat until melted and the sauce is smooth and creamy. Season with pepper. • Put a large pot of salted water to boil over high heat. • Cook the gnocchi in small batches in the boiling water until they rise to the surface, 2–3 minutes each batch. Scoop out with a slotted spoon and place in a heated serving dish. • Pour the cheese sauce over the top. Toss gently and serve hot.

1 recipe potato gnocchi (see pages 334–335) or 1 pound (500 g) fresh storebought potato gnocchi

**Four-Cheese Sauce**

2 tablespoons butter

2 tablespoons all-purpose (plain) flour

Pinch of nutmeg

1¼ cups (300 ml) milk

Salt and freshly ground white pepper

8 ounces (250 g) Fontina cheese, freshly grated

4 ounces (125 g) Gorgonzola cheese, coarsely chopped

4 ounces (125 g) mascarpone cheese

1 cup (120 g) freshly grated Parmesan cheese

Freshly ground black pepper

Serves: 4–6
Preparation: 20 minutes
+ time to make gnocchi
Cooking: 30 minutes
Level: 2

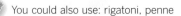

You could also use: rigatoni, penne

# GNOCCHI WITH BROCCOLI & PANCETTA

340

If using homemade gnocchi, prepare them first.
• Cook the broccoli in a large pan of salted boiling water until just tender, 6–8 minutes. Remove with a slotted spoon, reserving the cooking water. • Heat the oil in a frying pan over medium heat and sauté the garlic, chile, and pancetta until pale golden brown, 4–5 minutes. • Add the broccoli. Season with salt and pepper. Simmer for 10 minutes.
• Bring the reserved cooking water to a boil. Cook the gnocchi in small batches in the boiling water until they rise to the surface, 2–3 minutes each batch. Scoop out with a slotted spoon and add to the pan with the sauce. • Sprinkle with pecorino, toss gently, and serve hot.

| 1 | recipe potato gnocchi (see pages 334–335) or 1 pound (500 g) fresh storebought potato gnocchi |
| 1 | pound (500 g) broccoli, broken into small florets |
| ½ | cup (125 ml) extra-virgin olive oil |
| 4 | cloves garlic, finely chopped |
| 1 | red chile, seeded and finely chopped |
| 5 | ounces (150 g) diced pancetta |
| | Salt and freshly ground black pepper |
| ½ | cup (60 g) freshly grated pecorino cheese |

Serves: 4–6
Preparation: 25 minutes
  + time to make the gnocchi
Cooking: 25 minutes
Level: 1

You could also use: orecchiette, conchiglie, cavatappi

# STUFFED
# PASTA

# ANOLINI IN BEEF STOCK

**Filling:** Place the lard on the piece of beef and tie with kitchen string. Season with salt, pepper, and nutmeg. • Melt the butter in a large saucepan and sauté the meat over high heat until browned all over, 5–10 minutes. • Add the onion and sauté until softened, 3–4 minutes. • Pour in 1 cup (250 ml) of beef stock. Cover and simmer over low heat until the meat is very tender and falling apart, about 3 hours. • Chop the meat with its cooking juices in a food processor until smooth. • Transfer to a bowl and add the bread crumbs, Parmesan, and egg. Season with salt and pepper and refrigerate until ready to use.

**Pasta:** Prepare the pasta dough and let rest for 30 minutes. • **Step 1:** Divide the dough into 4 pieces. Roll it out quite thinly (to the second thinnest setting on your pasta machine). • Place balls of filling in rows 2 inches (5 cm) apart on half of each past sheet. Fold the other half of each sheet over the top. • **Step 2:** Press down gently between the blobs of filling with your fingertips to remove the air. • Use a plain or fluted pastry cutter or cookie cutter to cut out disks. Re-roll the scraps and repeat until all the filling and pasta is used. • Place on a floured cloth until ready to cook. • Bring the remaining 4 cups (1 liter) of beef stock to a boil over medium heat. • Add the pasta in 2–3 batches and simmer until al dente, 2–3 minutes each batch. • Ladle the pasta and stock into individual serving bowls. • Serve hot.

## Filling

2 ounces (60 g) lard or fatty bacon, cut in a thin strip

14 ounces (400 g) lean beef, in a single piece

Salt and freshly ground black pepper

Pinch of freshly grated nutmeg

¼ cup (60 g) butter

1 small onion, finely chopped

5 cups (1.25 liters) beef stock (see page 48)

½ cup (75 g) fine dry bread crumbs

½ cup (60 g) freshly grated Parmesan cheese

1 large egg

## Pasta

½ recipe fresh pasta dough (see page 242)

Serves: 4
Preparation: 1 hour + time to prepare the pasta dough
Cooking: 3½ hours
Level: 3

Anolini are small, round ravioli from Emilia-Romagna in central Italy. They are usually served in boiling beef stock, but they can also be served with sauces. Fillings are traditionally meat-based but can also be made with vegetables, cheese, or seafood. Do not roll the pasta too thin; roll to the second thinnest setting on your machine. It needs to be strong enough to hold the filling.

**1.** PREPARE the pasta dough and roll out into thin sheets. Place balls of filling in rows 2 inches (5 cm) apart on half of each past sheet. Fold the other half of each sheet over the top.

**2.** PRESS DOWN gently between the blobs of filling with your fingertips to remove the air. Use a plain or fluted pastry cutter or cookie cutter to cut out disks. Re-roll the scraps and repeat until all the filling and pasta are used.

**3.** ANOLINI are generally quite small, but you can make them any size you like. They can have smooth or fluted edges.

# POTATO & PUMPKIN ANOLINI WITH MEAT SAUCE

**Pasta:** Prepare the pasta dough and let rest for 30 minutes.

**Sauce:** Put the dried mushrooms in a small bowl of cold water and let soak for 15 minutes. Drain and chop finely. • Heat the oil in a medium saucepan over low heat and sauté the onion, carrot, celery with a pinch of salt for 15 minutes. • Add the garlic and mushrooms and cook for 2 minutes. • Add the beef and sauté over high heat until well browned. • Stir in the flour and cook for 2 minutes. • Pour in the wine and simmer until evaporated. • Stir in the tomatoes and parsley. Season with salt and pepper. Cover and simmer over low heat for 1 hour.

**Filling:** Preheat the oven to 400°F (200°C/gas 6). • Bake the pumpkin until tender, about 1 hour. Remove and let cool. • Use a tablespoon to scoop out the flesh. Transfer to a food processor and chop until smooth. • Boil the potatoes in lightly salted water in their skins until tender. • Drain and slip off the skins. Mash in a large bowl with the butter, Parmesan, nutmeg, salt, and pepper until smooth. • Stir in the pumpkin. • Divide the pasta dough into four pieces. Roll it out quite thinly. • Prepare the anolini following the instructions on page 347. Place on a floured cloth until ready to cook. • Put a large pot of salted water to boil over high heat. • Cook the pasta in 2–3 batches in the boiling water until al dente, 2–3 minutes each batch. • Scoop out with a slotted spoon, drain well, and serve hot with the meat sauce and extra Parmesan.

**Pasta**

½   recipe plain fresh pasta dough (see page 242)

**Sauce**

½   ounce (15 g) dried porcini mushrooms

¼   cup (60 ml) extra-virgin olive oil

1   onion, finely chopped

1   carrot, finely chopped

1   stalk celery, finely chopped

   Salt and freshly ground black pepper

1   clove garlic, finely chopped

8   ounces (250 g) ground (minced) beef

1   tablespoon all-purpose (plain) flour

½   cup (125 ml) dry red wine

1   pound (500 g) canned tomatoes, with juice

1   tablespoon finely chopped fresh parsley

**Filling**

12   ounces (350 g) winter squash or pumpkin, cut in pieces but not peeled

1   pound (500 g) potatoes

1½  tablespoons butter

2   tablespoons Parmesan + extra to serve

   Pinch of freshly grated nutmeg

Serves: 4–6
Preparation: 1 hour + time to make the pasta
Cooking: 1³/4 hours
Level 3

# MUSHROOM ANOLINI WITH BUTTER & HERBS

**Pasta:** Prepare the pasta dough and let rest for 30 minutes.

**Filling:** Soak the mushrooms in a small bowl of warm water for 1 hour. Drain the mushrooms, reserving the liquid. Chop the mushrooms finely.
• Heat the oil in a large frying pan over high heat. Add the garlic, rosemary, and bay leaf and sauté for 1 minute. • Add the pork, shallot, and mushrooms and sauté for 2 minutes. Add the brandy and simmer until evaporated. • Cook over medium heat for 10 minutes, stirring often, and adding a little of the mushroom liquid if the sauce dries out.
• Discard the bay leaf and rosemary. Transfer the mixture to a food processor and chop finely.
• Transfer to a bowl and add the parsley, egg, and Parmesan. Season with salt and pepper. • Divide the pasta dough into four pieces. Roll it out quite thinly.
• Prepare the anolini following the instructions on page 347. Place on a floured cloth until ready to cook. • Put a large pot of salted water to boil over high heat. • Cook the pasta in the boiling water in 2–3 batches until al dente, 2–3 minutes each batch.
• Scoop out with a slotted spoon, drain well, and transfer to a serving dish.

**To Serve:** Sprinkle with the Parmesan and marjoram and drizzle with the butter. • Serve immediately.

## Pasta
- 1/2 recipe plain fresh pasta dough (see page 242)

## Filling
- 1 ounce (30 g) dried porcini mushrooms
- 2 tablespoons extra-virgin olive oil
- 1 clove garlic, finely chopped
- 1 sprig fresh rosemary
- 1 bay leaf
- 8 ounces (250 g) ground (minced) pork
- 1 shallot, finely chopped
- 2 tablespoons brandy
- 1 tablespoon finely chopped parsley
- 1 small egg
- 4 tablespoons freshly grated Parmesan cheese

  Salt and freshly ground black pepper

## To Serve
- 8 tablespoons freshly grated Parmesan cheese
- 3 sprigs fresh marjoram, finely chopped
- 1/3 cup (90 g) melted butter

Serves: 4
Preparation: 1 hour + time to prepare the pasta dough
Cooking: 1 hour
Level: 3

# PECORINO ANOLINI WITH FAVA BEAN SAUCE

**Sauce:** Melt the butter in a small saucepan over low heat. Add the leek and sauté for 10 minutes. • Add the fava beans. Season with salt and pepper and pour in the beef stock. Cover and simmer over low heat for about 1 hour, stirring often, adding more stock if the beans begin to dry.

**Pasta:** Prepare the pasta dough and let rest for 30 minutes.

**Filling:** Strain the ricotta through a fine-mesh sieve into a medium bowl. Add the pecorino and season with salt, pepper, and nutmeg. Refrigerate until ready to use. • Divide the pasta dough into four pieces. Roll it out quite thinly. • Prepare the anolini following the instructions on page 347. Place on a floured cloth until ready to cook. • Put a large pot of salted water to boil over high heat. • Cook the pasta in the boiling water in 2–3 batches until al dente, 2–3 minutes each batch. • Scoop out with a slotted spoon, drain well, and transfer to a serving dish. • Serve hot with the fava bean sauce and a little extra pecorino cheese.

### Sauce

- 1/3 cup (90 g) butter
- 1 leek, thinly sliced
- 12 ounces (350 g) fresh hulled fava (broad) beans
  Salt and freshly ground black pepper
- 1 1/4 cups (300 ml) beef stock (see page 48) + extra, as required

### Pasta

- 1/2 recipe plain fresh pasta dough (see page 242)

### Filling

- 5 ounces (150 g) fresh ricotta cheese, drained
- 1 3/4 cups (200 g) coarsely grated young pecorino cheese + extra to serve
  Salt and freshly ground white pepper
  Pinch of freshly grated nutmeg

Serves: 4
Preparation: 45 minutes + time to make the pasta dough
Cooking: 1 1/2 hours
Level: 3

# ORIENTAL ANOLINI

**Pasta:** Sift both flours into a mound on a clean work surface. Make a well in the center and add the oil and half of the water. Stir with a fork until the flour is all absorbed, adding extra water as required. Knead until smooth and silky, 10–15 minutes. Let rest for 1 hour.

**Filling:** Place the cabbage in a large bowl and rub in 2–3 pinches of salt. Set aside for 1 hour. • Squeeze the cabbage to remove excess water. • Return to the bowl and add the pork, lemon grass, carrot, scallions, light soy sauce, sherry, cornstarch, ginger, and sugar. Use your hands to mix well. Refrigerate until ready to use. • Divide the pasta dough into four pieces. Roll it out quite thinly. • Prepare the anolini following the instructions on page 347. If liked, use a fork to mark each anolino around the edges (see photograph). Place on a floured cloth until ready to cook. • Put a large pan of salted water to boil over high heat. • Place the ravioli in an oriental steamer over the boiling water and steam for 10 minutes. • Serve hot with the dark soy sauce.

## Pasta

- 1 cup (150 g) all-purpose (plain) flour
- ⅓ cup (50 g) hard wheat (durum wheat) flour
- 1 tablespoon peanut oil
- ⅓ cup (90 ml) warm water

## Filling

- 8 ounces (250 g) cabbage, thinly sliced
- Salt
- 8 ounces (250 g) ground (minced) pork
- 2 tablespoons finely chopped lemon grass
- 1 small carrot, finely chopped
- 3 scallions (spring onions), finely chopped
- 1 tablespoon light soy sauce
- 2 tablespoons sherry
- 1 tablespoon cornstarch (cornflour)
- 1 teaspoon finely chopped fresh ginger
- Pinch of sugar
- Dark soy sauce, to serve

Serves: 4
Preparation: 45 minutes
+ 1 hour to rest
Cooking: 10 minutes
Level: 3

# RICOTTA & MINT ANOLINI WITH VEGETABLE SAUCE

**Pasta:** Prepare the pasta dough and let rest for 30 minutes.

**Filling:** Strain the ricotta through a fine-mesh sieve into a bowl. • Mix in the pecorino, egg, and mint. Season with salt and pepper. • Place the mixture in a pastry bag fitted with a smooth tip and refrigerate until ready to use.

**Sauce:** Heat the oil in a large frying pan over medium heat. Add the garlic and sauté until pale gold, 2–3 minutes. • Add the zucchini and sauté over medium heat for 5 minutes. • Add the tomatoes and parsley and simmer for 2 minutes. Season with salt and pepper. • Divide the pasta dough into four pieces. Roll it out quite thinly. • Prepare the anolini following the instructions on page 347. Place on a floured cloth until ready to cook. • Put a large pot of salted water to boil over high heat. • Cook the pasta in 2–3 batches in the boiling water until al dente, 2–3 minutes each batch. • Scoop out with a slotted spoon, drain well, and transfer to a serving dish. • Spoon the zucchini sauce over the top. Garnish with the basil and serve hot.

**Pasta**

| | |
|---|---|
| ¹⁄₂ | recipe plain fresh pasta dough (see page 242) |

**Filling**

| | |
|---|---|
| 1 | pound (500 g) fresh ricotta cheese, drained |
| ³⁄₄ | cup (90 g) freshly grated pecorino cheese |
| 1 | large egg |
| 2 | tablespoons finely chopped fresh mint |
| | Salt and freshly ground white pepper |

**Sauce**

| | |
|---|---|
| ¹⁄₄ | cup (60 ml) extra-virgin olive oil |
| 2 | cloves garlic, finely chopped |
| 1 | pound (500 g) zucchini (courgettes), cut in matchsticks |
| 3 | tomatoes, peeled and coarsely chopped |
| 1 | tablespoon finely chopped fresh parsley |
| | Salt and freshly ground black pepper |
| | Fresh basil, to garnish |

Serves: 4
Preparation: 45 minutes
  + time to prepare the
  pasta dough
Cooking: 45 minutes
Level: 3

# PECORINO & PEAR ANOLINI WITH BUTTER & CINNAMON

**Pasta:** Prepare the pasta dough and let rest for 30 minutes.

**Filling:** Peel the pears and drizzle with the lemon juice to prevent them from turning black. Cut in small cubes. • Put the water in a medium saucepan with the sugar and pears. Cover with a piece of parchment paper (directly on the pears) and simmer gently for 15–20 minutes, stirring occasionally. The pears should be tender but not mushy. Remove from the heat. • Stir in the pecorino and season generously with black pepper. • Divide the pasta dough into four pieces. Roll it out quite thinly. • Prepare the anolini following the instructions on page 347. Place on a floured cloth until ready to cook. • Put a large pot of salted water to boil over high heat. • Cook the pasta in batches in the boiling water until al dente, 2–3 minutes each batch. • Scoop out with a slotted spoon, drain well, and transfer to a serving dish.

**Sauce:** Melt the butter in a small saucepan with the marjoram and a pinch of salt. • Drizzle the butter mixture over the pasta, sprinkle with the pecorino, and dust with the cinnamon. • Serve hot.

**Pasta**

½  recipe plain fresh pasta dough (see page 242)

**Filling**

3  firm, ripe pears (Kaiser are good)

Freshly squeezed juice of ½ lemon

½  cup (120 ml) water

1  tablespoon sugar

¾  cup (90 g) freshly grated pecorino cheese

Freshly ground black pepper

**Sauce**

½  cup (120 g) butter

1  sprig marjoram

Salt

½  cup (60 g) freshly grated aged pecorino cheese

½  teaspoon ground cinnamon

Serves: 4
Preparation: 45 minutes + time to make the pasta dough
Cooking: 25–30 minutes
Level: 3

# FILLED PASTA IN BEEF STOCK

**Pasta:** Prepare the pasta dough and let rest for 30 minutes.

**Filling:** Mix the ricotta, Parmesan, egg, lemon zest, chives, and bread crumbs in a medium bowl. Season with salt and pepper and refrigerate until ready to use. • **Step 1:** Divide the pasta dough into four pieces. Roll it through the machine one notch at a time down to the second thinnest setting. • Cut the pasta sheets into 4-inch (10-cm) wide strips. Put blobs of filling at regular intervals (about 2 inches/5 cm apart) down one side of each strip. • **Step 2:** Slightly flatten the blobs of filling. Fold the pasta sheet over on itself to cover the blobs of filling. • **Step 3:** Press down lightly between the blobs of filling with your fingertips to remove excess air. • **Step 4:** Use a fluted or plain pastry cutter to cut out the ravioli. • Put the beef stock in a medium saucepan over high heat. Cover and bring to a boil. • Cook the pasta in 2–3 batches in the boiling stock until al dente, 2–3 minutes each batch. • Ladle the pasta and stock into serving bowls and garnish with the basil. • Serve hot.

**Pasta**

1 recipe plain fresh pasta dough (see page 242)

**Filling**

12 ounces (350 g) ricotta (or other fresh creamy cheese)

1¼ cups (150 g) freshly grated Parmesan cheese

1 large egg

Finely grated zest of ½ organic lemon

1 tablespoon finely chopped fresh chives

2 tablespoons fine dry bread crumbs

Salt and freshly ground white pepper

**To Serve**

5 cups (1.25 liters) beef stock (see page 48)

Fresh basil leaves

Serves: 4–6
Preparation: 45 minutes + time to prepare the pasta dough
Cooking: 20 minutes
Level: 3

Ravioli are generally square or rectangular, with all four sides fluted or three fluted sides and one straight (where the pasta has been folded over). They are usually about 2 inches (5 cm) long. Ravioli can have vegetable, cheese, seafood, or meat fillings and can be served in boiling stock or with sauces.

361

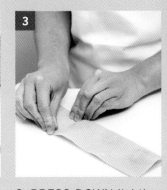

**1.** CUT the pasta sheets into 4-inch (10-cm) wide strips. Put blobs of filling at regular intervals (about 2 inches/5 cm apart) down one side of each strip.

**2.** SLIGHTLY FLATTEN the blobs of filling. Fold the pasta sheet over on itself to cover the blobs of filling.

**3.** PRESS DOWN lightly between the blobs of filling with your fingertips to remove excess air.

**4.** USE a fluted or plain pastry cutter to cut out the ravioli.

**5.** THE RAVIOLI will have three fluted edges and one plain edge where they have been folded. Flute the fourth side too, if liked.

# RICOTTA RAVIOLI WITH CONSOMMÉ

364

**Pasta:** Prepare the pasta dough and let rest for 30 minutes.

**Filling:** Mix the speck, egg yolk, Parmesan, and ricotta in a bowl. Season with salt and pepper. Refrigerate until ready to use. • Divide the pasta dough into four pieces. Roll it out quite thinly. • Prepare the ravioli following the instructions on page 361. • Place on a floured cloth until ready to cook.

**Consommé:** Place the beef, carrot, leek, celery, and egg white in a medium saucepan and add 2 cups (500 ml) of the stock. Bring to a boil, stirring gently until the liquid begins to evaporate. Stop stirring and wait for the egg white to come to the surface, filtering all impurities. Simmer for a few minutes, then strain through a fine mesh sieve without breaking the egg white. • Return to the heat and bring to a boil. Remove from the heat and add the wine. • Place the remaining 4 cups (1 liter) of beef stock over high heat. Cover and bring to a boil. • Cook the pasta in batches in the boiling stock until al dente, 2–3 minutes each batch. • Scoop out with a slotted spoon, drain well, and place in the clarified stock. • Ladle into serving bowls and serve hot.

**Pasta**

1   recipe plain fresh pasta dough (see page 242)

**Filling**

4   ounces (120 g) speck or smoked bacon, finely chopped

1   large egg yolk

5   tablespoons freshly grated Parmesan cheese

8   ounces (150 g) fresh ricotta cheese, drained

    Salt and freshly ground white pepper

**Consommé**

2   ounces (60 g) ground (minced) beef

½   carrot, finely chopped

½   leek, finely chopped

½   stalk celery, finely chopped

1   large egg white

6   cups (1.5 liters) beef stock (see page 48), fat skimmed off the top

2   cups (500 ml) sparkling dry white wine

Serves: 4–6
Preparation: 1 hour + time to prepare the pasta dough
Cooking: 30 minutes
Level: 3

# BROCCOLI RAVIOLI WITH ANCHOVY SAUCE

**Pasta:** Prepare the pasta dough and let rest for 30 minutes.

**Filling:** Peel the broccoli stalks and chop into small cubes. Divide the heads into florets. Place the stalks in a steamer and sprinkle with salt. Cook for 10 minutes. • Add the florets and steam until tender, about 5 minutes. • Transfer to a food processor and chop until smooth. • Place the mixture in a large frying pan and cook, stirring often, over medium-low heat for to remove any extra moisture. • Mix the mashed potatoes, broccoli, garlic, oil, parsley, red pepper flakes, and salt in a bowl. • Refrigerate until ready to use.

**Sauce:** Heat the oil in a medium frying pan over low heat. Add the onion and a pinch of salt, cover, and simmer for 10 minutes. • Add the anchovies and garlic and stir until the anchovies have dissolved into the oil. • Pour in the wine and cook until evaporated. • Divide the pasta dough into four pieces. Roll it out quite thinly. • Prepare the ravioli following the instructions on page 361. • Place on a floured cloth until ready to cook. • Put a large pot of salted water to boil over high heat. • Cook the pasta in 2–3 batches in the boiling water until al dente, 2–3 minutes each batch. Drain well and transfer to a serving dish. • Drizzle with the anchovy sauce and sprinkle with the bread crumbs and pecorino. • Serve hot.

**Pasta**

1  recipe plain fresh pasta dough (see page 242)

**Filling**

2½  pounds (1.25 kg) broccoli

12  ounces (350 g) boiled floury potatoes, mashed

2  cloves garlic, finely chopped

2  tablespoons extra-virgin olive oil

1  tablespoon finely chopped fresh parsley

½  teaspoon dried red pepper flakes

Salt

**Sauce**

¼  cup (60 ml) extra-virgin olive oil

½  onion, finely chopped

8  salt-cured anchovy fillets, finely chopped

3  cloves garlic, finely chopped

¼  cup (60 ml) dry white wine

6  tablespoons fine dry bread crumbs, toasted

6  tablespoons freshly grated aged pecorino cheese

Serves: 4–6
Preparation: 45 minutes
   + time to prepare the pasta dough
Cooking: 45 minutes
Level: 3

# EGGPLANT RAVIOLI WITH TOMATO SAUCE

**Pasta:** Prepare the pasta dough and let rest for 30 minutes.

**Filling:** Preheat the oven to 400°F (200°C/gas 6).
• Bake the eggplant for 30–40 minutes, until tender when pressed with a fingertip. • Cut the eggplant in half and use a tablespoon to scoop out the flesh. Place in a bowl. Season with salt and let rest for 30 minutes. • Put the eggplant in a clean cloth and squeeze gently to remove excess water. • Return to a bowl and mash with a fork. Season with pepper, parsley, oregano, and basil. Add the egg, Parmesan, and bread crumbs to make a firm dough (about the same as meatballs). Refrigerate until ready to use.
• Divide the pasta dough into four pieces. Roll it out quite thinly. • Prepare the ravioli following the instructions on page 361. • Place on a floured cloth until ready to cook. • Put a large pot of salted water to boil over high heat.

**Sauce:** Heat the oil in a large frying pan over medium heat and sauté the garlic until it turns pale gold. • Discard the garlic. Add the tomatoes and cook over high heat for 3 minutes. Season with salt, pepper, and oregano. • Cook the pasta in 2–3 batches in the boiling water until al dente, 2–3 minutes each batch. • Scoop out with a slotted spoon, drain well, and place in a heated serving dish. Sprinkle with the mozzarella and spoon the tomato sauce over the top. • Serve hot garnished with the basil.

**Pasta**

1   recipe plain fresh pasta dough (see page 242)

**Filling**

1   eggplant (aubergine), weighing about 12 ounces (350 g)

Salt and freshly ground black pepper

1   tablespoon finely chopped fresh parsley

Pinch of oregano

5   leaves fresh basil, torn

1   large egg

4   tablespoons freshly grated Parmesan cheese

4   tablespoons fine dry bread crumbs

**Sauce**

¼   cup (60 ml) extra-virgin olive oil

1   clove garlic, crushed with the back of a knife but whole

2½   pounds (1.25 kg) ripe tomatoes, peeled, seeds gently squeezed out, cut in small cubes

Salt and freshly ground black pepper

Pinch of oregano

5   ounces (150 g) fresh mozzarella cheese, cut in small cubes

Fresh basil, to garnish

Serves: 4–6
Preparation: 1¹/₂ hours
+ time to prepare the pasta dough
Cooking: 45 minutes
Level: 3

# SWEET RAVIOLI

**Pasta**

1   recipe plain fresh pasta dough (see page 242)

**Filling**

4   tablespoons golden raisins (sultanas)

¼   cup (60 g) butter

1   onion, finely chopped
    Salt and freshly ground black pepper

14   ounces (400 g) mashed potatoes

1   teaspoon ground cinnamon

6   tablespoons finely chopped walnuts
    Finely grated zest of ½ organic lemon

1   teaspoon dried mint

1   tablespoon sugar

**To Serve**

¾   cup (90 g) freshly grated smoked ricotta cheese (or other smoked cheese)

⅓   cup (90 g) melted butter

**Pasta:** Prepare the pasta dough and let rest for 30 minutes.

**Filling:** Soak the golden raisins in a small bowl of cold water for 30 minutes. Drain well. • Melt the butter in a medium saucepan over medium heat. Add the onion and a pinch of salt and sweat over low heat for 10 minutes. • Mix the mashed potatoes, onion, cinnamon, golden raisins, walnuts, lemon zest, mint, and sugar in a medium bowl. Season with salt and pepper and refrigerate until ready to use. • Divide the pasta dough into four pieces. Roll it out quite thinly. • Prepare the ravioli following the instructions on page 361. • Place on a floured cloth until ready to cook. • Put a large pot of salted water to boil over high heat. • Cook the pasta in 2–3 batches in the boiling water until al dente, 2–3 minutes each batch. • Scoop out with a slotted spoon, drain well, and place in a heated serving dish.

**To Serve:** Sprinkle with the ricotta and drizzle with the butter. • Serve immediately.

Serves: 4–6
Preparation: 1¹/2 hours
    + time to prepare the pasta dough
Cooking: 15–20 minutes
Level: 3

■ ■ ■ *This is a traditional recipe from Friuli, in the northeast of Italy. If you can't get the smoked ricotta cheese, replace with another aged, smoked cheese.*

# CANDIED CITRON PEEL RAVIOLI WITH BUTTER & NUTMEG

**Pasta:** Prepare the pasta dough and let rest for 30 minutes.

**Filling:** Combine the citron peel, almonds, lemon zest, ricotta, and egg in a medium bowl. Season with salt and pepper and mix well. • Divide the pasta dough into four pieces. Roll it out quite thinly. • Prepare the ravioli following the instructions on page 361. • Place on a floured cloth until ready to cook. • Put a large pot of salted water to boil over high heat. • Cook the pasta in 2–3 batches in the boiling water until al dente, 2–3 minutes each batch. • Scoop out with a slotted spoon, drain well, and transfer to a serving dish.

**To Serve:** Drizzle with the butter, sprinkle with the sugar, and dust with the nutmeg. • Serve hot.

**Pasta**

1   recipe plain fresh pasta dough (see page 242)

**Filling**

3   ounces (90 g) candied (glacé) citron peel, finely chopped

²⁄₃ cup (100 g) finely ground almonds

Finely grated zest of ¹⁄₂ organic lemon

4   ounces (120 g) ricotta cheese, drained

1   small egg

Salt and freshly ground white pepper

**To Serve**

¹⁄₃ cup (90 g) melted butter

1   tablespoon sugar

Pinch of freshly grated nutmeg

Serves: 4–6
Preparation: 45 minutes + time to prepare the pasta dough
Cooking: 20 minutes
Level: 3

■ ■ ■ *The traditional version of this recipe uses candied (glacé) citron peel, but if preferred you can use candied lemon, orange, or grapefruit peel instead.*

# RICOTTA & PECORINO RAVIOLI

**Pasta:** Prepare the pasta dough and let rest for 30 minutes.

**Filling:** Mix the ricotta, butter, Parmesan, beef stock, egg, nutmeg, salt, and pepper in a medium bowl. Refrigerate until ready to use. • Divide the pasta dough into four pieces. Roll it out quite thinly.
• Prepare the ravioli following the instructions on page 361. • Place on a floured cloth until ready to cook. • Put a large pot of salted water to boil over high heat.

**Sauce:** Melt the butter with the beef stock in a small saucepan. Simmer over low heat for 3–4 minutes. • Pour in the cream and simmer for 10 minutes. • Cook the pasta in 2–3 batches in the boiling water until al dente, 2–3 minutes each batch.
• Scoop out with a slotted spoon, drain well, and transfer to a serving dish. • Pour the sauce over the top and sprinkle with the pecorino. • Garnish with the marjoram and serve hot.

■ ■ ■ *Traditionally, both the filling and the sauce contained the brownings from a roasting pan instead of beef stock. If you have some on hand use them instead of the stock. Remember too that if you don't have fresh homemade stock on hand you can use a bouillon cube to make the stock.*

374

**Pasta**

1    recipe plain fresh pasta dough (see page 242)

**Filling**

12   ounces (350 g) fresh ricotta cheese, drained

¼    cup (60 g) melted butter

3    tablespoons freshly grated Parmesan cheese

3    tablespoons beef stock (see page 48)

1    small egg

     Pinch of freshly grated nutmeg

     Salt and freshly ground white pepper

**Sauce**

¼    cup (60 g) butter

3    tablespoons beef stock (see page 48)

¾    cup (200 ml) heavy (double) cream

2    ounces (60 g) pecorino cheese, in thin flakes

     Fresh marjoram to garnish

Serves: 4–6
Preparation: 45 minutes
     + time to prepare the pasta dough
Cooking: 20 minutes
Level: 3

# SEAFOOD RAVIOLI

**Pasta:** Prepare the pasta dough and let rest for 30 minutes.

**Filling:** Heat the oil and garlic in a large frying pan over medium heat. Add the fish fillets and cook, stirring gently, for 2 minutes. • Add the vermouth and sherry, season with salt and pepper, and simmer until the alcohol is evaporated. • Remove from the heat and finely chop the fish and cooking juices. • Dust the scallops lightly with flour. • Melt the butter in a small pan over medium heat and sauté the scallops until tender, 3–4 minutes. Season with salt and remove from the heat. • Combine the fish mixture and scallops in a medium bowl. Season with salt and pepper. Stir in the egg and parsley. • Divide the pasta dough into four pieces. Roll it out quite thinly. • Prepare the ravioli following the instructions on page 361. • Place on a floured cloth until ready to cook. • Put a large pot of salted water to boil over high heat.

**Sauce:** Heat the oil in a large frying pan over medium heat. Add the fish fillets and shrimp. Sauté gently for 2 minutes. Add the vermouth and cook until evaporated. • Stir in the tomatoes, season with salt and pepper, and simmer for 2 minutes. • Cook the pasta in 2–3 batches in the boiling water until al dente, 2–3 minutes each batch. • Scoop out with a slotted spoon, drain well, and transfer to the pan with the sauce. Add the butter and 4 tablespoons of cooking water. • Sprinkle with the parsley, stir gently, and serve immediately.

## Pasta

1 recipe plain fresh pasta dough (see page 242)

## Filling

3 tablespoons extra-virgin olive oil

1 clove garlic, peeled

1 pound (500 g) firm, white fish fillets, chopped

1 tablespoon dry vermouth

1 tablespoon sherry

Salt and freshly ground white pepper

4 tablespoons all-purpose (plain) flour

8 ounces (250 g) scallops, coarsely chopped

1½ tablespoons butter

1 small egg

1 tablespoon finely chopped fresh parsley

## Sauce

2 tablespoons extra-virgin olive oil

8 ounces (250 g) firm, white fish fillets

8 ounces (250 g) small shrimp (prawns), shelled

2 tablespoons dry vermouth

12 ounces (350 g) peeled and chopped tomatoes

2 tablespoons butter

1 tablespoon finely chopped fresh parsley

Serves: 4–6
Preparation: 1 hour + time to prepare the pasta dough
Cooking: 15–20 minutes
Level: 3

# MIXED SALMON RAVIOLI WITH MUSHROOMS

**Pasta:** Prepare the pasta dough and let rest for 30 minutes.
**Filling:** Melt the butter in a large frying pan over medium-high heat. Add the salmon and sear well.
• Add the Martini and simmer until evaporated.
• Let cool, then chop in a food processor. • Transfer to a bowl and add the egg yolks, cream, bread crumbs, Parmesan, and dill. Season with salt and pepper. • Chill in the refrigerator until ready to use.
**Sauce:** Heat the oil in a large frying pan over medium heat. Add the garlic and sauté for 2 minutes. Add the mushrooms and a pinch of salt. Cover and simmer over low heat until tender, 5–10 minutes. • Stir in the flour and simmer for 2 minutes. Pour in the stock. Cover and simmer over low heat for 15 minutes. • Remove from the heat and add the dill. • Divide both pasta doughs in half. Roll each piece out quite thinly. Cut into 4-inch (10-cm) wide sheets. Cut each sheet down the center lengthwise. • Put blobs of filling at regular intervals down the center of half of the pasta strips. Cover each strip with a piece of pasta of the other color.
• Press down lightly between the blobs of filling with your fingertips to remove excess air. Use a fluted or plain pastry cutter to cut out the ravioli. Place on a clean floured. • Put a large pot of salted water to boil over high heat. • Cook the pasta in 2–3 batches in the boiling water until al dente, 2–3 minutes each batch. • Scoop out with a slotted spoon, drain well, and place in the pan with the sauce. • Serve hot.

## Pasta

- ½ recipe plain fresh pasta dough (see page 242)
- ½ recipe spinach pasta dough (see pages 276–7)

## Filling

- 2 tablespoons butter
- 8 ounces (250 g) fresh salmon fillets, chopped
- 2 tablespoons dry Martini
- 2 small egg yolks
- 2 tablespoons fresh cream
- 2 tablespoons fine dry bread crumbs
- 2 tablespoons freshly grated Parmesan cheese
- 1 tablespoon finely chopped fresh dill
  Salt and freshly ground white pepper

## Sauce

- 5 tablespoons (75 ml) extra-virgin olive oil
- 2 cloves garlic, finely chopped
- 1 pound (500 g) champignons, sliced
  Salt
- 1 tablespoon all-purpose (plain) flour
- 1⅓ cups (300 ml) fish stock
- 1 tablespoon finely chopped fresh dill

Serves: 4
Preparation: 1 hour + time to prepare the pasta doughs
Cooking: 25–35 minutes
Level: 3

# CHRISTMAS AGNOLOTTI

380

**Pasta:** Prepare the pasta dough using the flour, egg, egg yolks, and water in the usual way (see page 242) and let rest for 30 minutes.

**Filling:** Chop the meat and mortadella in a food processor until very finely chopped. • Stir in the Parmesan, egg, cream, and bread crumbs. Season with salt, pepper, and nutmeg. • Divide the pasta dough into four pieces. Roll it out quite thinly (to the second thinnest setting on a pasta machine). Cut into long strips about 2$^1$/$_2$ inches (6 cm) wide. • **Step 1:** Shape heaped teaspoons of filling into balls. Place at regular intervals (about 1$^1$/$_2$ inches/ 4 cm apart) down one side of each strip. • **Step 2:** Fold the pasta over on itself. Squeeze between each blob of filling as you continue to roll the pasta over on itself. • **Step 3:** Use a fluted pastry cutter to trim the extra strip of pasta to about $^1$/$_2$ inch (1 cm).

**Step 4:** Fold the pasta over again so that a thin strip of pasta extends. Cut between the blobs of filling. Place on a floured cloth until ready to cook.

**Sauce:** Combine the cheese, milk, egg yolks, and butter in a double boiler over barely simmering water. • Stir until the cheese has melted. Whisk until the sauce is thick and creamy. Do not overcook as the eggs can curdle. • Remove from the heat and season with salt and pepper. Keep warm, stirring often until ready to use. • Put a large pot of salted water to boil over high heat. • Cook the pasta in 2–3 batches in the boiling water until al dente, 3–4 minutes each batch. • Drain and serve hot with the sauce.

## Pasta

2   cups (300 g) all-purpose flour

1   large fresh egg

3   large fresh egg yolks

    Few tablespoons cold water

## Filling

12   ounces (350 g) roasted meat (pork, beef, or chicken), fat removed

4   ounces (125 g) mortadella

1   cup (125 g) freshly grated Parmesan cheese

1   small egg

$^1$/$_2$   cup (120 ml) heavy (double) cream

2   handfuls fresh bread crumbs, soaked in milk and squeezed dry

    Salt and freshly ground black pepper

    Pinch of nutmeg

## Sauce

5   ounces (150 g) Fontina cheese, cut into cubes and soaked in 3$^1$/$_2$ tablespoons milk in the refrigerator for 2 hours

3   large egg yolks

2   tablespoons butter

    Salt and freshly ground white pepper

Serves: 4–6
Preparation: 1$^1$/$_2$ hours
   + 2 hours to soak cheese
   & time to prepare the
   pasta dough
Cooking: 20 minutes
Level: 3

Agnolotti are a type of ravioli from Piedmont in the northwest. They usually have a roasted or braised meat filling and are served in boiling stock or with a simple butter and sage sauce. These special agnolotti, known as *Agnolotti con plin,* in Italian, are traditionally served at Christmas. The dough is a darker yellow than normal because more egg yolks are used.

**1.** CUT the pasta sheets into 2$^{1}/_{2}$-inch (6-cm) wide strips. Put balls of filling at regular intervals (about 1$^{1}/_{2}$ inches/4 cm apart) down one side of each strip.

**2.** FOLD the pasta over on itself. Squeeze gently between each blob of filling as you continue to roll the pasta over on itself.

**3.** USE a fluted pastry cutter to trim the extra strip of pasta to about $^{1}/_{2}$ inch (1 cm) from the edge.

**4.** FOLD the pasta over again so that a thin strip of pasta extends. Cut between the blobs of filling.

**5.** THE FINISHED AGNOLOTTI are quite small and have a distinctive strip of fluted pasta along one edge.

# CHEESE & PEAR CAPPELLETTI

384

**Pasta:** Prepare the pasta dough and let rest for 30 minutes.

**Filling:** Mix the pecorino, ricotta, pear, egg, salt, and pepper in a medium bowl. • **Step 1:** Divide the dough into three pieces. Roll it out quite thinly (down to the second thinnest setting on a pasta machine). • Cut the dough into 2$^1$/2-inch (6-cm) squares. • **Step 2:** Place a heaped teaspoon of filling at the center of each square of pasta and fold into a triangle shape. • **Step 3:** Wrap the triangular-shaped piece of pasta around your index finger and seal the ends. • **Step 4:** Slip the finished pasta off your finger and repeat the process with the remaining squares of pasta and filling. • Place on a floured cloth until ready to cook. • Put a large pot of salted water to boil over high heat. • Cook the pasta in 2–3 batches in the boiling water until al dente, 3–4 minutes each batch. • Scoop out with a slotted spoon, drain well, and transfer to individual serving dishes.

**To Serve:** Sprinkle with the pecorino, drizzle with the butter, and season with pepper. • Serve immediately.

### Pasta

1    recipe plain fresh pasta dough (see page 242)

### Filling

2    cups (250 g) coarsely grated pecorino cheese

8    ounces (250 g) fresh ricotta cheese, drained

1    small pear, peeled, cored, and coarsely grated

1    small egg

    Salt and freshly ground white pepper

### To Serve

4    tablespoons coarsely grated pecorino cheese

6    tablespoons (90 ml) melted butter

    Freshly ground black pepper

Serves: 4–6
Preparation: 1 hour + time to prepare the pasta dough
Cooking: 10–15 minutes
Level: 3

## ■ PREPARING CAPPELLETTI (CAPPELLACCI)

Cappelletti ("little hats"), also known as cappellacci, are made from small, individually cut squares of fresh pasta. They are then filled and folded into triangles and twisted into their classic shape.

**1.** ROLL the pasta into sheets on a floured work surface. Use a plain pastry cutter to cut into strips and then into $2^1/_2$-inch (6-cm) squares.

**2.** PLACE a heaped teaspoon of filling at the center of each square of pasta and fold into a triangle shape.

**3.** WRAP the triangular-shaped piece of pasta around a finger and seal the ends.

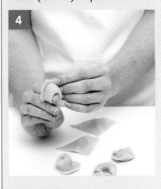

**4.** SLIP the finished pasta off your finger and repeat the process with the remaining squares of pasta and filling.

**5.** CAPPELLETTI have sharp pointed pieces of pasta sticking up at the top, unlike tortellini which are rounded.

# CAPPELLACCI WITH EGGPLANT & CHOCOLATE

**Pasta:** Prepare the pasta dough and let rest for 30 minutes.

**Sauce:** Heat the oil in a medium saucepan and add the tomatoes, onion, garlic, basil, and sugar. Season with salt. Cover and simmer over low heat for 40 minutes. If the sauce is too liquid, uncover and cook until it reduces a little.

**Filling:** Preheat the oven to 350°F (180°C/gas 4).
• Cut the eggplant in half lengthwise. Use a sharp knife to make deep cuts crosswise in the flesh, without piercing the skin. • Bake for about 1 hour, until tender. • Let the eggplant cool, then use a tablespoon to scoop out the flesh. • Heat the oil in a large frying pan over medium heat. Add the onion and sauté until softened, 3–4 minutes. • Add the tomato, eggplant, and red pepper flakes. Simmer for 10 minutes. Season with salt and remove from the heat. • Stir in the bread crumbs, cocoa, ricotta, and chocolate. • Chop in a food processor.
• Prepare the cappellacci following the instructions on page 385. • Put a large pot of salted water to boil over high heat. • Spoon the hot tomato sauce into four individual serving dishes. • Cook the pasta in 2–3 batches in the boiling water until al dente, 3–4 minutes each batch. • Scoop out with a slotted spoon, drain well, and transfer to the serving dishes.
• Drizzle with the butter and serve immediately.

**Pasta**

1 recipe plain fresh pasta dough (see page 242)

**Sauce**

1 tablespoon extra-virgin olive oil

1 pound (500 g) tomatoes, peeled and chopped

½ small onion, finely chopped

1 clove garlic, finely chopped

4 leaves fresh basil, torn

Pinch of sugar

Salt

¼ cup (60 g) melted butter

**Filling**

1 medium eggplant (aubergine), with skin

1 tablespoon extra-virgin olive oil

1 tablespoon finely chopped white onion

1 ripe tomato, peeled and cut in small cubes

¼ teaspoon dried red pepper flakes

3 tablespoons fine dry bread crumbs

1 tablespoon unsweetened cocoa powder

5 ounces (150 g) ricotta cheese, drained

1 ounce (30 g) dark chocolate, grated

Serves: 4
Preparation: 1 hour + time to prepare the pasta dough
Cooking: 1 hour
Level: 3

# HALF MOONS

**Pasta**

1     recipe plain fresh pasta dough (see page 242)

**Filling**

4     ounces (120 g) day-old bread, crusts removed

½     cup (120 ml) dry white wine

2     artichokes

     Freshly squeezed juice of 1 lemon

3     tablespoons extra-virgin olive oil

½     clove garlic, finely chopped

1     tablespoon finely chopped fresh mint

     Salt and freshly ground black pepper

4     cups (1 liter) cold water

1     small onion, finely chopped

3     ounces (90 g) smoked ham

2     cups (250 g) freshly grated Parmesan cheese

1     large egg

**To Serve**

½     cup (120 ml) butter

1     tablespoon finely chopped fresh mint

**Pasta:** Prepare the pasta dough and let rest for 30 minutes.

**Filling:** Soak the bread in the wine. • Clean the artichokes and place in a bowl of cold water with the lemon juice. • Slice thinly and place in a frying pan with 2 tablespoons of oil, the garlic, mint, salt, and pepper. Pour in the water, cover, and simmer until the artichokes are tender, 10–15 minutes. • In a small frying pan, sweat the onion with the remaining 1 tablespoon of oil and salt for 10 minutes. • Add the ham and simmer for 3–4 minutes. • Chop both mixtures with a large knife. • Place in a bowl and mix in the Parmesan and egg. Season with salt and pepper. • **Step 1:** Divide the dough into three pieces. Roll it out quite thinly (down to the second thinnest setting on a pasta machine). Use a smooth pastry or cookie cutter about 3 inches (7.5 cm) in diameter to cut out disks of pasta. • **Step 2:** Shape heaped teaspoons of filling in balls. Put one at the center of each disk of pasta. Fold into half moon shapes. • Put a large pot of salted water to boil over high heat. • Cook the pasta in 2–3 batches in the boiling water until al dente, 2–3 minutes each batch. • Scoop out with a slotted spoon, drain well, and transfer to a serving dish.

**To Serve:** Melt the butter and mint in a small saucepan. Drizzle over the pasta. • Serve hot.

Serves: 4–6
Preparation: 1 hour + time to prepare the pasta dough
Cooking: 40 minutes
Level: 3

Use a round pastry or cookie cutter to make half-moon shaped ravioli. With just a little extra folding these can become exquisite little tortellini ("little cakes") or slightly larger tortelloni. Tortelloni can be so large that you only need to serve 3 or 4 per person. Tortellini differ from cappelletti ("little hats,"), because they have rounded rather than pointed edges.

**1.** ROLL the pasta into sheets on a floured work surface. Use a smooth 3-inch (7.5-cm) pastry or cookie cutter to cut out disks of pasta.

**2.** SHAPE heaped teaspoons of filling in balls. Put one at the center of each disk. Fold the pasta over to seal in a half-moon shape.

**3.** TO PREPARE TORTELLINI, continue by folding the edges of the half-moon pasta back on themselves.

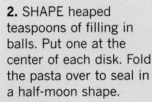

**4.** FINISH by twisting the pasta around your index finger and sealing the ends.

**5.** SLIDE the tortellini off your finger.

**6.** YOU CAN MAKE large tortelloni, by using a larger cutter for the disks and more filling.

# TORTELLINI WITH MEAT SAUCE

**Pasta:** Prepare the pasta dough and let rest for 30 minutes.

**Filling:** Dry-fry the pork in a nonstick frying pan: begin by cooking over high heat, turning the meat once to seal. Reduce the heat and simmer for 4–5 minutes until cooked through. Season with salt and remove from heat. • Chop the pork with the mortadella and prosciutto in a food processor until finely ground. • Add the egg and Parmesan. Season with salt, pepper, and nutmeg. Transfer to a bowl and refrigerate for 2 hours. • Prepare the tortellini following the instructions on page 391.

**Sauce:** Sauté the onion, carrot, and celery in the butter in a large saucepan over medium heat until softened, 5–7 minutes. • Add the pork, beef, and chicken livers. Moisten with the wine and cook until it has evaporated. • Stir in the tomatoes, salt, and pepper. • Cover and simmer gently for 2 hours. • Put a large pot of salted water to boil over high heat. • Cook the pasta in 2–3 batches in the boiling water until al dente, 2–3 minutes each batch. • Scoop out with a slotted spoon, drain well, and transfer to a serving dish. Spoon the sauce over the top and toss gently. • Serve hot.

**Pasta**

| | |
|---|---|
| 1 | recipe plain fresh pasta dough (see page 242) |

**Filling**

| | |
|---|---|
| 5 | ounces (150 g) lean sliced pork |
| | Salt |
| 4 | ounces (120 g) mortadella |
| 4 | ounces (120 g) prosciutto |
| 1 | small egg, lightly beaten |
| 4 | tablespoons freshly grated Parmesan cheese |
| | Freshly ground black pepper |
| 1/8 | teaspoon nutmeg |

**Sauce**

| | |
|---|---|
| 1 | onion, finely chopped |
| 1 | carrot, finely chopped |
| 1 | stalk celery, finely chopped |
| 2 | tablespoons butter |
| 12 | ounces (350 g) ground lean pork |
| 8 | ounces (250 g) ground lean beef |
| 2 | chicken livers, chopped |
| 1 | cup (250 ml) dry red wine |
| 1 | (14-ounce/400-g) can tomatoes, with juice |
| | Salt and freshly ground black pepper |

Serves: 4–6
Preparation: 45 minutes + time to prepare the pasta dough
Cooking: 2 hours
Level: 3

# TORTELLINI WITH ONION CONFIT

**Pasta:** Prepare the pasta dough and let rest for 30 minutes.

**Filling:** Dry-fry the pork in a nonstick frying pan: begin by cooking over high heat, turning the meat once to seal. Reduce the heat and simmer for 4–5 minutes until cooked through. Season with salt and remove from heat. • Chop the pork with the mortadella and prosciutto in a food processor until finely ground. • Add the egg and Parmesan. Season with salt, pepper, and nutmeg. Transfer to a bowl and refrigerate for 2 hours. • Prepare the tortellini following the instructions on page 391.

**Onion Confit:** Sauté the onions in the butter in a medium saucepan over medium heat until softened, 3–4 minutes. • Stir in the sugar and simmer for 2 minutes. • Add the thyme, wine, and vinegar. Simmer, stirring frequently, until the mixture reduces and thickens, about 40 minutes. • Stir in the peas and simmer gently until tender. • Put a large pot of salted water to boil over high heat. • Cook the pasta in 2–3 batches in the boiling water until al dente, 2–3 minutes each batch. • Scoop out with a slotted spoon, drain well, and transfer to a the pan with the sauce. Toss gently. • Garnish with the parsley and serve hot.

**Pasta**

1 recipe plain fresh pasta dough (see page 242)

**Filling**

5 ounces (150 g) lean sliced pork

Salt

4 ounces (125 g) mortadella

4 ounces (125 g) prosciutto (Parma ham)

1 large egg, lightly beaten

3 tablespoons freshly grated Parmesan cheese

Freshly ground black pepper

1/8 teaspoon nutmeg

**Onion Confit**

2 large onions, thinly sliced

2 tablespoons butter

2 teaspoons sugar

4 sprigs fresh thyme, leaves removed and stalks discarded

1 cup (250 ml) dry red wine

2 tablespoons red wine vinegar

1 cup (150 g) frozen peas

2 tablespoons finely chopped fresh parsley

Serves: 4–6
Preparation: 45 minutes
+ time to prepare the pasta dough
Cooking: 2 hours
Level: 1

# TRIANGULAR RAVIOLI WITH TUNA & BEANS

**Pasta:** Prepare the pasta dough and let rest for 30 minutes.

**Filling:** Chop the beans in a food processor until smooth. • Mix the mashed potatoes, bean purée, oil, salt, and pepper in a medium bowl. • **Step 1:** Divide the dough into three pieces. Roll it out quite thinly (down to the second thinnest setting on a pasta machine). • Use a plain pastry cutter to cut into strips and then into squares about 2 1/2 inches (6 cm) square. • **Step 2:** Place a teaspoon of filling in the center of each piece of pasta. • **Step 3:** Fold the pasta over the filling to form triangles, pressing the edges down well to seal. • **Step 4:** Lightly flour the tines (prongs) of a fork and press down firmly around the edges to seal. • Place the ravioli on a clean dry cloth and sprinkle with hard wheat flour. Let rest until ready to cook.

**Sauce:** Heat the chile-flavored oil and garlic in a small saucepan. • Add the tuna, breaking it up with a fork. Cook until heated through, about 5 minutes. • Put a large pot of salted water to boil over high heat. • Cook the pasta in 2–3 batches in the boiling water until al dente, about 3–4 minutes each batch. • Scoop out with a slotted spoon, drain well, and transfer to a serving dish. • Spoon the sauce over the top, sprinkle with the scallion and parsley, and serve immediately.

## Pasta

1 recipe plain fresh pasta dough (see page 242)

## Filling

1 cup (200 ml) canned cannellini

12 ounces (350 g) mashed potatoes

1 tablespoon extra-virgin olive oil

Salt and freshly ground black pepper

## Sauce

2 tablespoons chile-flavored extra-virgin olive oil

1 clove garlic, crushed

8 ounces (250 g) canned tuna, drained

1 scallion (spring onion), finely chopped

Fresh parsley, to garnish

Serves: 4–6
Preparation: 45 minutes
 + time to prepare the pasta dough
Cooking: 15–20 minutes
Level: 3

Triangle-shaped ravioli are prepared from individual squares of pasta dough. Cut the pasta dough into squares about 2–3 inches (5–7.5 cm) each side. They can be stuffed with vegetable, meat, or seafood fillings. If liked, even large squares of pasta can be cut and filled so that you serve just 3 or 4 large triangles to each guest.

**1.** ROLL the pasta out into sheets on a floured work surface. Use a plain pastry cutter to cut into strips and then into squares.

**2.** PLACE a teaspoon of filling at the center of each square of pasta.

**3.** TO PREPARE THE TRIANGLES, fold the pasta over the filling, pressing the edges down ro seal.

**4.** LIGHTLY FLOUR the tines (prongs) of a fork and press down firmly around the edges to seal.

**5.** TRIANGULAR-SHAPED filled pasta can be made in all sizes, from tiny to large.

# OPEN RAVIOLI WITH BELL PEPPERS

**Pasta:** Prepare the pasta dough and let rest for 30 minutes. • Put a large pot of salted water to boil over high heat. Add the oil. • Divide the pasta into four pieces. Roll each piece through a pasta machine one notch at a time down to the thinnest setting. Cut into sheets about 5 inches (13 cm) square. • Blanch the sheets of pasta one at a time in the boiling water. Remove with a slotted spoon. Transfer to a large bowl of cold water. Dip into the water then remove. Gently squeeze out the excess water. Place on a clean kitchen towel and keep warm until ready to serve.

**Filling:** Heat the oil in a large frying pan over low heat and simmer the onion, carrot, and celery with a pinch of salt for 15 minutes. • Add the pancetta and cook for 5 minutes. • Increase the heat to medium and add the bell peppers. Season with salt and pepper. Cover and simmer until tender, 15–20 minutes. • Stir in the butter. • Spoon a layer of filling into four heated serving plates and cover with a piece of pasta. Cover with a layer of sauce and sprinkle with half the Parmesan. Top with a layer of pasta, placed to form a star-shape in each dish, and the remaining sauce. • Sprinkle with the remaining Parmesan, garnish with the parsley, and serve immediately.

**Pasta**

- ½ recipe plain fresh pasta dough (see page 242)
- 1 tablespoon extra-virgin olive oil

**Filling**

- ¼ cup (60 ml) extra-virgin olive oil
- 1 white onion, finely chopped
- ½ carrot, finely chopped
- ½ stalk celery, finely chopped
- Salt and freshly ground black pepper
- 3½ ounces (100 g) pancetta, cut in cubes
- 1 pound (500 g) yellow bell peppers (capsicums), cut in julienne strips
- 2 tablespoons butter
- 1 cup (120 g) freshly grated Parmesan cheese
- 1 tablespoon finely chopped fresh parsley

Serves: 4
Preparation: 30 minutes + time to make the pasta dough
Cooking: 50 minutes
Level: 2

# LARGE STRIPED RAVIOLI

**Pasta:** Prepare the four types of pasta dough and let rest for 30 minutes.

**Filling:** Mix the ricotta, eggs, and Parmesan in a bowl until smooth and creamy. Season with salt and pepper. • **Step 1:** Divide the plain pasta dough into four pieces. Roll each piece through a pasta machine down to the second thinnest setting. Cut into sheets about 4 x 6 inches (10 x 15 cm). • Divide the colored pasta doughs into two pieces and roll each piece through the machine down to the thinnest setting. Cut into $1/2$ x 6-inch (1 x 15-cm) strips. Place the strips of colored pasta on the plain pasta. • **Step 2:** Roll through the pasta machine at the third thinnest setting so that the colored pasta sticks to the plain pasta. • You will have 16 squares of striped pasta.

**Step 3:** Divide the filling into eight and spread over eight pieces of pasta, leaving a $3/4$-inch (2-cm) border around the edges. Cover with the remaining pieces of pasta, pressing down on the edges to seal. Place on a clean floured cloth until ready to cook.

**Sauce:** Cook the cauliflower to a boil in a medium saucepan with the vinegar and a pinch of salt until tender, 10–15 minutes. Drain and chop in a food processor with the oil and herbs. • Put a large pot of salted water to boil over high heat. Add the oil. • Cook the pasta in 3–4 batches in the boiling water until al dente, 3–4 minutes each batch. • Scoop out carefully with a slotted spoon, drain well, and place in serving dishes with the cauliflower sauce. • Serve hot garnished with marjoram and wild fennel.

## Pasta

1   recipe plain fresh pasta dough (see page 242)

$1/3$   recipe spinach pasta dough (see pages 276–7)

$1/3$   recipe beet pasta dough (see page 294)

$1/3$   recipe squid ink pasta dough (see page 300)

## Filling

1   pound (500 g) ricotta cheese, drained

2   small eggs

$1^{1}/2$ cups (180 g) freshly grated Parmesan cheese

   Salt and freshly ground black pepper

## Sauce

2   pounds (1 kg) cauliflower, cut in small florets, stems in small cubes

2   tablespoons white wine vinegar

   Salt

$1/4$   cup (60 ml) extra-virgin olive oil

2   sprigs marjoram, finely chopped + extra to garnish

2   sprigs wild fennel, finely chopped + extra to garnish

Serves: 8
Preparation: 1 hour + time to prepare the pasta doughs
Cooking: 40 minutes
Level: 3

## PREPARING STRIPED FRESH PASTA

To make the dough for striped pasta you will need to prepare the four different types of pasta first. Make one quantity of plain pasta and three small quantities of spinach pasta, tomato pasta, and squid ink pasta.

**1.** ROLL the pasta dough into sheets about 4 x 6 inches (10 x 15 cm). Cut the colored sheets into strips about $^1/_2$ x 6 inches (1 x 15 cm) wide and lay on the plain pasta.

**2.** ROLL the sheet very carefully through the pasta machine at the third thinnest setting. Do not roll any thinner than this.

**3.** USE the striped pasta to make an eyecatching lasagna or special filled shapes.

# SWISS CHARD & RICOTTA ROLL

**Pasta:** Prepare the pasta dough and let rest for 30 minutes.

**Filling:** Melt the butter in a large frying pan over medium-low heat and sauté the Swiss chard for 10 minutes. • Season with salt and remove from the heat. Let cool. • Strain the ricotta and mix in the cooled Swiss chard with the Parmesan, lemon zest, salt, and pepper. • Divide the dough into three pieces. Roll it through the machine one notch at a time down to the second thinnest setting. Trim the pieces to obtain neat rectangles. • Spread the sheets of dough with even layers of filling, leaving a border around the edges. Roll the sheets of pasta up carefully and wrap in clean pieces of muslin (cheesecloth). Tie the ends with kitchen string. • Place a large pan of water over high heat. Cover and bring to a boil. • Cook the pasta in the gently simmering water for 20 minutes. • Remove the rolls from the water and unwrap the muslin. Cut in thick slices and drizzle with the melted butter. • Serve immediately.

**Pasta**

1    recipe plain fresh pasta dough (see page 242)

**Filling**

2    tablespoons butter

1¼  pounds (625 g) cooked Swiss chard, squeezed dry and finely chopped

    Salt and freshly ground white pepper

12  ounces (350 g) fresh ricotta cheese, drained

¾  cup (90 g) freshly grated Parmesan cheese

1    teaspoon finely grated organic lemon zest

½  cup (120 g) melted butter

Serves: 4–6
Preparation: 1 hour + time to prepare the pasta dough
Cooking: 30–40 minutes
Level: 3

# BAKED
# PASTA

# ANELLINI PASTA BAKE

412

Heat 2 tablespoons of oil in a large frying pan over medium heat. Add the onion and sauté until softened, 3–4 minutes. • Add the beef and pork and sauté until browned all over, 5–7 minutes. • Pour in the wine and let it evaporate. • Stir in the peas, tomatoes, and water. Season with salt. Cover and simmer over low heat for 1 hour. • Put a large pot of salted water to boil over high heat. • Cook the pasta in the boiling water for half the time indicated on the pasta package. • Drain and add to the meat sauce. Stir in the grated pecorino. • Preheat the oven to 425°F (220°C/gas 7). • Butter a large baking pan and sprinkle with the bread crumbs. Spoon in half the pasta and top with the cubes of pecorino. Cover with the remaining pasta, smoothing the top. • Put the ciabatta bread in a bowl with the remaining 2 tablespoons of oil and the dried herbs and toss well. Sprinkle over the pasta in the dish. • Bake for 20–25 minutes, until the bread is golden brown and crisp. • Serve hot.

4 tablespoons (60 ml) extra-virgin olive oil

1 onion, finely chopped

8 ounces (250 g) beef, cut into small cubes

8 ounces (250 g) pork, cut into small cubes

1 cup (250 g) dry red wine

2 cups (300 g) frozen peas

1 pound (500 g) peeled and chopped tomatoes

2 cups (500 ml) hot water

Salt

1 pound (500 g) anellini (small pasta rings)

1 cup (120 g) freshly grated pecorino cheese

$1/3$ cup (50 g) fine dry bread crumbs

$2/3$ cup (150 g) pecorino cheese, cut into small cubes

6 slices ciabatta bread, crumbled or torn

1 tablespoon dried Italian herbs

Serves: 6–8
Preparation: 30 minutes
Cooking: 1$1/2$ hours
Level: 1

You could also use: pennette, penne, sedani

# BAKED TOMATOES WITH PASTA FILLING

414

Cut the top off each tomato (with its stalk) and set aside. Use a teaspoon to hollow out the insides of each tomato. Put the pulp in a bowl. • Place a basil leaf in the bottom of each hollow shell. • Preheat the oven to 350°F (180°C/gas 4).• Put a large pot of salted water to boil over high heat. • Cook the pasta in the boiling water for half the time indicated on the pasta package. • Combine the pasta with the tomato pulp. Add the parsley and 2 tablespoons of the oil. Season with salt and pepper. • Stuff the hollow tomatoes with the pasta mixture. • Grease an ovenproof dish just large enough to hold the tomatoes snugly with the remaining 1 tablespoon of oil and carefully place the tomatoes in it. Cover each tomato with its top. • Bake for 40–45 minutes, until the tomatoes are tender and the pasta is fully cooked. • Serve hot or at room temperature.

8 **medium tomatoes**

8 **leaves fresh basil**

8 **tablespoons ditaloni rigati or other small, tubular pasta**

2 **tablespoons finely chopped fresh parsley**

3 **tablespoons extra-virgin olive oil**

**Salt and freshly ground black pepper**

**Serves: 4–8**
**Preparation: 20 minutes**
**Cooking: 45–50 minutes**
**Level: 2**

■ ■ ■ *Choose eight round tomatoes of about the same size. Make sure they have no blemishes and that they still have their stalks attached.*

You could also use: risone, tubetti, conchigliette

# BAKED PASTA WITH CHEESE

416

**Pasta:** Preheat the oven to 400°F (200°C/gas 6).
• Butter a large baking dish. • Put a large pot of salted water to boil over high heat. • Cook the pasta in the boiling water for half the time indicated on the package. • Drain and transfer to a large bowl. Toss with the oil to prevent it from sticking.

**Béchamel Sauce:** Melt the butter in a small saucepan over medium heat and add the flour. Simmer for 1–2 minutes. Remove from the heat and add the milk all at once. Stir thoroughly, return to the heat, and bring to a boil, stirring constantly. As soon as the sauce comes to a boil, decrease the heat to low, and season with salt, pepper, and nutmeg. Simmer for 5 minutes, stirring constantly.

**To Serve:** Mix three-quarters of the pasta into the Béchamel together with 1 cup (120 g) of the pecorino. • Spoon this creamy pasta mixture into the baking dish. Cover with the sliced cheese. Top with the remaining pasta and sprinkle with the remaining pecorino. • Bake until bubbling and golden brown, 35–40 minutes. • Serve hot.

**Pasta**

1    pound (500 g) sedani
1    tablespoon extra-virgin olive oil

**Béchamel Sauce**

¼    cup (60 g) butter
⅓    cup (50 g) all-purpose (plain) flour
2    cups (500 ml) milk
     Salt and freshly ground white pepper
¼    teaspoon freshly grated nutmeg

**To Serve**

1¼   cups (150 g) freshly grated pecorino cheese
5    ounces (150 g) caciocavallo or other firm, tasty cheese, thinly sliced

Serves: 4–6
Preparation: 30 minutes
Cooking: 45–50 minutes
Level: 2

You could also use: penne, farfalle, rigatoni, maccheroni

# BAKED PASTA WITH PEAS & MEAT SAUCE

418

Heat 3 tablespoons of oil in a large frying pan over medium heat. Add half the onion and parsley and sauté until the onion is softened, 3–4 minutes. • Add the beef and sausages and sauté until browned all over, 5–7 minutes. • Pour in the wine and simmer until it evaporates. • Stir in the tomatoes and water. Season with salt. Cover and simmer over low heat for 1 hour. • Heat 1 tablespoon of oil in a large frying pan and sauté the remaining onion until softened. Stir in the peas. Cover and simmer for 15 minutes. • Cook the pasta in a large pan of salted, boiling water until just al dente. • Drain and add to the meat sauce. Sprinkle with pecorino. • Preheat the oven to 425°F (220°C/gas 7). • Butter a deep 11-inch (28-cm) springform pan and sprinkle it with half the bread crumbs. Spoon in half the pasta and top with the ricotta salata and cooked peas. Cover with the remaining pasta, smoothing the top. Sprinkle with the remaining bread crumbs and drizzle with the remaining 1 tablespoon of oil. • Bake for 20–25 minutes. • Let rest for 5 minutes, then loosen and remove the pan sides and bottom. • Serve hot.

| | |
|---|---|
| 5 | tablespoons (75 ml) extra-virgin olive oil |
| 1 | tablespoon finely chopped fresh parsley |
| 1 | onion, finely chopped |
| 12 | ounces (350 g) beef, cut into small cubes |
| 2 | Italian sausages, peeled and crumbled |
| 1 | cup (250 ml) dry red wine |
| 1 | pound (500 g) tomatoes, peeled and chopped |
| 2 | cups (500 ml) boiling water |
| | Salt |
| 2 | cups (300 g) frozen peas |
| 1 | pound (500 g) anellini (small pasta rings) |
| 2 | cups (250 g) freshly grated pecorino cheese |
| 2/3 | cup (100 g) fine dry bread crumbs |
| 2/3 | cup (150 g) ricotta salata cheese, cut into small cubes |

Serves: 4–6
Preparation: 45 minutes
Cooking: 1 1/2 hours
Level: 2

You could also use: pennette, mezze maniche, sedani

# CALABRIAN BAKED PASTA

Preheat the oven to 350°F (180°C/gas 4). • Grease a large deep baking dish with a little of the oil. • Blanch the tomatoes in a large pan of salted boiling water for 2 minutes. Drain, reserving 1/2 cup (120 ml) of the cooking water, and slip off their skins. Chop finely. • Transfer the tomatoes and their juices to a large bowl with the basil. Season with salt and pepper. • Peel the potatoes and slice 1/4-inch (5-mm) thick. • Place a layer of tomatoes on the bottom of the prepared baking dish. Cover with a layer of raw pasta, followed by layers of potatoes, olives, and onion. Repeat until all the ingredients are in the pan. Drizzle each layer with oil and sprinkle with pecorino and oregano. Pour in the reserved cooking water. • Sprinkle with the bread crumbs and drizzle with the remaining oil. Cover the dish with aluminum foil. • Bake until the pasta and potatoes are just tender, about 50 minutes. Remove the foil and finish baking, 10–15 minutes. • Serve hot.

420

½ cup (125 ml) extra-virgin olive oil

3 pounds (1.5 kg) firm-ripe tomatoes

10 leaves fresh basil, torn

Salt and freshly ground black pepper

1 pound (500 g) potatoes

1 pound (500 g) conchiglie

2 cups (200 g) black olives, pitted

1 large onion, thinly sliced

1 cup (120 g) freshly grated pecorino cheese

1 tablespoon finely chopped fresh oregano

1 cup (75 g) fine dry bread crumbs

Serves: 6–8
Preparation: 15 minutes
Cooking: 1 hour
Level: 1

You could also use: penne, fusilli, rigatoni

# BAKED PASTA WITH MEATBALLS

**Meatballs:** Mix the beef, sausages, parsley, egg, cheese, garlic, salt, and pepper in a large bowl. Stir in the bread crumbs and form into balls the size of walnuts. • Heat the oil in a deep frying pan until very hot. Fry the meatballs in small batches until crisp and browned, 5–7 each batch. • Drain on paper towels.

**Sauce:** Heat the oil in a medium saucepan over low heat. Add the onion, cover, and simmer until softened, about 10 minutes. • Add the tomatoes and basil and season with salt and pepper. Cook, uncovered, over medium-low heat until the oil separates from the tomatoes, 25–30 minutes. • Preheat the oven to 350°F (180°C/gas 4). • Put a large pot of salted water to boil over high heat. • Cook the pasta in the boiling water for half the time indicated on the pasta package. • Drain and transfer to a large bowl. Toss with half the sauce. Transfer half of the pasta mixture to a large baking dish. Top with half the mozzarella and half the meatballs. Cover with the remaining pasta mixture. Cover with the remaining meatballs and mozzarella. Finish with the remaining sauce and sprinkle with the Parmesan. • Bake for 30–35 minutes, until the cheese is bubbling and golden brown. • Serve hot.

## Meatballs

- 8 ounces (250 g) lean ground (minced) beef
- 2 Italian sausages, crumbled
- 1 tablespoon finely chopped fresh parsley
- 1 large egg
- 2 tablespoons freshly grated Parmesan cheese
- 1 clove garlic, finely chopped

  Salt and freshly ground black pepper
- 2 tablespoons fresh bread crumbs
- 1 cup (250 ml) olive oil, for frying

## Sauce

- ¼ cup (60 ml) extra-virgin olive oil
- 1 large onion, finely chopped
- 2 pounds (1 kg) peeled plum tomatoes, pressed through a fine mesh strainer (passata)
- 1 tablespoon fresh basil

  Salt and freshly ground black pepper
- 1 pound (500 g) penne
- 1 pound (500 g) mozzarella cheese, thinly sliced
- ½ cup (60 g) freshly grated Parmesan cheese

Serves: 6–8
Preparation: 65 minutes
Cooking: 65–80 minutes
Level: 2

You could also use: fusilli, rigatoni, tortiglioni

# FARFALLE PASTA & CHICKEN BAKE

Heat the oil in a large frying pan over medium heat. Add the onion and sauté until softened, 3–4 minutes. Season with salt and pepper. • Pierce the sausages and blanch in boiling water for 3 minutes. Drain, remove the casings, and crumble the meat. • Add the sausage meat, ham, and shredded chicken to the onion in the pan. Simmer over medium-low heat for 10 minutes, adding stock if the mixture starts to stick to the pan. • Add the eggs, and season with salt and pepper, and set aside. • Meanwhile, put a large pot of salted water to boil over high heat. • Cook the pasta in the boiling water for half the time indicated on the pasta package. • Preheat the oven to 350°F (180°C/gas 4). • Butter a baking dish and sprinkle with bread crumbs. • Arrange the pasta in the baking dish. Spoon the tomato sauce over the top and sprinkle with the cheese. • Bake until golden brown, 35–40 minutes. • Serve hot.

¼ cup (60 ml) extra-virgin olive oil

1 large onion, finely chopped

Salt and freshly ground black pepper

2 Italian sausages

1 cup (150 g) diced smoked ham

3 cups (400 g) leftover roast or grilled chicken, shredded.

1 cup (250 ml) vegetable stock (optional), homemade or bouillon cube

3 hard-boiled eggs, crumbled

1 pound (500 g) farfalle

2 cups (500 ml) homemade (see recipe on page 182) or storebought tomato pasta sauce

1 cup (120 g) freshly grated pecorino or Parmesan cheese

Serves: 6–8
Preparation: 45 minutes
Cooking: 50–60 minutes
Level: 2

You could also use: spaghettini, spaghetti, linguine

# BAKED RIGATONI

Heat the oil in a large frying pan over medium heat. Add the onion and garlic and sauté until softened, 3–4 minutes. Season with salt and pepper. • Add the sausage meat, salami, and beef to the onion and simmer over low heat for 30 minutes. • Put a large pot of salted water to boil over high heat. • Cook the pasta in the boiling water for half the time indicated on the pasta package. • Drain well and let cool a little. • Preheat the oven to 350°F (180°C/gas 4). Butter a large baking dish. • Use a teaspoon to fill the pasta with the meat sauce. • Arrange the pasta in the baking dish. Spoon the tomato sauce over the top and sprinkle with the Parmesan. • Bake until golden brown, 35–40 minutes. • Serve hot garnished with a few leaves of fresh parsley.

¼ cup (60 ml) extra-virgin olive oil

1 large onion, finely chopped

2 cloves garlic, finely chopped

Salt and freshly ground black pepper

3 Italian sausages, peeled and crumbled

1 cup (150 g) diced salami

1 pound (500 g) ground (minced) beef

3 cups (750 ml) homemade (see recipe on page 190) or storebought tomato pasta sauce

1 pound (500 g) large rigatoni pasta

1 cup (125 g) freshly grated Parmesan cheese

Fresh parsley to garnish

Serves: 6–8
Preparation: 1 hour
Cooking: 80 minutes
Level: 2

You could also use: conchiglione

# BAKED SPAGHETTI WITH CHICKEN & SPINACH

428

Put a large pot of salted water to boil over high heat. • Cook the pasta in the boiling water for half the time indicated on the pasta package. • Drain and set aside. • Preheat the oven to 400°F (200°C/gas 6). • Heat the oil in large saucepan over medium heat. Add the garlic and onion and sauté until softened, 3–4 minutes. • Add the chicken and sauté until browned, 5–10 minutes. • Put the tomatoes, basil, salt, chile, parsley, garlic, and 1 cup (120 g) of the Parmesan in a food processor. Pulse until chunky, not smooth. • Add to the chicken mixture. Simmer for 15 minutes. • Remove from the heat and stir in the spinach and pasta. • Place the mixture in a baking dish. Sprinkle the remaining 1/2 cup (60 g) of Parmesan. Bake for 20–25 minutes, until golden brown. • Serve hot.

| 1 | pound (500 g) spaghetti |
| 2 | tablespoons extra-virgin olive oil |
| 6 | garlic cloves, smashed |
| 1 | red onion, chopped |
| 4 | boneless, skinless chicken breast halves, coarsely chopped |
| 2 | (14-ounce/400-g) cans tomatoes, with juice |
| | Fresh basil leaves |
| 1/4 | teaspoon salt |
| 1 | small dried chile, crumbled |
| 1/4 | cup fresh parsley |
| 4 | garlic cloves |
| 1 1/2 | cups (180 g) freshly grated Parmesan cheese |
| 4 | cups (200 g) fresh spinach |

Serves: 6
Preparation: 30 minutes
Cooking: 55–60 minutes
Level: 1

You could also use: penne, ruote, rigatoni

# BAKED TAGLIATELLE WITH SHRIMP & WHITE WINE

**Pasta:** If using homemade pasta, prepare it first.
**Sauce:** Preheat the oven to 400°F (200°C/gas 6).
• Cook the shrimp in 4 cups (1 liter) of boiling water for 5 minutes. Remove with a slotted spoon. • Use a pair of sharply pointed scissors to cut down the center of their backs. Pull the sides of the shell apart and take out the flesh, keeping it as intact as possible, and set aside. • Return the shells and heads to the stock and continue boiling until it has reduced by two-thirds.
• Heat the oil and 4 tablespoons (60 g) of butter in a large frying pan over medium heat. Add the garlic and onion and sauté until softened, 3–4 minutes. • Add the reserved shrimp flesh and wine and cook until the wine has evaporated. Season with salt. Remove from the heat. • Melt the remaining 2 tablespoons of butter in a small saucepan. Stir in the flour and keep stirring to prevent lumps forming as you add first the hot milk and then 2 cups (500 ml) of strained hot shrimp stock. Continue cooking and stirring until the sauce is thick and glossy, 5–10 minutes. • Put a large pot of salted water to boil over high heat. • Cook the pasta in the boiling water for 1 minute (or half the time indicated on the package). • Drain and add to the pan. Pour in the sauce and stir gently while cooking over low heat.
• Transfer to a large baking dish. Sprinkle with the Parmesan and parsley, and bake for 15–20 minutes, until a golden crust has formed on top. • Serve hot.

You could also use: penne, farfalle, linguine

**Pasta**

1    **recipe tagliatelle (see pages 242–5) or 14 ounces (400 g) storebought tagliatelle**

**Sauce**

1½   **pounds (750 g) whole raw shrimp (prawns)**

3    **tablespoons extra-virgin olive oil**

6    **tablespoons (90 g) butter**

1    **clove garlic, finely chopped**

1    **small onion, finely chopped**

½   **cup (120 ml) dry white wine**

    **Salt**

3    **tablespoons all-purpose (plain) flour**

1    **cup (250 ml) hot milk**

1    **cup (150 g) freshly grated Parmesan cheese**

2    **tablespoons finely chopped fresh parsley**

Serves: 6
Preparation: 40 minutes
Cooking: 1 hour
Level: 3

# BAKED SPINACH TAGLIATELLE

432

**Pasta:** If using homemade pasta, prepare it first.

**Béchamel Sauce:** Melt the butter in a medium saucepan, then stir in the flour and nutmeg. Cook for 3–4 minutes, stirring constantly, then add the milk all at once. Season with salt and pepper. Bring to a boil, stirring constantly. • Simmer over low heat for 5 minutes, stirring almost continuously. Remove from the heat.

**Sauce:** Melt the butter in a large frying pan over medium heat. Add the prosciutto and sauté until crisp, 2–3 minutes. • Drain the mushrooms, reserving the water. • Chop the mushrooms coarsely and add to the prosciutto. Cook over medium heat until the mushrooms are tender, gradually adding the reserved water, about 5 minutes. • Season with salt and pepper. • Put a large pot of salted water to boil over high heat. • Preheat the oven to 375°F (190°C/gas 5). • Butter a large baking dish. • Cook the pasta in the boiling water for 1 minute. • Drain well and place in a large bowl. • Carefully stir in the sauce, almost all the Béchamel, and 3 tablespoons of Parmesan. Place in the baking dish, top with the remaining Béchamel, and sprinkle with the remaining cheese. • Bake for 30–35 minutes, until golden brown. • Serve hot.

## Pasta

1 recipe spinach pasta tagliatelle (see pages 276–7) or 14 ounces (400 g) storebought spinach tagliatelle

## Béchamel Sauce

3 tablespoons (45 g) butter

$\frac{1}{3}$ cup (50 g) all-purpose (plain) flour

Pinch of freshly grated nutmeg

$2\frac{2}{3}$ cups (650 ml) milk

Salt and freshly ground white pepper

## Sauce

4 tablespoons (60 g) butter,

$\frac{1}{2}$ cup (60 g) prosciutto, finely chopped

2 ounces (60 g) dried mushrooms, soaked in 1 cup (250 ml) warm water for 15 minutes

Salt and freshly ground white pepper

4 tablespoons freshly grated Parmesan cheese

Serves: 4–6
Preparation: 45 minutes + time to prepare the pasta
Cooking: 50–60 minutes
Level: 3

You could also use: whole-wheat or spinach penne, fusilli

# BAKED PUMPKIN PAPPARDELLE

434

**Pasta:** If using homemade pasta, prepare it first.
**Sauce:** Preheat the oven to 400°F (200°C/gas 6).
• Oil a large baking dish. • Heat the oil in a large
frying pan over medium heat. Add the pancetta and
garlic and sauté until pale gold, 3–4 minutes. • Add
the pumpkin and wine and simmer for 10 minutes.
• Put a large pot of salted water to boil over high
heat. • Cook the pasta in the boiling water for 1
minute (or half the time indicated on the package).
• Drain and add to the pumpkin. Simmer over
medium heat for 2 minutes. • Add the parsley and
season with pepper. Discard the garlic. • Transfer
the mixture to the prepared dish. Top with the
cheese. • Bake until the cheese is bubbling and
lightly browned, 10–15 minutes. • Serve hot.

**Pasta**

1   recipe pappardelle
    (see pages 242–5)
    or 14 ounces (400 g)
    storebought
    pappardelle

**Sauce**

¼   cup (60 ml) extra-
    virgin olive oil

1   cup (125 g) diced
    pancetta or bacon

1   clove garlic, lightly
    crushed but whole

12  ounces (350 g)
    pumpkin flesh, thinly
    sliced

½   cup (120 ml) dry white
    wine

1   tablespoon finely
    chopped fresh parsley

    Freshly ground black
    pepper

2   cups (250 g) freshly
    grated Fontina cheese

Serves: 4–6
Preparation: 15 minutes
    + time to prepare the
    pasta
Cooking: 30–35 minutes
Level: 1

You could also use: spaghettini, spaghetti, linguine

# BAKED TAGLIOLINI WITH MEAT SAUCE

**Pasta:** If using homemade pasta, prepare it first.
**Béchamel Sauce:** Melt the butter in a medium saucepan over medium heat. Add the flour and cook for 1 minute, stirring constantly. • Add the stock, cream, endives, and Marsala, and season with salt and pepper. Simmer for 10 minutes, stirring constantly. Remove from the heat and set aside.

**To Serve:** Put a large pot of salted water to boil over high heat. • Preheat the oven to 350°F (180°C/gas 4). • Butter six to eight individual ovenproof dishes. • Cook the pasta in the boiling water for 1 minute, or half the time indicated on the package. • Drain well and place in a large bowl. Add the Parmesan, Béchamel sauce, and meat sauce. Stir carefully until well mixed. • Divide the pasta mixture evenly among the ovenproof dishes. • Place a large pan half filled with cold water in the oven and carefully place the small dishes in the large pan. Bake for 15–20 minutes. • Serve hot.

## Pasta

1    recipe tagliolini (see pages 242–5) or 14 ounces (400 g) storebought tagliolini

## Béchamel Sauce

¼    cup (60 g) butter

4    tablespoons all-purpose (plain) flour

$1^{2}/_{3}$ cups (400 ml) beef stock (see page 48)

½    cup (120 ml) heavy (double) cream

5    leaves Belgian endives, cut in thin strips and cooked for 2–3 minutes in hot butter

1    tablespoon Marsala wine

     Salt and freshly ground white pepper

## To Serve

¾    cup (90 g) freshly grated Parmesan

1    quantity meat sauce (see Baked Cannelloni, page 442)

Serves: 6–8
Preparation: 30 minutes
+ time to make the pasta & meat sauce
Cooking: 35–45 minutes
Level: 2

You could also use: spaghetti, penne

# BAKED TAGLIATELLE NESTS

**Pasta:** If using homemade pasta, prepare it first.
**Filling:** Melt the butter in a medium saucepan, then stir in the flour and nutmeg. Cook for 3–4 minutes, stirring constantly, then add the milk all at once. Season with salt and pepper. Bring to a boil, stirring constantly. • Simmer for 5 minutes, stirring almost continuously, then remove from the heat. • Put a large pot of salted water to boil over high heat.
• Cook the pasta in the boiling water for 1 minute or for half the time indicated on the package.
• Drain well and place in a large bowl. • Carefully stir in the sauce, mozzarella, ham, Parmesan, and the egg. Season with salt and pepper and stir until well mixed. • Line a baking sheet lined with aluminum foil. Spread with the filling to about $2/3$-inch (2-cm) thick. Let rest in a dry place for at least 4 hours, until firm.
**To Serve:** Preheat the oven to 400°F (200°C/gas 6).
• Use a cookie cutter or glass to cut the mixture into $2^1/2$-inch (6-cm) disks. • Sprinkle a baking sheet with the bread crumbs or line it with foil.
• Place the disks of pasta on the prepared sheet and sprinkle with the butter and Parmesan. • Bake for 10–15 minutes, until golden brown. • Serve hot.

**Pasta**

1 recipe tagliatelle (see pages 242–5) or 14 ounces (400 g) storebought tagliatelle

**Filling**

5 tablespoons (75 g) butter

$1/2$ cup (75 g) all-purpose (plain) flour

Pinch of freshly ground nutmeg

3 cups (750 ml) milk

Salt and freshly ground white pepper

8 ounces (250 g) mozzarella cheese, cut in small cubes

5 ounces (150 g) ham, cut in small cubes

$3/4$ cup (90 g) freshly grated Parmesan cheese

1 large egg

**To Serve**

2 tablespoons butter, cut up

4 tablespoons freshly grated Parmesan cheese

Serves 4–6
Preparation: 1 hour
+ time to prepare the pasta + 4 hours to rest
Cooking: 30 minutes
Level: 3

# BAKED PASTA WITH VEGGIES

440

**Pasta:** If using homemade pasta, prepare it first. Place a large pan of water over high heat with the coarse sea salt. Cover and bring to a boil. • Preheat the oven to 350°F (180°C/gas 4).

**Cream Sauce:** Melt the butter in a medium saucepan over medium heat and add the flour. Cook for 1 minute, stirring constantly. Pour in the stock and cream. Season with salt and pepper. Bring to a boil and simmer for 10 minutes, stirring constantly.

**Filling:** Cook the vegetables in salted, boiling water for 5 minutes. • Drain and place in a bowl of cold water to cool. • Melt 3 tablespoons of butter in a large frying pan. Drain the vegetables thoroughly and add to the pan. Cook for 5 minutes over low heat. Season with salt and pepper and remove from the heat. • Put a large pot of salted water to boil over high heat. • Cook the pasta in the boiling water for 1 minute or for half the time indicated on the package. • Drain well and toss with the remaining 2 tablespoons of butter. • Cover the bottom of each of eight small ovenproof dishes with a layer of pasta. • Mix the pasta into the remaining cream sauce. Add the vegetables, pecorino, and egg. Mix well, then divide evenly among the ovenproof dishes. • Bake for 25–30 minutes, until golden brown. • Turn out onto serving plates and serve hot.

You could also use: plain tagliatelle

**Pasta**

½ recipe tagliatelle (see pages 242–5) or 7 ounces (200 g) storebought tagliatelle

½ recipe spinach pasta tagliatelle (see pages 276–7) or 7 ounces (200 g) storebought spinach tagliatelle

**Cream Sauce**

5 tablespoons (75 g) butter

½ cup (75 g) all-purpose (plain) flour

1¼ cups (300 ml) beef stock (see page 48)

1²⁄₃ cups (400 ml) single (light) cream

Salt and freshly ground white pepper

**Filling**

12 ounces (350 g) mixed vegetables, cut in small cubes (a mix of peas, carrots, and green beans is ideal)

6 tablespoons (90 g) butter

Salt and freshly ground white pepper

¾ cup (90 g) freshly grated pecorino cheese

1 large egg

Serves: 8
Preparation: 1 hour + time to make the pasta
Cooking: 1 hour
Level: 3

# BAKED CANNELLONI

**Pasta:** Prepare the pasta dough.

**Meat Sauce:** Heat the oil in a medium saucepan over high heat. Add the onion, celery, carrot, and parsley and sauté until softened, 3–4 minutes.
• Add the sausages and cook over medium-low heat until the fat in the sausages has melted. • Increase the heat and sauté the beef until browned all over, about 5 minutes. • Add the chicken livers and cook for 3 minutes. • Sprinkle with the flour and cook for 3 minutes. • Pour in the Marsala and cook until evaporated. • Stir in the tomatoes and stock. Season with salt and pepper. Cover and simmer over low heat for 1 hour, stirring often.

**Pasta:** Divide the pasta dough into six pieces. Roll it through a pasta machine one notch at a time down to the second thinnest setting. Let dry on a lightly floured cloth for 30 minutes. • Cut the dough into 4 x 7-inch (10 x 18-cm) rectangles. • Blanch the rectangles of pasta as you would for lasagna, following the instructions on page 453.

**Béchamel Sauce:** Melt the butter in a medium saucepan, then stir in the flour and nutmeg. Cook for 3–4 minutes, stirring constantly, then add the milk all at once. Season with salt and pepper. Bring to a boil, stirring constantly. • Simmer for 5 minutes, stirring almost continuously, then remove from the heat.

**Filling:** Melt 4 tablespoons (60 g) of butter in a small frying pan over medium heat. Add the onion

**Pasta**

1    recipe plain fresh pasta dough (see page 242)

**Meat Sauce**

2    tablespoons extra-virgin olive oil

1    onion, finely chopped

1    stalk celery, finely chopped

1    carrot, finely chopped

1    tablespoon finely chopped fresh parsley

4    Italian sausages, crumbled

4    ounces (125 g) ground (minced) beef

5    ounces (150 g) chicken livers, finely chopped

1    tablespoon all-purpose (plain) flour

½    cup (120 ml) dry Marsala wine

1    cup (250 g) canned tomatoes, with juice

½    cup (120 ml) beef stock (see page 48)

    Salt and freshly ground black pepper

**Béchamel Sauce**

3    tablespoons (45 g) butter

⅓ cup (50 g) all-purpose (plain) flour

Pinch of freshly grated nutmeg

2⅔ cups (650 ml) milk

Salt and freshly ground white pepper

**Filling**

6 tablespoons (90 g) butter

½ onion, finely chopped

10 ounces (300 g) lean ground (minced) beef

¾ cup (90 g) finely chopped ham

3 ounces (90 g) ground (minced) chicken breast

⅓ cup (90 ml) dry white wine

⅓ cup (90 ml) beef stock (see page 48)

3 tablespoons Béchamel sauce (see above)

1 small egg

4 tablespoons freshly grated Parmesan cheese

⅛ teaspoon freshly grated nutmeg

Serves: 6
Preparation: 1¹/₂ hours + time to make the pasta
Cooking: 2 hours
Level: 3

and sauté until softened, 3–4 minutes. • Increase the heat to high and sauté the beef, ham, and chicken until browned all over, about 5 minutes. • Pour in the wine and cook until evaporated. • Pour in the stock and season with salt and pepper. Stir well. • Add the 3 tablespoons of the Béchamel sauce and cook for 15 minutes, stirring often. • Remove from the heat and set aside.

**To Assemble & Bake:** Preheat the oven to 400°F (200°C/gas 6). • Butter a baking dish. • Transfer the meat sauce to a food processor and chop finely. • Mix in the egg, Parmesan, and nutmeg. • Spread a small amount of filling on each of the pasta rectangles and roll them up. • Lay the cannelloni in a single layer in the prepared baking dish. Cover with the Béchamel, meat sauce, and dot with the remaining 2 tablespoons of butter. • Bake for 15–20 minutes, until the sauces are bubbling. • Let rest for 10 minutes before serving.

# CANNELLONI WITH MUSHROOM MEAT SAUCE

**Pasta:** Prepare the pasta dough.

**Meat Sauce:** Soak the mushrooms in a small bowl of milk for 1 hour. Drain and chop finely. • Melt the butter in a large frying pan over medium heat. Add the onion and prosciutto and sauté until softened, 3–4 minutes. • Add the mushrooms and cook for 2 minutes. • Add the beef and chicken and sauté over medium-high heat until well browned, about 5 minutes. • Pour in the wine and simmer until evaporated. • Pour in the stock, cover, and simmer over low heat for 30 minutes. When the meat sauce is cooked, stir in 2 tablespoons of the Béchamel.

**Pasta:** Divide the pasta dough into five pieces. Roll it through a pasta machine one notch at a time down to the thinnest setting. Let dry on a lightly floured cloth for 30 minutes.

**To Assemble & Bake:** Preheat the oven to 450°F (225°C/ gas 7). • Butter a large baking dish • Cut the pasta dough into 4 x 7-inch (10 x 18-cm) rectangles. • Blanch the rectangles of pasta as you would for lasagna, following the instructions on page 453. • Spread the pieces of pasta with the meat sauce. Roll the pasta up and place the rolls in the dish. Cover with Béchamel and tomato sauce. Sprinkle with Parmesan and chopped butter.

• Bake for 15 minutes, until the top is golden brown.

• Serve hot.

## Pasta

1   recipe plain fresh pasta dough (see page 242)

## Meat Sauce

1   ounce (30 g) dried porcini mushrooms,

2   tablespoons butter

1   small onion, finely chopped

2½   ounces (75 g) prosciutto, finely chopped

8   ounces (250 g) ground (minced) beef

4   ounces (125 g) ground (minced) chicken

½   cup (120 ml) dry white wine

½   cup (100 ml) beef stock (see page 48)

¾   cup (90 g) freshly grated Parmesan cheese

  Salt and freshly ground black pepper

1   recipe Béchamel sauce (see pages 442–3)

6   tablespoons tomato sauce

¾   cup (90 g) freshly grated Parmesan cheese

1   tablespoon butter

Serves: 6
Preparation: 1 hour + time to make the pasta & to soak the mushrooms
Cooking: 1½ hours
Level: 3

# SICILIAN CANNELLONI

**Pasta:** Prepare the pasta dough.

**Meat Sauce:** Sauté the pancetta in the oil in a Dutch oven (casserole) over medium heat until crisp, about 5 minutes. • Add the beef, onion, celery, garlic, parsley, cinnamon, rosemary, and bay leaf. • Pour in the wine followed by the tomatoes and basil. Season with salt and pepper and bring to a boil. Cover and simmer over low heat until the meat is tender, adding water if the sauce begins to stick to the pan, about 2 hours. • Discard the cinnamon stick, rosemary, and bay leaf. • Remove from the heat and process the meat with 3 tablespoons of the cooking juices in a food processor.

**To Assemble & Bake:** Preheat the oven to 375°F (190°C/gas 5). • Cut the pasta dough into 4 x 7-inch (10 x 18-cm) rectangles. • Blanch the rectangles of pasta as you would for lasagna, following the instructions on page 453. • Spread the meat sauce over the pasta and roll up tightly into rolls from the long side. • Arrange in a baking dish and cover with the meat sauce.

**Topping:** Beat the eggs with the salt and pepper and 2 tablespoons caciocavallo. Sprinkle the remaining caciocavallo over the meat sauce. Pour the eggs over the top. • Bake for 30–35 minutes, until the top is brown. • Serve hot.

## Pasta

1   recipe plain fresh pasta dough (see page 242)

## Meat Sauce

3/4   cup (100 g) diced pancetta

1/3   cup (90 ml) extra-virgin olive oil

1   pound (500 g) stewing beef, in a single piece

1   red onion, chopped

1   stalk celery, chopped

2   cloves garlic, chopped

2   tablespoons finely chopped fresh parsley

1   stick cinnamon

1   sprig rosemary

1   bay leaf

1/4   cup (60 ml) red wine

3   pounds (1.5 kg) peeled plum tomatoes, pressed through a fine mesh strainer (passata)

1   sprig fresh basil

  Salt and freshly ground black pepper

## Topping

2   large eggs

  Salt and freshly ground black pepper

1 3/4   cups (200 g) freshly grated caciocavallo or ricotta salata cheese

Serves 6
Preparation: 2 1/2 hours + 30 minutes to rest the dough
Cooking: 2 1/2 hours
Level: 3

# CANNELLONI WITH TOMATOES & CHEESE

450

Preheat the oven to 350°F (180°C/gas 4). • Butter a baking dish. • Mix the ricotta, half the pecorino, half the basil, and the egg and egg yolk in a large bowl. Season with salt and pepper and mix well. • Arrange half of the tomato slices in the prepared baking dish. Drizzle with 2 tablespoons of oil and season with salt, pepper, and the remaining chopped basil. Sprinkle with 2 tablespoons of pecorino. • Spoon the ricotta mixture into the cannelloni. Arrange the cannelloni on top of the tomatoes, one next to the other. Season with salt and pepper and drizzle with 2 tablespoons oil. Sprinkle with 2 tablespoons of pecorino. • Place the mozzarella on top of the cannelloni. Cover with the remaining halved tomatoes. Drizzle with the remaining oil and season with salt and pepper. Cover with aluminum foil and bake for 20 minutes. • Remove the foil and sprinkle with the remaining pecorino. Bake for 25–30 minutes, until golden brown. • Serve hot garnished with the extra whole basil leaves.

2   cups (500 ml) fresh ricotta cheese, drained

1 ¼ cups (150 g) freshly grated pecorino cheese

1   tablespoon finely chopped fresh basil + extra whole leaves, to garnish

1   egg + 1 egg yolk
    Salt and freshly ground black pepper

2   pounds (1 kg) tomatoes, thickly sliced

½   cup (125 ml) extra-virgin olive oil

12  ounces (350 g) storebought dried cannelloni tubes

5   ounces (150 g) mozzarella, diced

Serves: 4–6
Preparation: 45 minutes
Cooking: 40 minutes
Level: 2

You could also use: fresh pasta cannelloni

# CLASSIC LASAGNA

452

**Pasta:** Prepare the pasta dough. Shape into a ball, wrap in a clean kitchen towel and let rest for 30 minutes. • Divide the pasta into six equal pieces. **Step 1:** Roll the pasta dough through a pasta machine down to the second thinnest setting. Alternatively, roll out on a lightly floured work surface to fairly thin. • Cut into 6 x 8-inch (15 x 20-cm) rectangles. • **Step 2:** Bring a large pot of water to a boil. Add 1 tablespoon of sea salt and 1 tablespoon of oil. Add the lasagna sheets carefully one at a time and blanch for 3–5 seconds. • Scoop the sheets of pasta out using a large slotted spoon. • **Step 3:** Transfer to a large bowl of cold water with the remaining 1 tablespoon of salt and 1 tablespoon of oil. Dip into the cold water then remove with the slotted spoon. If the water warms up, add a few ice cubes. • **Step 4:** Squeeze the excess water from each sheet. Lay out on a clean damp cloth. Make sure they do not overlap as they will stick together. **Béchamel Sauce:** Melt the butter in a medium saucepan over medium heat. Stir in the flour, salt, and nutmeg. Simmer over low heat, stirring constantly, for 1–2 minutes. • Remove from the heat and add the milk all at once. Stir well and return to the heat. Bring to a boil, then simmer over low heat, stirring constantly, until thickened, about 5 minutes. **To Assemble & Bake:** Preheat the oven to 400°F (200°C/gas 6). • Butter a large baking dish. • Arrange four layers of pasta in the dish, alternating with meat sauce, Béchamel, and Parmesan. • Bake for 20–30 minutes, until bubbling and golden. • Serve hot.

**Pasta**

1   recipe plain fresh pasta dough (see page 242)

2   tablespoons coarse sea salt

2   tablespoons olive oil

**Béchamel Sauce**

3   tablespoons butter

3   tablespoons all-purpose (plain) flour

1/4   teaspoon salt

1/4   teaspoon ground nutmeg

2   cups (500 ml) milk

1   recipe meat sauce (see page 446)

1   cup (120 g) freshly grated Parmesan cheese

Serves: 6
Preparation: 1 hour + time for the pasta & meat sauce
Cooking: 35–45 minutes
Level: 3

The sheets of pasta for lasagna have to be blanched for a few seconds in boiling water, then cooled in cold water and gently squeezed. Blanch the sheets in 3 quarts (3 liters) of boiling water with 1 tablespoon of coarse sea salt and 1 tablespoon of olive oil. Cool in the same quantity of cold water, salt, and oil.

**1.** ROLL each piece of dough through the pasta machine down to the second thinnest setting. Cut into 6 x 8-inch (15 x 20-cm) rectangles.

**2.** BRING a large pot of water to a boil. Add 1 tablespoon of sea salt and oil. Blanch the sheets one at a time for 3–5 seconds. Remove with a slotted spoon.

**3.** TRANSFER to a large bowl of cold water with the remaining oil and sea salt. Dip into the cold water, then remove.

**4.** SQUEEZE the excess water gently from each sheet. Lay the sheets out in a single layer on a damp cloth.

# LASAGNA WITH PESTO

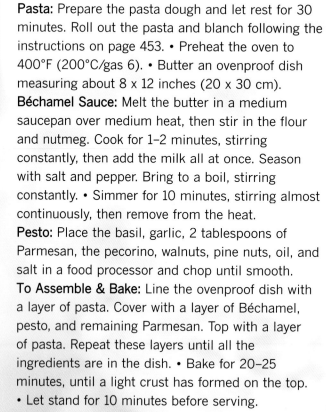

**Pasta:** Prepare the pasta dough and let rest for 30 minutes. Roll out the pasta and blanch following the instructions on page 453. • Preheat the oven to 400°F (200°C/gas 6). • Butter an ovenproof dish measuring about 8 x 12 inches (20 x 30 cm).

**Béchamel Sauce:** Melt the butter in a medium saucepan over medium heat, then stir in the flour and nutmeg. Cook for 1–2 minutes, stirring constantly, then add the milk all at once. Season with salt and pepper. Bring to a boil, stirring constantly. • Simmer for 10 minutes, stirring almost continuously, then remove from the heat.

**Pesto:** Place the basil, garlic, 2 tablespoons of Parmesan, the pecorino, walnuts, pine nuts, oil, and salt in a food processor and chop until smooth.

**To Assemble & Bake:** Line the ovenproof dish with a layer of pasta. Cover with a layer of Béchamel, pesto, and remaining Parmesan. Top with a layer of pasta. Repeat these layers until all the ingredients are in the dish. • Bake for 20–25 minutes, until a light crust has formed on the top. • Let stand for 10 minutes before serving.

**Pasta**

1   recipe plain fresh pasta dough (see page 242)

**Béchamel Sauce**

5   tablespoons (75 g) butter

½   cup (75 g) all-purpose (plain) flour

Pinch of freshly grated nutmeg

4   cups (1 liter) milk

Salt and freshly ground white pepper

**Pesto**

3   bunches fresh basil

1   clove garlic

¾   cup (90 g) freshly grated Parmesan cheese

2   tablespoons freshly grated pecorino romano cheese

2   walnuts, shelled

3   tablespoons pine nuts

¾   cup (180 ml) extra-virgin olive oil

1   teaspoon salt

Serves: 6
Preparation: 1 hour + time to make the pasta
Cooking: 35–40 minutes
Level: 3

# LASAGNA WITH MUSHROOMS & CHEESE

**Pasta:** Prepare the pasta dough and let rest for 30 minutes. • If liked, prepare the parsely-patterned pasta sheets following the instructions on the facing page. • Blanch the sheets of lasagna following the instructions on page 453.

**Filling:** Separate the mushroom stalks from the heads. Chop the stalks into cubes and slice the heads. • Heat 4 tablespoons (60 ml) of oil in a large frying pan over high heat and cook the mushroom heads for 4 minutes. Set aside. • Heat the remaining 2 tablespoons of oil in the same pan and add the stalks and a pinch of salt. Cover and cook over medium heat until tender. • Melt 4 tablespoons (60 g) of butter over medium heat. Stir in the flour and nutmeg. Cook for 1–2 minutes, stirring constantly, then add the milk all at once. Season with salt and pepper. Bring to a boil, stirring constantly. Simmer for 5 minutes, then set aside. • Stir in the Parmesan. • Chop the mushroom stalks with two-thirds of the sauce in a food processor.

**To Assemble & Bake:** Preheat the oven to 400°F (200°C/gas 6). • Butter a 10 x 14 inch (25 x 35 cm) baking dish. • Use a quarter of the pasta to line the dish. Cover with one-third of the ham, one-third of the sliced cheese, one-third of the sliced mushrooms, and one-third of the mushroom sauce. Repeat these layers twice and top with half the pasta. Spread with the plain sauce (without mushrooms) and cover with the parsley-patterned sheets of pasta, if using. • Chop the remaining 3 tablespoons of butter and sprinkle over the top. Cover with a sheet of aluminum and bake for 30 minutes. • Let stand for 20 minutes before serving.

**Pasta**

| | |
|---|---|
| 1 | recipe plain fresh pasta dough (see page 242) |
| 6 | large leaves flat-leaf parsley, damp (optional) |

**Filling**

| | |
|---|---|
| 1¹/₂ | pounds (750 g) mushrooms (porcini or white mushrooms) |
| 6 | tablespoons (90 ml) extra-virgin olive oil |
| | Salt and freshly ground white pepper |
| 7 | tablespoons (100 g) butter |
| ²/₃ | cup (100 g) all-purpose (plain) flour |
| | Pinch of freshly grated nutmeg |
| 6 | cups (1.5 liters) milk |
| ³/₄ | cup (90 g) freshly grated Parmesan cheese |
| 8 | ounces (250 g) ham |
| 7 | ounces (200 g) cheese (Fontina, Edam, or similar), thinly sliced |

Serves: 6
Preparation: 1 hour + time
  to make the pasta
Cooking: 1¹/₂ hours
Level: 3

## ■ PREPARING FRESH PASTA WITH HERB MOTIFS

With just a little extra time and effort you can create some very attractive designs for sheets of pasta. These can be used to add a special touch to lasagna (be sure to place the decorated sheet of pasta on top) and for many filled pasta dishes too.

**1.** PLACE an attractively shaped, slightly damp flat-leaf parsley leaf at one end of a lasagna sheet. Fold the other end over the top.

**2.** ROLL the sheet through the pasta machine at the second thinnest setting and then again at the thinnest setting.

**3.** YOU WILL END UP with an attractive green parsley leaf motif at the center of the sheet of lasagna.

# LASAGNA WITH SPRING VEGETABLES

**Pasta:** Prepare the pasta dough and let rest for 30 minutes. Roll out the pasta and blanch following the instructions on page 453. • Preheat the oven to 400°F (200°C/gas 6). • Butter an ovenproof dish measuring about 8 x 12 inches (20 x 30 cm).

**Béchamel Sauce:** Melt the butter in a small saucepan over medium heat, then stir in the flour and nutmeg. Cook for 1–2 minutes, stirring constantly, then add the milk all at once. Season with salt and pepper. Bring to a boil, stirring constantly. • Simmer for 8–10 minutes, stirring almost continuously, then set aside to cool a little.

**Filling:** Stir the pesto into the Béchamel sauce. • Mix the tomatoes, potatoes, green beans, and mozzarella in a large bowl.

**To Assemble & Bake:** Cover the bottom of the ovenproof dish with a layer of the mixed Béchamel and basil sauce. Cover with a layer of pasta followed by a layer of vegetables and mozzarella. Sprinkle with Parmesan. Repeat this layering process until all the ingredients are in the baking dish, finishing with a layer of Béchamel and Parmesan. • Bake for 45 minutes, until golden brown on top. • Let stand for about 15 minutes before serving.

**Pasta**

1 recipe plain fresh pasta dough (see page 242)

**Béchamel Sauce**

3½ ounces (100 g) butter

²/₃ cup (100 g) all-purpose (plain) flour

Pinch of freshly grated nutmeg

1½ quarts (1.5 liters) milk

Salt and freshly ground white pepper

**Filling**

5 tablespoons pesto

2 pounds (1 kg) tomatoes, peeled and coarsely chopped

1 pound (500 g) potatoes, boiled and cut in cubes

14 ounces (400 g) green beans, boiled in lightly salted water and cut in short pieces

8 ounces (250 g) mozzarella cheese, sliced

¾ cup (90 g) freshly grated Parmesan cheese

Serves: 6
Preparation: 1 hour + time to prepare the pasta
Cooking: 1 hour
Level: 3

# LASAGNA WITH RADICCHIO

**Pasta:** Prepare the pasta dough and let rest for 30 minutes. Roll out the pasta and blanch following the instructions on page 453.

**Filling:** Drain the mushrooms and chop finely.
• Heat the butter in a large saucepan and add the onion and mushrooms. Cover and cook over low heat for 15 minutes. • Add the radicchio. Season with salt, cover, and simmer over medium heat for 10 minutes. • Pour in the Marsala and cook until evaporated. • Cook for 5 minutes. Set aside.

**Béchamel Sauce:** Melt the butter in a medium saucepan. Stir in the flour and nutmeg. Cook for 3–4 minutes, stirring constantly, then add the milk all at once. Season with salt and pepper. Bring to a boil, stirring constantly. • Simmer for 5 minutes, stirring almost continuously. Remove from heat. • Stir the Parmesan, Fontina, and egg yolks into the Béchamel. Season with salt and pepper. • Preheat the oven to 400°F (200°C/gas 6). • Butter a 10 x 14 inch (25 x 35 cm) baking dish. • Cover the bottom and sides with a layer of lasagna sheets. Leave enough pasta hanging over the edges to fold over the lasagna in the pan. Spoon in a third of the radicchio mixture and cover with another layer of pasta. Add another third of radicchio mixture and then fold the overhanging pieces of pasta over the filling. Cover with another layer of pasta and the remaining radicchio mixture.

**Topping:** Dot with the butter and sprinkle with the Parmesan. • Bake for 35–40 minutes, until golden brown. • Let rest for 10 minutes before serving.

**Pasta**

1 recipe plain fresh pasta dough (see page 242)

**Filling**

1 ounce (30 g) dried porcini mushrooms, soaked in water for 2 hours

2 tablespoons butter

1 small onion, finely chopped

Salt and freshly ground black pepper

1 pound (500 g) red radicchio, finely chopped

½ cup (125 ml) dry Marsala wine

**Béchamel Sauce**

5 tablespoons (75 g) butter

½ cup (75 g) all-purpose (plain) flour

Pinch of freshly grated nutmeg

3¼ cups (800 ml) milk

Salt and freshly ground white pepper

½ cup (60 g) freshly grated Parmesan

½ cup (60 g) freshly grated Fontina cheese

2 large egg yolks

**Topping**

3 tablespoons butter

4 tablespoons freshly grated Parmesan

Serves: 6–8
Preparation: 50 minutes
+ time to make the pasta
Cooking: 1½ hours
Level: 3

# GARBANZO BEAN LASAGNA

**Pasta:** Sift both flours onto a clean work surface and gradually stir in the eggs using a fork. Follow the instructions on page 242 to mix the dough, then knead for 20 minutes. Wrap the dough in plastic wrap (cling film) and let rest for 30 minutes. • Divide the dough into five pieces. Roll it through a pasta machine one notch at a time down to the thinnest setting. Cut with a knife into rectangles about 4 x 6 inches (10 x 15 cm). Let dry on a lightly floured cloth for 30 minutes. • Blanch the sheets of lasagna following the instructions on page 453. • Preheat the oven to 350°F (180°C/gas 4). • Butter an ovenproof dish measuring about 8 x 12 inches (20 x 30 cm). **Filling:** Blanch the beans in salted, boiling water for 2–3 minutes. Drain well. • Heat the oil in a large frying pan and sauté the onion until softened, 3–4 minutes. • Add the zucchini, carrots, bell pepper, and beans. Season with salt and sauté over high heat for about 8 minutes. • Pour in the cream and bring to a boil. Cook for 1–2 minutes, then remove from the heat. • Place the ricotta in a large bowl and season with salt and pepper. • Cover the bottom of the ovenproof dish with a layer of pasta. Spread with a layer of ricotta and cover with a layer of vegetables. Sprinkle with the Parmesan. Repeat this layering process until all the ingredients are in the dish, finishing with a layer of vegetables and Parmesan. • Bake for 30 minutes, until golden brown on top. • Let stand for 15 minutes before serving.

**Pasta**

1 cup (150 g) garbanzo bean (chickpea) flour

1 cup (150 g) all-purpose (plain) flour

3 very fresh large eggs

**Filling**

4 ounces (125 g) green beans, cut in short lengths

6 tablespoons (90 ml) extra-virgin olive oil

1 onion, finely chopped

3 medium zucchini (courgettes), cut in small cubes

2 carrots, cut in small cubes

1 red bell pepper (capsicum), cut in small squares

Salt and freshly ground white pepper

1 cup (250 ml) single (light) cream

1 pound (500 g) fresh ricotta cheese, drained

3/4 cup (90 g) freshly grated Parmesan

Serves: 6
Preparation: 1 hour + time to make the pasta
Cooking: 1 hour
Level: 3

# MUSHROOM LASAGNA

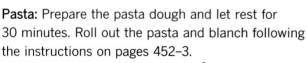

**Pasta:** Prepare the pasta dough and let rest for 30 minutes. Roll out the pasta and blanch following the instructions on pages 452–3.

**Filling:** Chop the mushrooms into 3/4-inch (2-cm) cubes. • Heat the oil in a large frying pan over high heat and sauté the garlic and rosemary for 2 minutes. • Add the mushrooms and cook until all the water they release has evaporated, about 5 minutes. • Cover and simmer over medium-low heat until tender, about 5 minutes. Season with salt and pepper and remove from the heat. Stir in the parsley.

**To Assemble & Bake:** Preheat the oven to 350°F (180°C/gas 4). • Butter an ovenproof dish measuring about 10 x 14 inches (25 x 35 cm). • Place the mascarpone in a medium bowl and stir in the egg yolks and almost all the Parmesan. Season with salt and pepper. Refrigerate until ready to use. • Cover the bottom and sides of the ovenproof dish with a layer of lasagna sheets. Spoon in a quarter of the mushroom mixture followed by one-fifth of the mascarpone mixture. Cover with another layer of pasta and repeat until there are four layers in the dish. Finish with the remaining mascarpone and sprinkle with the remaining Parmesan. • Bake for 30–40 minutes, until the top is golden brown. Let rest for 15 minutes before serving.

**Pasta**

1   recipe plain fresh pasta dough (see page 242)

**Filling**

2½ pounds (1.2 kg) mixed mushrooms

¼   cup (60 ml) extra-virgin olive oil

2   cloves garlic, finely chopped

1   sprig fresh rosemary

Salt and freshly ground white pepper

2   tablespoons finely chopped fresh parsley

1½ pounds (750 g) mascarpone cheese

6   large egg yolks

1   cup (125 g) freshly grated Parmesan cheese

Serves: 6–8
Preparation: 45 minutes + time to make the pasta
Cooking: 1 hour
Level: 3

# SEAFOOD LASAGNA

**Pasta:** Prepare the pasta dough and let rest for 30 minutes. Roll out the pasta and blanch following the instructions on pages 452–3.

**Filling:** Heat the oil in a large frying pan and sauté the garlic and half the parsley for 3 minutes. • Add the wine and cook until evaporated. • Add the shrimps, mixed shellfish, fish, and squid. Season with salt and pepper and cook over medium heat for 10 minutes. Add the remaining parsley just before removing from the heat. • Preheat the oven to 350°F (180°C/gas 4). • Butter an 8 x 12 inch (20 x 30 cm) baking dish.

**To Assemble & Bake: Fish Sauce:** Melt the butter in a medium saucepan and stir in the flour. Pour in the stock and simmer for 10 minutes, stirring almost constantly. • Cover the bottom of the ovenproof dish with a layer of pasta. Spread with a layer of fish sauce and cover with a layer of filling. Repeat this layering process until all the ingredients are in the dish. • Bake for 20 minutes, until golden brown on top. • Let stand for 10 minutes before serving.

470

**Pasta**

1  recipe plain fresh pasta dough (see page 242)

2  tablespoons extra-virgin olive oil (to cook the pasta)

**Filling**

4  tablespoons extra-virgin olive oil

2  cloves garlic, finely chopped

2  tablespoons finely chopped fresh parsley

½  cup (125 ml) dry white wine

12  ounces (350 g) shrimp (prawns), peeled

12  ounces (350 g) mixed clams, mussels, and scallops, shelled

1  small white firm-textured fish (weighing about 14 oz/400 g), cleaned

8  ounces (250 g) chopped squid

**Fish Sauce**

6  tablespoons (90 g) butter, cut up

½  cup (75 g) all-purpose (plain) flour

Salt and freshly ground white pepper

4  cups (1 liter) fish or vegetable stock

Serves: 4–6
Preparation: 50 minutes + time to prepare the pasta
Cooking: 1 hour
Level: 2

# POTATO GNOCCHI & LEEK GRATIN

472

If using homemade gnocchi, prepare them first.
• Preheat the oven to 400°F (200°C/gas 6).
• Grease one large or 4–6 individual ovenproof
dishes. • Melt the butter in a large frying pan over
medium heat. Add the leeks and sauté until they
begin to soften, 3–4 minutes. • Add the water and
simmer until the leeks are tender, about 5 minutes.
• Add the cognac and cook over high heat until it
evaporates, 2–3 minutes. • Lower the heat and
sprinkle with the cornstarch. Stir in the cream and
simmer, stirring often, until thickened, about 5
minutes. Stir in the nutmeg and season with salt
and pepper. Set aside. • Cook the gnocchi in
batches in a large pot of salted boiling water until
the rise to the surface, 2–3 minutes each batch.
• Scoop out with a slotted spoon, drain well, and
place in the prepared baking dish(es). Spoon the
leek sauce over the top. Sprinkle with the
Parmesan. • Bake for 8–10 minutes, until the
cheese is bubbling and golden brown. • Serve hot.

| | |
|---|---|
| 1 | recipe potato gnocchi (see pages 334–335) or 1 pound (500 g) fresh storebought potato gnocchi |
| 2 | tablespoons butter |
| 5 | small leeks, thinly sliced |
| 3 | tablespoons (45 ml) water |
| 2 | tablespoons cognac |
| 1 | tablespoon cornstarch (cornflour) |
| 1¼ | cups (300 ml) heavy (double) cream |
| ¼ | teaspoon freshly grated nutmeg |
| | Salt and freshly ground black pepper |
| ¾ | cup (90 g) freshly grated Parmesan cheese |

Serves: 4–6
Preparation: 30 minutes
   + time to make gnocchi
Cooking: 35–40 minutes
Level: 2

# GNOCCHI ALLA ROMANA

Bring the milk to a boil in a large saucepan over medium heat. • Gradually sprinkle in the semolina, stirring constantly to prevent lumps from forming. • Simmer, stirring constantly, until the mixture is thick, 10–15 minutes. • Remove from the heat and season with salt. • Stir in $1/4$ cup (60 g) of butter, the egg yolks, half the Parmesan, and the Gruyère. • Spread the mixture out to a thickness of $1/2$-inch (1-cm) on a lightly floured work surface. Let cool, about 1 hour. • Use a small glass or cookie cutter (not larger than 2 inches/5 cm) to cut out rounds. • Preheat the oven to 350°F (180°C/gas 4). • Butter four individual baking dishes (or one large baking dish). • Use the pieces leftover after cutting out the disks to form a first layer in the dish(es). Sprinkle with some Parmesan. Lay the rounds over the top, one overlapping the next. • Melt the remaining $1/4$ cup (60 g) butter and pour over the top. Sprinkle with the remaining $1/2$ cup (60 g) of Parmesan and season with white pepper. • Bake 25–30 minutes, until golden. • Serve hot.

| | |
|---|---|
| 4 | cups (1 liter) milk |
| $1^2/3$ | cups (250 g) semolina |
| | Salt and freshly ground white pepper |
| $1/2$ | cup (120 g) butter |
| 2 | large egg yolks |
| 1 | cup (125 g) freshly grated Parmesan cheese + extra, to serve |
| 6 | tablespoons freshly grated Gruyère cheese |

Serves: 4
Preparation: 10 minutes
  + 1 hour to cool
Cooking: 45 minutes
Level: 2

■ ■ ■ *These simple gnocchi come from Rome and are surprisingly good. Made with semolina (from durum wheat), milk, eggs, and cheese, these gnocchi pre-date the more widely known ones made from potato, probably by many centuries.*

# NOODLES

# TYPES OF NOODLES

## DRIED RICE VERMICELLI

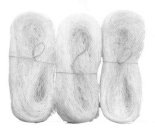

Thin translucent white noodles made from rice flour and packaged in blocks. Soak in boiling water before use. They expand when fried and are often used as a garnish.

## DRIED EGG NOODLES

Dried egg noodles are made of wheat flour and egg and are available in many shapes and sizes. Cook in boiling water for 4–5 minutes. Often flavored with shrimp.

## SINGAPORE EGG NOODLES

Thin egg noodles made of wheat flour and egg. They are available fresh or dried.

## FRESH RICE NOODLES

Available in varying thicknesses. These noodles are steamed and lightly oiled then sealed into packages. They have a silky, slippery texture and are used in soups and stir-fries.

## SOBA NOODLES

A Japanese noodle made from buckwheat flour. They are usually served chilled with a dipping sauce, or in hot stock as a soup. For cold dishes, be sure to rinse the noodles in cold water after cooking.

## HOKKIEN NOODLES

Yellow wheat and egg noodles originally from southern China but now very popular in Singapore, Malaysia, and Indonesia. Sold fresh or vacuum-packed and chilled.

A huge variety of different noodles are eaten all over Asia, but especially in China, Japan, Korea, and Southeast Asian countries such as Singapore, Malaysia, Thailand, and Indonesia. Generally speaking, wheat flour noodles come from northern China and Japan while rice noodles are from southern China and Southeast Asia. Given the variety of noodles available, it is usually best to follow the cooking instructions on the package.

### CHINESE WHEAT NOODLES

Some Chinese noodles are made of wheat flour, salt, and water, without eggs. They are more delicate than egg noodles. Cook in boiling water for 5–10 minutes. They keep well.

### RAMEN NOODLES

A Japanese wheat noodle. They come in many shapes and sizes. They are often cooked and served in meat stock. Outside of Japan, instant or quick-cooking ramen noodles are better known.the cooking instructions on the package.

### UDON NOODLES

A popular Japanese noodle made from wheat flour. They are usually eaten hot in soups during the winter, and chilled with shredded nori or other toppings and dipping sauce during the summer.

### CELLOPHANE NOODLES

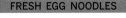

Also known as glass or bean thread noodles, these very thin noodles are made from mung bean starch. They become almost transparent when cooked by soaking in hot water.

### FRESH EGG NOODLES

These noodles come in every shape and size imaginable: flat, round, thick, thin, fresh, or dried. Made of wheat flour and egg, the fresh noodles are cooked for 2–3 minutes in boiling water.

### RICE STICK NOODLES

Rice stick noodles are flat dried noodles. They come in various widths and are used in everything from spring rolls, salads, and soups to stir-fries and braised dishes.

# CHICKEN & NOODLE RICE PAPER ROLLS

480

Put the noodles in a medium bowl and let stand in boiling water for 5 minutes, or follow the instructions on the package. • Drain well and chop coarsely. • Mix the noodles, chicken, carrot, bean sprouts, pea shoots, cilantro, and mint in a large bowl. • Mix the sweet chili sauce and lemon juice in a small bowl. • Pour over the chicken mixture and toss well. • Dip each rice paper sheet in hot water until just softened. • Place on a clean work surface and top with a little of the chicken mixture. • Roll up the rice paper sheets, tucking in the ends as you go. • Serve with the sweet chili sauce on the side.

| | |
|---|---|
| 2 | ounces (60 g) dried rice vermicelli |
| 2 | cups (200 g) barbecued or roast chicken breasts, shredded |
| 1 | carrot, coarsely grated |
| 1 | cup (50 g) fresh bean sprouts |
| 1 | cup (50 g) pea shoots or snow pea sprouts, trimmed |
| 2 | tablespoons coarsely chopped fresh cilantro (coriander) |
| 2 | tablespoons coarsely chopped fresh mint |
| 2 | tablespoons Thai sweet chili sauce + extra to serve |
| 2 | tablespoons freshly squeezed lemon juice |
| 12 | large round rice paper wrappers |

Serves: 6–8
Preparation: 15–20 minutes
Level: 1

■■■ *Rice paper sheets are made from rice flour, salt, and water. They are used to wrap spring rolls before frying but can also be used to wrap fillings without being cooked. They are widely available in Asian food stores and supermarkets.*

 You could also use: cellophane noodles

# DUCK & NOODLE RICE PAPER ROLLS

482

Put the noodles in a medium bowl and let stand in boiling water for 5 minutes, or follow the instructions on the package. • Drain well and transfer to a large bowl. Chop the noodles coarsely. • Mix the noodles, duck, cucumber, cilantro, mint, sweet chili sauce, and lime juice in a large bowl. • Briefly dip a rice wrapper into a dish of hot water until it softens. • Place the wrapper on a clean work surface. Spoon the duck mixture onto the center and roll up tightly, tucking in the ends. • Repeat using remaining wrappers and filling. • Serve with the sweet chili sauce for dipping.

| | |
|---|---|
| 2 | ounces (60 g) dried rice vermicelli |
| 2 | cups (300 g) Chinese barbecued duck, shredded |
| 1 | cucumber, cut into thin lengths |
| 3 | tablespoons coarsely chopped fresh cilantro (coriander) |
| 1 | tablespoon coarsely chopped fresh mint |
| ¼ | cup (60 ml) Thai sweet chili sauce |
| 1 | tablespoon freshly squeezed lime juice |
| 12 | large round rice paper wrappers |
| | Thai sweet chili sauce, to serve |

Serves: 4–6
Preparation: 20 minutes
Cooking: 5 minutes
Level: 1

You could also use: cellophane noodles

# SOY NOODLE & TOFU SOUP

Bring the chicken stock to a boil in a large saucepan. • Stir in the soy sauce, mirin, oil, and brown sugar. • Add the noodles and choy sum stems and simmer for 1 minute. • Add the choy sum leaves and tofu. Simmer for 2 minutes. • Ladle the soup into individual serving bowls. • Top with the scallions and serve hot.

**484**

8   cup (2 liters) chicken stock (see page 498)

3   tablespoons dark soy sauce

2   tablespoons mirin or sweet sherry

1   teaspoon Asian sesame oil

2   teaspoons brown sugar

1   pound (500 g) fresh thin Chinese egg noodles

1   bunch baby choy sum or bok choy, stems sliced and leaves coarsely chopped

8   ounces (250 g) firm tofu, diced

3   scallions (spring onions), finely shredded

Serves: 4–6
Preparation: 10 minutes
Cooking: 5 minutes
Level: 1

You could also use: dried egg noodles, tagliatelle

# COCONUT & SHRIMP NOODLE SOUP

486

Place the noodles in a medium bowl, cover with boiling water, and soak until softened, 5–10 minutes, or follow the instructions on the package. • Drain and transfer to a large bowl. • Combine the chicken stock, coconut milk, and fish sauce in a medium saucepan over medium heat and bring to a boil. • Add the shrimp and simmer until cooked through, 3–4 minutes. • Add to the noodles and mint. • Toss gently and serve hot.

14 ounces (400 g) dried rice vermicelli

5 cups (1.25 liters) chicken stock (see page 498)

1 cup (250 ml) coconut milk

1 tablespoon Thai fish sauce

14 ounces (400 g) shrimp (prawns), peeled and deveined

3 tablespoons fresh mint leaves

Serves: 4
Preparation: 15 minutes
Cooking: 10–15 minutes
Level: 1

You could also use: cellophane noodles, angel hair pasta

# RAMEN NOODLES WITH SPICY SALMON

Prepare the noodles following the instructions on the package. Divide among four soup bowls. • Bring the chicken stock to a gentle simmer in a large soup pot. Add the salmon and simmer for 2 minutes. • Add the chiles, scallions. and soy sauce, and simmer until the salmon is firm to the touch, 2–3 minutes. • Lift a piece of salmon into each soup bowl and pour the stock in over the top. • Garnish each bowl with cilantro and a squeeze of lime juice. • Serve hot.

| | |
|---|---|
| 8 | ounces (250 g) ramen noodles |
| 6 | cups (1.5 liters) chicken stock (see page 498) |
| 4 | (5-ounce/150-g) skinless salmon fillets |
| 2 | red chiles, seeded and thinly sliced |
| 6 | scallions (spring onions), sliced |
| 1 | tablespoons light soy sauce |
| 2 | tablespoons fresh cilantro (coriander) |
| 1 | lime, quartered |

Serves: 4
Preparation: 15 minutes
Cooking: 5 minutes
Level: 1

You could also use: dried rice vermicelli, cellophane noodles

# SHRIMP LAKSA

Put the noodles in a large bowl and pour in enough boiling water to cover. Let stand until softened, about 5 minutes. Drain well and refresh under cold water. • Heat the oil in a large soup pot over medium heat. Add the shallots and sauté until softened, 3–4 minutes. • Stir in the chile paste and sauté for 1 minute. • Add the coconut milk and chicken stock. Bring to a simmer then add the shrimp, sugar snap peas, and bean sprouts. Simmer until the shrimp are cooked, 2–3 minutes. • Divide the noodles among four soup bowls and pour the laksa mixture over the top. • Garnish with the scallions, cilantro, and a squeeze of lime juice. • Serve hot.

| | |
|---|---|
| 12 | ounces (350 g) rice stick noodles |
| 1 | tablespoon vegetable oil |
| 2 | shallots, diced |
| 1 | tablespoon chile paste or sambal olelek |
| 1 | (14-ounce/400-g) can coconut milk |
| 2 | cups (500 ml) chicken stock (see page 498) |
| 12 | ounces (350 g) raw, peeled giant shrimp (king prawns) |
| 1 | cup (150 g) sugar snap peas, halved lengthways |
| 1 | cup (50 g) bean sprouts |
| 2 | scallions (spring onions), shredded |
| | Fresh cilantro (coriander) leaves |
| | Lime wedges, to serve |

■■■ *Laksa soup comes from Singapore and Malaysia and a mixture of Chinese and Malay influences. There are many different laksa soups, most of which are spicy and thick with noodles and coconut milk.*

Serves: 4
Preparation: 15 minutes
Cooking: 10 minutes
Level: 2

You could also use: spaghettini, spaghetti, linguine

# SEAFOOD LAKSA

8 ounces (250 g) hokkein noodles

8 ounces (250 g) rice stick noodles

1 tablespoon peanut oil

¼ cup (60 g) laksa paste

3 cups (750 ml) coconut milk

2 cups (500 ml) fish stock

1 stalk lemongrass, bruised

3 kaffir lime leaves, finely sliced

1 pound (500 g) shrimp (prawns), deveined and shelled, with tails on

1 pound (500 g) firm white fish fillets, such as snapper, cod, halibut, whiting, monkfish, cut into 1-inch (2.5-cm) pieces

8 ounces (250 g) scallops

8 black mussels, cleaned

2 cups (100 g) mung bean sprouts

Fresh cilantro (coriander) leaves

Fresh mint leaves

6 teaspoons sambal oelek (chile paste)

492

Combine both noodles in a medium bowl, cover with boiling water, and set aside to soften, 5–10 minutes. • Heat the oil in a large soup pot over medium-low heat. • Add the laksa paste and stir until fragrant, 1–2 minutes. Add the coconut milk, fish stock, lemongrass, and kaffir lime leaves and bring to a boil. • Add the shrimp, fish, scallops, and mussels, cover, and simmer until the seafood is cooked, 3–5 minutes. Discard any unopened mussels. • Meanwhile, divide the noodles among four to six large soup bowls and top with bean sprouts, cilantro, and mint. • Ladle the laksa mixture over the noodles, distributing the seafood evenly. • Garnish each bowl with 1 teaspoon of chile paste and serve hot.

Serves: 4–6
Preparation: 20–24 minutes
Cooking: 10 minutes
Level: 2

■■■ *Laksa paste is available in many Asian food stores and from online suppliers.*

You could also use: dried egg noodles, tagliatelle, dried rice vermicelli

# PORK & SHRIMP NOODLE SOUP

494

Heat the oil in a large frying pan over medium heat. Add the shallots and three-quarters of the garlic and sauté until golden, about 5 minutes. • Add the reserved shrimp heads and shells and the sambal oelek and sauté for 2–3 minutes more. • Add the chicken stock, bring to a boil, cover, and simmer for 15 minutes. • Meanwhile, mix the pork with the fish sauce, sugar, and remaining garlic in a bowl. Shape into truffle-size balls. • Bring a large pan of unsalted water to a boil. Add the egg noodles and simmer until tender, 2–3 minutes, or according to the time on the package. Drain. • Strain the stock through a fine-mesh sieve, return to the pan, and bring back to a simmer. • Add the pork balls and simmer for 2 minutes. Add the shrimp and simmer until just cooked, 2–3 minutes. Remove from the heat. • Divide the noodles among four bowls. Top with the bean sprouts and spinach. Ladle in the soup, dividing the pork balls and shrimp evenly. • Serve hot.

| 1 | tablespoon peanut oil |
| 4 | shallots, coarsely chopped |
| 4 | cloves garlic, finely chopped |
| 12 | ounces (350 g) large, shrimp (prawns), peeled and deveined, reserve the heads and shells |
| 1 | tablespoon sambal oelek (chile paste) |
| 6 | cups (1.5 liters) chicken stock (see page 498) |
| 8 | ounces (250 g) lean ground (minced) pork |
| 1 | teaspoon Thai fish sauce |
| 1 | teaspoon brown sugar |
| 8 | ounces (250 g) fresh or dried egg noodles |
| 2 | cups (100 g) fresh bean sprouts |
| 1 | cup (50 g) baby spinach leaves |

Serves: 4
Preparation: 20 minutes
Cooking: 30 minutes
Level: 2

You could also use: hokkien noodles, rice stick noodles, cellophane noodles

# THAI FISH CURRY

Cook the hokkien noodles in plenty of boiling water until tender. Refer to the package for exact cooking time. • Drain and set aside. • Place a wok over high heat. • Cook the curry paste until aromatic, about 30 seconds. • Pour in the coconut milk and lime juice and bring to a boil. • Decrease the heat to low. Add the fish and simmer until cooked, 2–3 minutes. • Add the noodles and simmer for 1–2 minutes. • Serve hot.

14 ounces (400 g) fresh hokkien noodles

2 tablespoons Thai green curry paste

1³/4 cups (400 ml) coconut milk

1 tablespoon freshly squeezed lime juice

12 ounces (350 g) firm-textured white fish (such as cod or haddock), cut into small pieces

Serves: 4
Preparation: 5 minutes
Cooking: 5–10 minutes
Level: 1

You could also use: Singapore egg noodles, fresh or dried egg noodles

# CHICKEN NOODLE SOUP

**Chicken Stock**

| | |
|---|---|
| 1 | (4-pound/2-kg) whole chicken |
| 2 | carrots, cut in half |
| 2 | stalks celery, cut in half |
| 3 | onions, quartered |
| 2 | bay leaves |
| 10 | cups (2.5 liters) water |

**Soup**

| | |
|---|---|
| 1 | tablespoon vegetable oil |
| 2 | carrots, cut in small cubes |
| 1 | stalk celery, finely chopped |
| 1 | onion, finely chopped |
| 1 | leek, sliced |
| 2 | cloves garlic, finely chopped |
| 8 | ounces (250 g) dried egg noodles |
| 2 | teaspoons finely grated fresh ginger |
| | Salt and freshly ground black pepper |
| | Fresh parsley leaves |
| 2 | scallions (spring onions), sliced |

**Chicken Stock:** Put the chicken in a large soup pot with the carrots, celery, onions, and bay leaves. Add the water and bring to a boil. Skim off any foam and simmer for about 1 hour. Top up the water so that you keep about the same amount. • Remove the chicken and strain the stock, discarding the vegetables. • Set the stock and chicken aside until required.

**Soup:** Heat the oil in a large soup pot over medium heat. Add the carrots, celery, onion, leek, and garlic and sauté until tender, about 5 minutes. • Add the strained stock and bring to a boil. Reduce the heat to low and simmer for 10 minutes. • Meanwhile, remove the skin and strip the meat from the chicken. Tear the meat into bite-size pieces and add to the soup. • Add the noodles and ginger and simmer for 4–5 minutes, until the noodles are tender. • Season with salt and pepper and garnish with the parsley and scallions.

Serves: 6–8
Preparation: 30 minutes
Cooking: $1^1/_2$ hours
Level: 1

You could also use: ramen noodles, dried egg noodles, tagliatelle

# CHICKEN UDON NOODLE SOUP

Bring the chicken stock to a boil in a large soup pot. Add the chicken. • Decrease the heat to medium and simmer until cooked, 12–15 minutes. • Remove the chicken from the pot and shred it finely. • Bring the stock back to a boil over high heat. • Add the soy sauce and dashi granules. Stir until the granules have dissolved. • Add the noodles and broccoli. Simmer until tender, about 4 minutes. • Add the chicken and return to a boil. • Ladle the soup into individual serving bowls. • Add the eggs and scallions. Serve hot.

| | |
|---|---|
| 8 | cups (2 liters) chicken stock (see page 498) |
| 2 | boneless skinless chicken breasts |
| 2 | tablespoons dark soy sauce |
| ½ | teaspoon dashi granules or miso paste |
| 8 | ounces (250 g) dried udon noodles |
| 1 | bunch kai-lan or Chinese broccoli, cut into short lengths |
| 3 | hard-boiled eggs, shelled and quartered lengthwise |
| 2 | scallions (spring onions), thinly sliced |

Serves: 4
Preparation: 10 minutes
Cooking: 20 minutes
Level: 1

■■■ *Dashi is a basic stock used in Japanese cooking. It is made from boiled seaweed and dried fish. Instant dashi granules are available at Asian food stores and from online suppliers.*

You could also use: hokkein noodles, Chinese wheat noodles

# QUICK CHICKEN LAKSA WITH NOODLES

Cook the hokkien noodles in plenty of boiling water until tender. Refer to the package for the exact cooking time. • Drain and set aside. • Place a wok over high heat. • Cook the laksa paste for 30 seconds until aromatic. • Pour in the coconut milk and chicken stock and bring to a boil. • Add the chicken and simmer until tender and cooked through, 5–7 minutes. • Add the noodles and cook for 2 minutes. • Serve hot.

14 ounces (400 g) fresh hokkien noodles

1 cup (250 ml) laksa paste

1²/₃ cups (400 ml) coconut milk

1½ cups (375 ml) chicken stock (see page 498)

2 boneless skinless chicken breast halves, thinly sliced

**Serves: 4**
**Preparation: 10 minutes**
**Cooking: 15 minutes**
**Level: 1**

■ ■ ■ *Laksa paste is available in some Asian food stores and from online suppliers.*

You could also use: Chinese wheat noodles, spaghetti

# THAI COCONUT CHICKEN & NOODLES

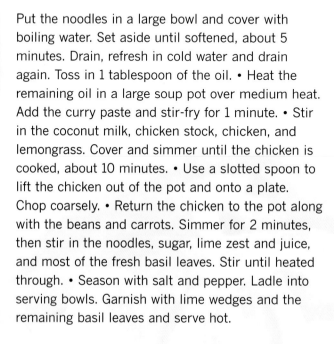

504

Put the noodles in a large bowl and cover with boiling water. Set aside until softened, about 5 minutes. Drain, refresh in cold water and drain again. Toss in 1 tablespoon of the oil. • Heat the remaining oil in a large soup pot over medium heat. Add the curry paste and stir-fry for 1 minute. • Stir in the coconut milk, chicken stock, chicken, and lemongrass. Cover and simmer until the chicken is cooked, about 10 minutes. • Use a slotted spoon to lift the chicken out of the pot and onto a plate. Chop coarsely. • Return the chicken to the pot along with the beans and carrots. Simmer for 2 minutes, then stir in the noodles, sugar, lime zest and juice, and most of the fresh basil leaves. Stir until heated through. • Season with salt and pepper. Ladle into serving bowls. Garnish with lime wedges and the remaining basil leaves and serve hot.

| | |
|---|---|
| 14 | ounces (400 g) dried medium egg noodles |
| 2 | tablespoons peanut oil |
| 2 | tablespoons Thai red curry paste |
| 1 | (14-ounce/400-ml) can reduced-fat coconut milk |
| 3 | cups (750 ml) boiling chicken stock (see page 498) |
| 2 | boneless skinless chicken breasts |
| 1 | stalk lemongrass, bruised |
| 5 | ounces (150 g) green beans, halved lengthwise |
| 2 | carrots, cut into thin sticks |
| 1 | teaspoon brown sugar |
| | Finely grated zest and juice of 1 lime + extra wedges, to serve |
| 1 | tablespoon fresh Thai or normal basil, to garnish |
| | Salt and freshly ground black pepper |

Serves: 4
Preparation: 15 minutes
Cooking: 15–20 minutes
Level: 1

You could also use: hokkien noodles, tagliatelle

# CHICKEN TOM YUM NOODLES

Cook the hokkien noodles in plenty of boiling water until tender. Refer to the package for the exact cooking time. • Drain and set aside. • Place a wok over high heat. • Cook the tom yum paste until aromatic, about 30 seconds. • Add the chicken stock and lime juice and bring to a boil. • Decrease the heat to low and add the chicken. Cook for 4 minutes until browned. • Add the noodles and cook for 2 minutes. • Serve hot.

1   **pound (500 g) fresh hokkien noodles**

3   **tablespoons tom yum paste**

4   **cups (1 liter) chicken stock (see page 498)**

1   **tablespoon freshly squeezed lime juice**

2   **boneless skinless chicken breast halves, thinly sliced**

**Serves: 6**
**Preparation: 10 minutes**
**Cooking: 15 minutes**
**Level: 1**

■ ■ ■ *Tom yum paste is made by crushing and stir-frying lemongrass, kaffir lime leaves, galangal, shallots, lime juice, fish sauce, tamarind, and chiles. It can be purchased from Asian food stores and online Thai food suppliers.*

You could also use: spaghetti

# CHICKEN NOODLE COCONUT LAKSA

Put the noodles in a large bowl and cover with boiling water. Set aside until softened, about 5 minutes. Drain, refresh in cold water and drain again. Set aside. • Preheat the overhead broiler (grill) in the oven to high. • Put the eggplant on a baking sheet, brush with the oil and season with salt and pepper. Broil (grill) until softened, 4–5 minutes each side. Drain on paper towels. • Stir-fry the curry paste in a large wok or frying pan over medium heat for 1 minute. Stir in the coconut milk and stock and bring to a simmer. • Add the chicken and lemongrass, cover, and simmer until the chicken is cooked, 12–15 minutes. Use a slotted spoon to lift the chicken out of the pot and onto a plate. Chop coarsely. • Return the chicken to the pot with the sugar snaps and eggplant. Simmer for 2 minutes, then stir in the noodles, sugar, and lime zest and juice. Stir until heated through. • Season with salt and pepper. Ladle into serving bowls. Garnish with lime wedges, cilantro, and basil and serve hot.

| | |
|---|---|
| 8 | ounces (250 g) dried medium rice noodles |
| 1 | medium eggplant (aubergine), halved lengthwise and cut into ¼ inch (5 mm) slices |
| 2 | tablespoons vegetable oil |
| | Salt and freshly ground black pepper |
| 2 | tablespoons Thai red curry paste |
| 1 | (14-ounce/400-ml) can reduced-fat coconut milk |
| 3 | cups (750 ml) hot chicken stock (see page 498) |
| 4 | small boneless skinless chicken breasts |
| 1 | stalk lemongrass, bruised |
| 1 | cup (150 g) sugar snap peas |
| 1 | teaspoon brown sugar |
| | Finely grated zest and juice of 1 lime + extra wedges to serve |
| | Fresh cilantro (coriander) and basil |

Serves: 4
Preparation: 10 minutes
Cooking: 15 minutes
Level: 1

You could also use: dried rice vermicelli

# PEKING DUCK & UDON NOODLE SOUP

Remove the flesh from the duck and coarsely shred it. • Combine the chicken stock and star anise in a large saucepan and bring to a boil over medium heat. • Add the udon noodles and simmer for 4 minutes. • Add the duck and simmer for 3 minutes. • Stir in the snow pea shoots. • Serve hot.

510

| 1 | storebought cooked Peking duck |
|---|---|
| 5 | cups (1.25 liters) chicken stock (see page 498) |
| 1 | star anise |
| 14 | ounces (400 g) udon noodles |
| 8 | ounces (250 g) snow pea shoots |

Serves: 4
Preparation: 10 minutes
Cooking: 10 minutes
Level: 1

■ ■ ■ *Peking ducks are available wherever there are Chinese markets and large ethnic populations. Snow pea shoots are available in natural food stores and Chinese markets.*

You could also use: ramen noodles, hokkein noodles

# VIETNAMESE NOODLE SOUP

Preheat the oven to 400°F (200°C/gas 6). • Put the beef bone, onion, garlic, and ginger in a roasting dish and bake for 1 hour. • Transfer to a large soup pot and add the water, cinnamon, cloves, and lemongrass. Bring to a boil, then simmer for 2 hours. • Strain through a fine-mesh sieve into a bowl, discarding the solids. You should have about 4 cups (1 liter) of stock. • Season with the fish sauce, salt, and sugar. Let cool overnight, then skim any fat from the top. • Cook the noodles in plenty of boiling water until just tender, about 2 minutes. Drain, cool under cold running water and divide among four serving bowls. • Put the stock into a large wok or pan and heat until simmering. Add the pak choi. • Thinly slice the steaks and add to the wok. Remove from the heat; the steak is only just cooked and should be very tender. • Divide the soup among the bowls of noodles, then top with the scallions. • Serve the bean sprouts, chiles, limes, and herbs at the table, with extra fish sauce, so that your guests can help themselves.

*■ ■ ■ This traditional Vietnamese soup is known as Pho bo tai in its homeland.*

| | |
|---|---|
| 1 | beef rib or shin bone, about 2 pounds (1 kg) |
| 1 | large onion, halved, with skin on |
| 3 | cloves garlic, unpeeled |
| 2 | ounces (60 g) fresh ginger, unpeeled and halved |
| 10 | cups (2.5 liters) water |
| 1 | cinnamon stick, broken in half |
| 2 | cloves |
| 1 | stalk lemongrass, bruised |
| 4 | tablespoons (60 ml) fish sauce + extra to serve |
| 1 | teaspoon salt |
| 1 | teaspoon sugar |
| 8 | ounces (250 g) dried rice noodles |
| 2 | heads pak choi, coarsely chopped |
| 2 | thick sirloin steaks |
| 4 | scallions (spring onions), sliced |
| 2 | cups (100 g) bean sprouts |
| 2 | small red chiles, sliced |
| 2 | limes, halved |
| | Small bunch of fresh Thai basil or tarragon |
| | Small bunch fresh cilantro (coriander) |

Serves: 4
Preparation: 30 minutes
    + 12 hours to cool
Cooking: 3 hours
Level: 2

You could also use: linguine

# BELL PEPPER & NOODLE STIR-FRY

514

Cook the noodles in plenty of boiling water until tender, 5–10 minutes. Refer to the package for the exact cooking time. • Drain and set aside. • Place a wok over high heat. • When it is very hot, add the sesame oil. • Add the bell peppers and eggplant. Stir-fry for 3 minutes. • Add the oyster sauce and noodles. Cook for 2 minutes. • Toss well and serve hot.

14 ounces (400 g) fresh or dried Chinese egg noodles

3 tablespoons Asian sesame oil

2 red bell peppers (capsicums), seeded and cut into thin strips

4 baby eggplants (aubergines), thinly sliced

3/4 cup (180 ml) oyster sauce

Serves: 4
Preparation: 10 minutes
Cooking: 10–15 minutes
Level: 1

You could also use: tagliatelle

# GINGER NOODLES WITH VEGETABLE RIBBONS

Cook the noodles in plenty of boiling water until tender, 5–10 minutes. Refer to the package for the exact cooking time. • Drain and set aside. • Place a wok over high heat. • When it is very hot, add the oil, carrots, zucchini, oyster sauce, and ginger. Stir-fry for 2 minutes. • Add the noodles and stir-fry for 2 minutes. • Toss well and serve hot.

1¼ pounds (600 g) fresh or dried Chinese egg noodles

2 tablespoons Asian sesame oil

2 medium carrots, cut lengthwise into thin ribbons

2 medium zucchini (courgettes), cut lengthwise into thin ribbons

½ cup (125 ml) oyster sauce

1 tablespoon freshly grated ginger

Serves: 4–6
Preparation: 10 minutes
Cooking: 10–15 minutes
Level: 1

You could also use: tagliatelle

# SOBA NOODLES WITH SNOW PEAS & BABY CORN

Cook the noodles in plenty of boiling water until tender, 5–7 minutes. • If using fresh baby corn, blanch it in boiling water for 2 minutes. • Add the snow peas and boil for 1 minute. • Drain and rinse under ice-cold water to stop the cooking process. • Drain the noodles and transfer to a large bowl. • Mix in the sesame oil and lemon juice. • Add the baby corn and snow peas. • Toss well and serve hot.

$1\frac{1}{4}$ **pounds (600 g) soba noodles**

12 **fresh or canned baby corn (sweetcorn), sliced in half lengthwise**

24 **snow peas (sugar peas/mangetout), trimmed**

3 **tablespoons Asian sesame oil**

3 **tablespoons freshly squeezed lemon juice**

**Serves: 4–6**
**Preparation: 5 minutes**
**Cooking: 10 minutes**
**Level: 1**

You could also use: whole-wheat (wholemeal) spaghetti

# SWEET SOY MUSHROOM & CASHEW NOODLES

**520**

Cook the noodles according to the instructions on the package. • Drain and set aside. • Mix the mushrooms and 2 tablespoons of kecap manis in a bowl. Toss well. • Heat a wok over high heat. • When it is very hot, add the cashews. Toast until golden, about 2 minutes. Remove from the pan and set aside. • Add the oil to the pan. • Stir-fry the onion until softened, about 3 minutes. • Add the mushroom mixture and stir-fry until the mushrooms have just softened, about 3 minutes. • Add the noodles and the remaining kecap manis. • Stir-fry for 2 minutes. • Add the bean sprouts and toasted cashews. Toss well and serve hot.

| | |
|---|---|
| 8 | ounces (250 g) dried rice noodles |
| 1 | pound (500 g) mushrooms, thickly sliced |
| ¼ | cup (60 ml) kecap manis |
| ½ | cup (80 g) cashews, coarsely chopped |
| 2 | tablespoons peanut oil |
| 1 | red onion, coarsely chopped |
| 3 | cups (150 g) fresh bean sprouts |

Serves: 4
Preparation: 15 minutes
Cooking: 10–15 minutes
Level: 1

■■■ *Kecap manis is a thick, Indonesian sweet soy sauce. It is available in Asian supermarkets and food stores.*

You could also use: spaghettini

# MUSHROOM & TOFU PAD THAI

**522**

Cover the noodles with boiling water in a medium bowl and soak until tender, 5–10 minutes. Refer to the time on the package. • Drain and set aside. • Mix the tamarind paste with the water. Stir in the soy sauce and palm sugar and set aside. • Heat 2 tablespoons of the oil in a wok or large frying panover medium-high heat. Stir-fry the tofu in batches until golden and almost crisp, 3–4 minutes per batch. Remove from the wok and set aside. • Heat the remaining 2 tablespoons of oil in the wok and stir-fry the garlic and shallots for 30 seconds. • Add the mushrooms and chiles and stir-fry until beginning to soften, 2–3 minutes. • Add the noodles and stir-fry for 2 minutes, then push to one side. • Add the eggs and allow to set, then scramble and mix with the noodles. • Add the tamarind mixture and stir well. • Add the scallions, carrot, and tofu and stir-fry for 2–3 minutes. • Divide among four to six serving bowls, sprinkle with the chives and cilantro, and serve hot with the lime wedges.

| | |
|---|---|
| 12 | ounces (350 g) wide rice stick noodles |
| 3 | tablespoons tamarind paste |
| 1 | tablespoon hot water |
| 3 | tablespoons dark soy sauce |
| 3 | tablespoons palm sugar (or light brown sugar) |
| 4 | tablespoons (60 ml) peanut oil |
| 1 | pound (500 g) firm tofu, cut into thin strips |
| 3 | cloves garlic, finely chopped |
| 2 | shallots, finely chopped |
| 12 | ounces (350 g) oyster mushrooms or plain white mushrooms, sliced |
| 2 | red chiles, seeded and finely chopped |
| 2 | large eggs, beaten |
| 4 | scallions (spring onions), thinly sliced |
| 1 | carrot, thinly sliced |
| | Handful fresh chives, snipped |
| | Fresh cilantro (coriander), coarsely chopped |
| 2 | limes, cut into wedges |

Serves: 4–6
Preparation: 15 minutes
Cooking: 15–20 minutes
Level: 1

You could also use: dried tagliatelle, dried pappardelle

# RICE NOODLES WITH MUSHROOMS & EGG

**524**

Cover the noodles with boiling water in a medium bowl and soak until tender, 5–10 minutes. Refer to the time on the package. • Drain and set aside. • Beat the eggs and 2 tablespoons of the soy sauce in a large bowl. • Heat 1 tablespoon of the oil in a large wok or frying pan. • Pour in the egg mixture. When the bottom has set, slide a wooden spatula under the eggs to loosen them from the pan. Shake the pan with a rotating movement to spread the eggs and cook until nicely browned on the underside and the top is set. • Remove from the heat and slice into strips. Set aside. • Sauté the mushrooms in the remaining 2 tablespoons of oil in a large frying pan over medium heat for 3 minutes. • Add the noodles, the remaining 2 tablespoons fo soy sauce, and egg strips. • Toss well and serve hot.

8   ounces (250 g) wide rice stick noodles

6   large eggs

4   tablespoons (60 ml) dark soy sauce

3   tablespoons Asian sesame oil

1   pound (500 g) shiitake mushrooms, stems trimmed and caps thinly sliced

Serves: 4
Preparation: 10–15 minutes
Cooking: 10–15 minutes
Level: 1

You could also use: dried egg noodles, tagliatelle

# SZECHUAN TOFU STIR-FRY

Prepare the noodles following the instructions on the package. Set aside. • Heat 2 tablespoons of the oil in a wok or deep frying pan and add the shallots, chiles, ginger, garlic, Szechuan peppercorns and a pinch of salt. Stir-fry for 1 minute, add the tofu and stir-fry for another 2 minutes. Remove from the heat and transfer to a plate. • Heat the remaining 1 tablespoon of oil and stir-fry the mangetout, corn, broccoli, and bean sprouts until starting to wilt, 3–5 minutes. Add the soy sauce and rice wine. • Stir in the tofu mixture and noodles and toss everything together until the noodles are heated through. • Drizzle with sesame oil and serve hot.

| | |
|---|---|
| 1 | pound (500 g) ramen noodles |
| 3 | tablespoons vegetable oil |
| 3 | shallots, thinly sliced |
| 2 | red chiles, thinly sliced |
| 1 | (1-inch/2.5-cm) piece fresh ginger, finely chopped |
| 3 | cloves garlic, thinly sliced |
| 1 | teaspoon crushed Szechuan peppercorns |
| | Salt |
| 8 | ounces (250 g) tofu, sliced |
| 8 | ounces (250 g) mangetout, halved |
| 5 | ounces (150 g baby corn (sweetcorn), halved lengthways |
| 8 | ounces (250 g) Chinese broccoli, thinly sliced |
| 2 | cups (100 g) bean sprouts |
| 2 | tablespoons light soy sauce |
| 2 | tablespoons Chinese rice wine |
| 2 | tablespoons Asian sesame oil, to drizzle |

Serves: 4–6
Preparation: 15–20 minutes
Cooking: 10–12 minutes
Level: 1

You could also use: hokkein noodles, fresh egg noodles, tagliatelle

# SOBA NOODLES WITH BLACK SESAME

528

Cook the soba noodles in plenty of boiling water for until tender, 5–7 minutes. • Drain and rinse under cold running water. • Place the noodles in a large bowl and set aside. • Mix the rice wine vinegar and soy sauce in a small bowl. • Pour the mixture over the noodles. • Add the cilantro and sesame seeds. • Toss well and serve at room temperature.

$1\frac{1}{4}$ **pounds (600 g) dried soba noodles**

$\frac{1}{3}$ **cup (90 ml) rice wine vinegar**

$\frac{1}{3}$ **cup (90 ml) soy sauce**

1 **cup (50 g) fresh cilantro (coriander) leaves**

3 **tablespoons black sesame seeds**

**Serves: 4–6**
**Preparation: 10 minutes**
**Cooking: 5–7 minutes**
**Level: 1**

■ ■ ■ *Black sesame seeds are prized for their earthy flavor. Replace with ivory-colored sesame seeds if that's what you have on hand. Both types are rich in protein and nutrients.*

You could also use: whole-wheat (wholemeal) spaghetti

# EGGPLANT NOODLE STIR-FRY

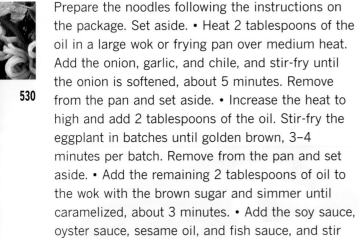

Prepare the noodles following the instructions on the package. Set aside. • Heat 2 tablespoons of the oil in a large wok or frying pan over medium heat. Add the onion, garlic, and chile, and stir-fry until the onion is softened, about 5 minutes. Remove from the pan and set aside. • Increase the heat to high and add 2 tablespoons of the oil. Stir-fry the eggplant in batches until golden brown, 3–4 minutes per batch. Remove from the pan and set aside. • Add the remaining 2 tablespoons of oil to the wok with the brown sugar and simmer until caramelized, about 3 minutes. • Add the soy sauce, oyster sauce, sesame oil, and fish sauce, and stir until heated through. • Add the noodles to the pan with the onion mixture and eggplant and toss well. Add the scallions and serve hot.

| | |
|---|---|
| 12 | ounces (350 g) ramen noodles |
| 6 | tablespoons (90 ml) peanut oil |
| 1 | red onion, finely chopped |
| 1 | clove garlic, crushed |
| 1 | red chile, seeded and thinly sliced |
| 8 | baby eggplants (aubergines), unpeeled, thinly sliced on the diagonal |
| 2 | tablespoons dark brown sugar |
| 2 | tablespoons light soy sauce |
| 2 | tablespoons oyster sauce |
| 1 | teaspoon Asian sesame oil |
| 1 | tablespoon Thai fish sauce |
| 2 | scallions (spring onions), white and tender green parts only, trimmed and chopped |

Serves: 4
Preparation: 15 minutes
Cooking: 15–20 minutes
Level: 1

You could also use: hokkein noodles, tagliatelle

Other Whipped
be Hydrogenated Oil

Redar
wip    15 Calories

# RICE NOODLES WITH SHRIMP & CILANTRO

532

Put the noodles in a medium bowl, cover with boiling water, and soak until softened, 5–10 minutes. • Drain and set aside. • Place a wok over high heat. • When it is very hot, add the sesame oil. • Add the shrimp and cook, turning often, until pink and cooked through, 3–4 minutes. • Add the lime juice and noodles and toss well. • Remove from the heat and toss with the cilantro. • Season with salt and serve hot.

14 **ounces (400 g) dried rice vermicelli**

⅓ **cup (90 ml) Asian sesame oil**

20 **large shrimp (prawn), peeled and deveined**

⅓ **cup (90 ml) freshly squeezed lime juice**

½ **cup (25 g) fresh cilantro (coriander) leaves**

**Salt**

**Serves: 4**
**Preparation: 10–15 minutes**
**Cooking: 5 minutes**
**Level: 1**

You could also use: cellophane noodles, angel hair pasta

# SHRIMP STIR-FRY

534

Prepare the noodles following the instructions on the package. Set aside. • Heat the oil in a wok or large frying pan over high heat. Add the shrimp and stir-fry for 3 minutes. • Add the turmeric, garlic, and chile and season with salt. • Stir-fry until the water from the shrimp has evaporated, then add the tomatoes, snow peas, and bell peppers. Stir-fry for 2 minutes. • Add the bean sprouts, water chestnuts, soy sauce, and oyster sauce. Stir-fry for 2 minutes. • Add the well-drained noodles and stir well. • Add the scallions, toss well, garnish with the cilantro, and serve hot.

12  ounces (350 g) ramen noodles

3  tablespoons peanut oil

1  pound (500 g) shrimp (prawns), shelled and deveined

½  teaspoon ground turmeric

2  cloves garlic, finely chopped

1  fresh red chile, seeded and finely chopped

Salt

8  cherry tomatoes, halved

4  ounces (125 g) snow peas (mangetout)

1  small red bell pepper (capsicum), seeded and thinly sliced

1  small green bell pepper (capsicum), seeded and thinly sliced

1  cup (50 g) bean sprouts

⅓  cup (60 g) canned water chestnuts, quartered

¼  cup (60 ml) dark soy sauce

1  tablespoon oyster sauce

4  scallions (green onions), sliced

Fresh cilantro (coriander) leaves

Serves: 4
Preparation: 15 minutes
Cooking: 10 minutes
Level: 1

You could also use: hokkein noodles, rice stick noodles

# CHILE & LIME SHRIMP NOODLE SALAD

Prepare the noodles according to the instructions on the package. • Drain and rinse under cold running water. • Place the noodles in a large bowl. • Add the shrimp, cilantro, mint, chile, and scallions. • Mix the lime juice, sweet chili sauce, sugar, and oil in a small bowl. • Pour the dressing over the noodle salad. • Toss gently and serve.

8   ounces (250 g) dried rice noodles

2   pounds (1 kg) cooked shrimp (prawns), peeled and deveined

1   cup (60 g) fresh cilantro (coriander) leaves

1   cup (50 g) fresh mint leaves

1   fresh red chile, seeded and thinly sliced

3   scallions (spring onions), thinly sliced

¼   cup (60 ml) freshly squeezed lime juice

⅓   cup (90 ml) Thai sweet chili sauce

2   teaspoons superfine (caster) sugar

2   tablespoons peanut oil

Serves: 4
Preparation: 20 minutes
Level: 1

You could also use: cellophane noodles, angel hair pasta, spaghettini

# THAI CRAB & RICE NOODLES

538

Place the noodles in a medium bowl, cover with boiling water, and soak until softened, 5–10 minutes. • Drain and transfer to a large bowl. • Thinly slice the scallions and cut the carrots into very thin strips (or use a julienne peeler). Add to the noodles with bean sprouts. • Mix the sweet chilli sauce and the lime juice together in a medium bowl. Season with salt and pepper. Toss through the noodles with crabmeat and chopped mint. • Divide among four to six bowls and serve hot.

| | |
|---|---|
| 1 | pound (500 g) rice stick noodles |
| 8 | scallions (spring onions) |
| 2 | carrots |
| 2 | cups (100 g) bean sprouts |
| 5 | tablespoons Thai sweet chile sauce |
| | Freshly squeezed juice of 1 lime |
| | Salt and freshly ground black pepper |
| 1 | (6-ounce/180-g) can white crabmeat, drained |
| | Handful of chopped fresh mint |

Serves: 4–6
Preparation: 15 minutes
Cooking: 10 minutes
Level: 1

You could also use: ramen noodles, dried egg noodles

# NOODLES WITH SQUID, TOMATO & BASIL

Place the noodles in a medium bowl, cover with boiling water and soak until softened, 5–10 minutes. • Drain and set aside. • Cut the squid into bite-size pieces. Lay the squid pieces flat, skin-side down, and score with a sharp knife in a crisscross pattern. • Place a wok over high heat. • When it is very hot, add the sesame oil. • Add the squid and stir-fry for 2 minutes, until it begins to change color and curl slightly. • Add the cherry tomatoes and cook for 1 minute. • Add the noodles and basil. Season with salt and pepper. • Toss well and serve hot.

| | |
|---|---|
| 1 | pound (500 g) wide rice stick noodles |
| 12 | ounces (350 g) squid, cleaned |
| | Salt and freshly ground black pepper |
| 3 | tablespoons Asian sesame oil |
| 24 | cherry tomatoes, quartered |
| 4 | tablespoons fresh basil leaves |

Serves: 4
Preparation: 15 minutes
Cooking: 5 minutes
Level: 1

You could also use: ramen noodles, tagliatelle, spaghetti, linguine

# SEARED TUNA WITH NOODLES

542

Place the tuna steaks in a bowl. Whisk the dark soy sauce, ginger, and garlic in a small bowl then drizzle over the tuna. Toss gently and set aside for 20 minutes. • Combine the chiles, light soy sauce, chopped cilantro stems, and lime juice in a small bowl and stir well. • Put the noodles in a bowl and cover with boiling water. Let stand until softened, then drain, rinse in cold water and drain again. • Put the noodles in a bowl and mix with the chopped cilantro and mint leaves. • Heat a grill pan (griddle) to high. • Drain the tuna, discarding the marinade, and cook for 2 minutes on each side. Slice the tuna. • Divide the noodles among four serving dishes. Top with the sliced tuna, drizzle with the dressing, and serve.

4 **(6-ounce/200-g) tuna steaks, about 1-inch (2.5-cm) thick**

¼ **cup (60 ml) dark soy sauce**

1 **teaspoon finely grated fresh ginger**

2 **cloves garlic, finely chopped**

2 **red chiles, seeded and finely chopped**

2 **tablespoons light soy sauce**

1 **cup (50 g) fresh cilantro (coriander), stems finely chopped, leaves chopped**

**Freshly squeezed juice of 2 limes**

8 **ounces (250 g) rice stick noodles**

**Bunch of fresh mint leaves, chopped**

Serves: 4
Preparation: 15 minutes
 + 20 minutes to
 marinate
Cooking: 10 minutes
Level: 2

You could also use: fresh or dried egg noodles, ramen noodles, tagliatelle

# SPICY SCALLOP & SNOW PEA NOODLES

544

Prepare the noodles according to the instructions on the package. • Drain and set aside. • Heat a wok over high heat. • When it is very hot, add the oil. • Add the chiles, garlic, lemongrass, scallions, snow peas, and asparagus. Stir-fry for 2 minutes. • Add the stock and scallops. • Cover and simmer until the scallops are cooked, about 2 minutes. • Add the noodles and basil. • Toss over medium-high heat for 2 minutes and serve hot.

| | |
|---|---|
| 1 | pound (500 g) fresh or dried round egg noodles |
| 1 | tablespoon peanut oil |
| 2 | small fresh red chiles, seeded and finely chopped |
| 2 | cloves garlic, finely chopped |
| 1 | stem lemongrass, trimmed, crushed, and thinly sliced |
| 3 | scallions (spring onions), thinly sliced |
| 5 | ounces (150 g) snow peas (mangetout) |
| 1 | bunch asparagus, cut into short lengths |
| 1/3 | cup (90 ml) fish stock or clam juice |
| 20 | large fresh scallops |
| 1 | cup (60 g) Thai basil or regular basil leaves |

Serves: 4
Preparation: 15 minutes
Cooking: 10 minutes
Level: 1

You could also use: ramen noodles, tagliatelle

# CHICKEN, VEGGIE & NOODLE STIR-FRY

Prepare the noodles according to the instructions on the package. • Drain and set aside. • Whisk the soy sauce, oyster sauce, and chilli sauce in a small bowl and set aside. • Put a large wok or frying pan over high heat. When hot, add the oil and chicken and stir-fry until golden and cooked through, about 5 minutes. • Add the scallions, ginger, bean sprouts, carrot, baby corn, and snow peas. Stir-fry for 1 minute. • Add the noodles and sauce to the wok and stir-fry until well mixed and heated through, 1–2 minutes. • Serve hot.

14 ounces (400 g) dried medium egg noodles

2 tablespoons light soy sauce

2 tablespoons oyster sauce

2 tablespoons Thai sweet chilli sauce

1 tablespoon peanut oil

2 boneless skinless chicken breasts, cut in thin strips

4 scallions (spring onions), sliced

2 teaspoons finely grated fresh ginger

4 cups (200 g) bean sprouts

1 large carrot, cut into matchsticks

4 ounces (125 g) baby corn (sweetcorn), halved lengthways

1 cup (150 g) snow peas (mangetout), finely sliced lengthways

Serves: 4
Preparation: 15 minutes
Cooking: 10–12 minutes
Level: 1

You could also use: ramen noodles, tagliatelle

# SPICY CHICKEN & LEMON NOODLES

548

Prepare the noodles following the instructions on the package. • Drain and set aside. • Toss the chicken in the cornstarch. Season generously with salt and pepper. • Put a large wok or frying pan over high heat. When hot, add the oil and chicken and stir-fry until golden and cooked through, 7–8 minutes. Remove the chicken and set aside. • Add the scallions, snow peas, bell peppers, and soy sauce to the pan and stir-fry for 2–3 minutes. • Return the chicken to the pan and add the lemon, honey, and chilli sauce. Stir-fry for 1–2 minutes. • Add the noodles and toss until heated through. • Top with the extra scallions and serve hot.

| | |
|---|---|
| 12 | ounces (350 g) thin egg noodles |
| 2 | boneless skinless chicken breasts, cut in small pieces |
| 2 | teaspoons cornstarch (cornflour) |
| | Salt and freshly ground black pepper |
| 2 | tablespoons Asian sesame oil |
| 8 | scallions (spring onions), shredded + extra to garnish |
| 1 | cup (150 g) snow peas (mangetout), shredded |
| 2 | red bell peppers (capsicums), sliced |
| 4 | tablespoons (60 ml) dark soy sauce |
| | Freshly squeezed juice of 2 lemons |
| 1 | tablespoon honey |
| 2 | tablespoons Thai sweet chilli sauce |

Serves: 4
Preparation: 10 minutes
Cooking: 15 minutes
Level: 1

You could also use: ramen noodles, spaghettini

# HOISIN CHICKEN WITH RICE NOODLES

Combine the chicken and $^1/_2$ cup (125 ml) of the hoisin sauce in a medium bowl. Let marinate for 1 hour. • Place the noodles in a medium bowl, cover with boiling water, and soak until softened, 5–10 minutes. • Drain and set aside. • Cook the snow peas in boiling water for 1 minute. • Drain and rinse under ice-cold water to stop the cooking process. • Place a grill pan over medium-high heat. • Grill the chicken on each side for 3–4 minutes, or until cooked through. • Slice the chicken thinly and set aside. • Mix the noodles, snow peas, peanuts, and remaining $^1/_4$ cup (60 ml) hoisin sauce in a large bowl. • Top with the chicken and serve hot.

2   boneless skinless chicken breasts, sliced

$^3/_4$   cup (180 ml) hoisin sauce

14   ounces (400 g) dried rice vermicelli

8   ounces (250 g) snow peas (mangetout), trimmed

$^1/_2$   cup (80 g) salted roasted peanuts

Serves: 4
Preparation: 15 minutes
  + 1 hour to marinate
Cooking: 4–5 minutes
Level: 1

You could also use: cellophane noodles, spaghettini

# STIR-FRIED CHICKEN & NOODLES WITH PLUM SAUCE

**552**

Prepare the noodles following the instructions on the package. • Drain and set aside. • Put a large wok or frying pan over high heat. When hot, add the oil and chicken and stir-fry until golden and cooked through, about 5 minutes. • Add the baby corn and pak choi. Stir-fry for 2 minutes with a dash of water, then add the noodles and plum sauce. • Toss until the noodles are heated through. • Garnish with the basil and serve hot.

14  ounces (400 g) fresh egg noodles

2  tablespoons peanut oil

2  boneless skinless chicken breasts, cut in thin strips

2  handfuls baby corn (sweetcorn)

4  pak choi, sliced

½  cup (120 ml) plum sauce

Fresh basil leaves, to garnish

Serves: 4
Preparation: 10 minutes
Cooking: 10–12 minutes
Level: 1

You could also use: ramen noodles, tagliatelle

# CHICKEN & HOKKEIN NOODLE STIR-FRY

Coat the chicken with $1/2$ cup (125 ml) the hoisin sauce in a large bowl. Cover with plastic wrap (cling film) and refrigerate for 1 hour. • Cook the noodles in a large pot of salted boiling water for about 5 minutes, or until al dente. • Drain and set aside. • Cook the broccoli in boiling water for 2 minutes. • Drain and set aside. • Place a wok over high heat. • When it is very hot, add the chicken and the remaining $1/2$ cup (125 ml) of hoisin sauce. Cook for 2 minutes. • Add the bell peppers and broccoli and cook for 2 minutes. • Add the noodles and cook for 1 minute. • Serve hot.

| | |
|---|---|
| 2 | boneless, skinless chicken breasts, cut into small pieces |
| 1 | cup (250 ml) hoisin sauce |
| 14 | ounces (400 g) fresh hokkien |
| 1 | bunch kai-lan or Chinese broccoli, cut into short lengths |
| 2 | red bell peppers (capsicums), seeded and cut into thin strips |

Serves: 4
Preparation: 10 minutes
+ 1 hour to marinate
Cooking: 12 minutes
Level: 1

You could also use: Singapore egg noodles

# SOY CHICKEN NOODLE SALAD

Coat the chicken with the soy sauce in a medium bowl. Cover with plastic wrap (cling film) and refrigerate for 1 hour. • Place a grill pan (griddle) over medium-high heat. • Grill the chicken until cooked through, about 5 minutes on each side. • Let rest in a warm place for 5 minutes. • Cover the noodles with boiling water in a medium bowl and soak for 5 minutes. • Drain and set aside. • Shred the chicken and put in a large bowl. Add the noodles, cucumber, and mint. • Toss well and serve warm or at room temperature.

| | |
|---|---|
| 2 | boneless, skinless chicken breasts |
| ¼ | cup (60 ml) dark soy sauce |
| 14 | ounces (400 g) dried rice vermicelli |
| 1 | cucumber, shaved lengthwise into ribbons |
| 2 | tablespoons leaves fresh mint |

Serves: 4
Preparation: 10 minutes
  + 1 hour to marinate
Cooking: 10 minutes
Level: 1

You could also use: cellophane noodles, spaghettini

# SOBA NOODLE DUCK SALAD

Cook the noodles according to the instructions on the package. • Drain and rinse under cold running water. • Place the noodles in a large bowl. • Add the duck, scallions, cucumber, and mizuna. • Whisk the rice vinegar, oil, soy sauce, ginger, sesame oil, sugar, and red pepper flakes in a small bowl. • Pour the dressing over the noodle salad. • Toss gently and serve.

■ ■ ■ *Mizuna is a leafy salad green grown in China and Japan. It has a sweet, slightly mustard-flavored tang. It can be found in Asian markets. If unavailable, replace with the same amount of arugula (rocket). Chinese barbecued duck can be found in Asian delicatessens.*

8 ounces (250 g) dried soba noodles

2 cups (300 g) shredded Chinese barbecued duck

3 scallions (spring onions), trimmed and thinly sliced

1 cucumber, thinly sliced

2 ounces (60 g) mizuna

¼ cup (60 ml) rice vinegar

2 tablespoons vegetable oil

1 tablespoon dark soy sauce

2 teaspoons finely grated fresh ginger

1 tablespoon Asian sesame oil

2 teaspoons superfine (caster) sugar

1 teaspoon dried red pepper flakes

Serves: 4
Preparation: 10 minutes
Cooking: 5 minutes
Level: 1

You could also use: whole-wheat (wholemeal) spaghetti, linguine

# CHICKEN NOODLES WITH SNAKE BEANS & PLUM SAUCE

Cook the noodles in plenty of boiling water until softened, about 5–10 minutes. • Drain and set aside. • Cook the snake beans in boiling water for 2 minutes. • Drain and rinse under ice-cold water to stop the cooking process. • Place a wok over high heat. • When it is very hot, add the sesame oil. • Add the chicken and stir-fry until tender, 4–5 minutes. • Stir in the plum sauce and beans. Cook for 2 minutes. • Add the noodles and cook for 2 minutes. • Toss well and serve hot.

14 ounces (400 g) Chinese dried wheat noodles

2 cups (200 g) snake beans, trimmed and cut into short lengths

3 tablespoons Asian sesame oil

2 boneless skinless chicken breasts, thinly sliced

3/4 cup (180 ml) storebought Chinese plum sauce

Serves: 4
Preparation: 10 minutes
Cooking: 15–20 minutes
Level: 1

■ ■ ■ *Snake beans go by a range of different names, including asparagus beans, pea beans, cowpeas, catjang, yard-long beans, and China peas. They have a refreshing delicate flavor. Substitute green beans if you can't find them.*

You could also use: spaghetti, linguine

# SPICY CHICKEN NOODLES WITH PEANUTS

562

Cook the hokkien noodles in plenty of boiling water until tender. Refer to the package for the exact cooking time. • Drain and set aside. • Combine the oil, chilli sauce, and dark soy sauce in a bowl. • Add the chicken to the bowl, season with pepper, and mix well. • Heat a wok or large frying pan over high heat. • Remove the chicken from the marinade (reserving the marinade), add to the wok, and stir-fry until lightly golden, 4–5 minutes. • Add the carrots, broccoli, cabbage, noodles, and reserved marinade. Stir-fry until heated through, 2–3 minutes. • Mix in the peanuts, drizzle with light soy sauce, and serve hot.

1   pound (500 g) hokkein noodles

2   tablespoons vegetable oil

4   tablespoons (60 ml) Thai sweet chilli sauce

4   tablespoons (60 ml) dark soy sauce

2   large boneless skinless chicken breasts, cut in thin strips

    Freshly ground black pepper

2   carrots, thinly sliced

1   small head broccoli, broken into small florets

1   small spring cabbage, thinly sliced

½   cup (80 g) salted roasted peanuts, coarsely chopped

    Light soy sauce, to serve

Serves: 4
Preparation: 10 minutes
Cooking: 10–12 minutes
Level: 1

You could also use: ramen noodles

# CHICKEN PAD THAI

Soak the noodles in a medium bowl of boiling water for 5–10 minutes. • Drain and set aside. • Place a wok over high heat. • When it is very hot, add 1 tablespoon of oil. • Beat the eggs lightly in a small bowl. Pour them into the wok. • Cook, stirring, until scrambled and cooked, about 2 minutes. • Remove from the pan and set aside. • Add the remaining oil to the wok and stir-fry the chicken for 3 minutes. • Add the garlic and scallions. Stir-fry for 1 minute. • Add the noodles, lime juice, fish sauce, brown sugar, soy sauce, and tofu. • Stir-fry for 3 minutes. • Add the bean sprouts and peanuts. • Garnish with the cilantro and lime wedges. Serve hot.

**564**

| | |
|---|---|
| 8 | ounces (250 g) rice stick noodles |
| 2 | tablespoons peanut oil |
| 2 | large eggs |
| 2 | boneless skinless chicken breasts, diced |
| 2 | cloves garlic, finely chopped |
| 4 | scallions (spring onions), thinly sliced |
| ¼ | cup (60 ml) freshly squeezed lime juice |
| ¼ | cup (60 ml) Asian fish sauce |
| 1 | tablespoon brown sugar |
| 1 | tablespoon light soy sauce |
| 8 | ounces (250 g) firm tofu, diced |
| 4 | cups (200 g) fresh bean sprouts |
| ⅓ | cup (50 g) roasted peanuts, chopped |
| | Fresh cilantro (coriander), to garnish |
| | Lime wedges, to serve |

■ ■ ■ *Pad Thai, which means "fried Thai style," is a traditional Thai dish made with stir-fried rice noodles, eggs, and fish sauce together with varying combinations of chicken, shrimp, tofu, vegetables, herbs, and peanuts.*

Serves: 4
Preparation: 20 minutes
Cooking: 10 minutes
Level: 1

You could also use: tagliatelle

# SPICY CHICKEN WITH HOKKEIN NOODLES & BOK CHOY

Cook the hokkien noodles in plenty of boiling water. Refer to the package for the exact cooking time.
• Drain and set aside. • Place a wok over high heat.
• When it is very hot, add the oil. • Stir-fry the chicken until cooked, 4–5 minutes. • Add the sweet chili sauce, soy sauce, bok choy, and noodles.
• Cook for 2 minutes. • Serve hot.

1 **pound (500 g) hokkien noodles**

2 **tablespoons peanut oil**

2 **boneless skinless chicken breasts, thinly sliced**

1/3 **cup (90 ml) Thai sweet chili sauce**

2 **tablespoons dark soy sauce**

1 **bunch baby bok choy, leaves separated and stems coarsely chopped**

Serves: 4
Preparation: 10 minutes
Cooking: 10 minutes
Level: 1

■■■ *Bok choy is a common Chinese leaf vegetable. It is widely available at Asian food markets. However, if you can't find it fresh, substitute with the same amount of fresh spinach or Swiss chard (silverbeet).*

You could also use: Chinese egg noodles, tagliatelle

# NOODLES WITH CHICKEN & VEGETABLES

Cook the noodles according to the instructions on the package. • Drain and set aside. • Place a wok over high heat. • When it is very hot, add 2 tablespoons of oil. • Stir-fry the chicken until cooked, about 5 minutes. • Remove from the pan and set aside. • Add the remaining oil and stir-fry the garlic, carrot, and cabbage for 1 minute. • Add the kecap manis, noodles, and chicken. • Stir-fry for 2 minutes. • Garnish with the scallions and serve hot.

| | |
|---|---|
| 14 | ounces (400 g) rice stick noodles |
| 3 | tablespoons peanut oil |
| 2 | boneless skinless chicken breasts, thinly sliced |
| 2 | cloves garlic, finely chopped |
| 1 | carrot, shredded |
| 8 | ounces (250 g) Chinese cabbage (wombok), coarsely shredded |
| ⅓ | cup (90 ml) kecap manis |
| 4 | scallions (spring onions), thinly sliced |

Serves: 4
Preparation: 15 minutes
Cooking: 10 minutes
Level: 1

■■■ *Kecap manis is a thick, Indonesian sweet soy sauce. It is available in Asian supermarkets and food stores.*

You could also use: tagliatelle

# CHICKEN, NOODLE & SUGAR SNAP STIR-FRY

Cook the noodles according to the instructions on the package. • Drain and set aside. • Heat a wok over high heat. • When it is very hot, add the oil. • Stir-fry the scallions and garlic for 1 minute. • Add the chicken, sugar snap peas, and oyster sauce. • Stir-fry for 3 minutes. • Add the noodles and cook for 2 minutes. • Toss well and serve hot.

14   ounces (400 g) ramen noodles

2   tablespoons peanut oil

4   scallions (spring onions), finely sliced

2   cloves garlic, finely chopped

2   cups (300 g) shredded cooked chicken

8   ounces (250 g) sugar snap peas, trimmed

1/3   cup (90 ml) Chinese oyster sauce

Serves: 4
Preparation: 10 minutes
Cooking: 6–7 minutes
Level: 1

You could also use: spaghetti

# BEEF & SPINACH STIR-FRY

Combine the beef with the soy sauce, apple juice, red pepper flakes, garlic, papaya, and tomatoes in a large nonreactive bowl. Use your hands to mix the ingredients for about 5 minutes to ensure all the spices are well absorbed. The heat from your hands will aid the tenderizing process. Let marinate for 2 hours. • Cook the noodles according to the instructions on the package. • Drain and set aside. • Heat a wok or large frying pan over high heat and add the oil. Stir-fry the celery and ginger until aromatic, about 1 minute. • Add the beef and the marinade. Stir occasionally until all the liquid has evaporated and the meat is tender, about 5 minutes. • Add the spinach and noodles. Stir-fry for another 2 minutes. • Serve hot.

| | |
|---|---|
| 2 | pounds (1 kg) beef tenderloin, cut into thin strips |
| 5 | tablespoons (75 ml) dark soy sauce |
| 5 | tablespoons (75 ml) apple juice |
| 1 | teaspoon dried red pepper flakes |
| 2 | cloves garlic, finely chopped |
| 1 | medium papaya (pawpaw), peeled and cut into small cubes |
| 10 | cherry tomatoes, halved |
| 12 | ounces (350 g) rice stick noodles |
| 3 | tablespoons peanut oil |
| 2 | stalks celery, sliced |
| 2 | tablespoons finely chopped fresh ginger |
| 5 | cups (250 g) baby spinach leaves |

Serves: 4–6
Preparation: 10 minutes
  + 2 hours to marinate
Cooking: 15 minutes
Level: 2

You could also use: cellophane noodles, spaghettini

# SATAY BEEF WITH RICE NOODLES

**Satay Sauce:** Heat the oil in a medium saucepan over medium-low heat. Add the garlic, chiles, and ginger and sauté until softened, about 5 minutes.
• Stir in the paprika, cayenne pepper, peanut butter, coconut milk, and sugar and bring to a boil. Decrease the heat, pour in the lime juice, fish sauce, and soy sauce and simmer until thickened, about 10 minutes. Keep warm.
**Beef:** Put the noodles in a medium bowl, cover with boiling water, and soak until softened, 5–10 minutes.
• Drain and set aside. • Place a wok over high heat.
• When it is very hot, add the sesame oil. • Add the beef and stir-fry for 2 minutes. • Add the bell peppers and stir-fry for 2 minutes. • Stir in the satay sauce and heat for 1 minute. • Add the noodles. • Toss well and serve hot.

**Satay Sauce**

1   tablespoon peanut oil

4   cloves garlic, finely chopped

2   small red chiles, seeded and finely chopped

1   tablespoon finely grated fresh ginger

1   teaspoon sweet paprika

1/2  teaspoon cayenne pepper

1   cup (250 g) crunchy peanut butter

2   cups (400 ml) canned coconut milk

1/4  cup (50 g) firmly packed soft brown sugar

1/4  cup (60 ml) freshly squeezed lime juice, strained

2   tablespoons Thai fish sauce

1   tablespoon soy sauce

**Beef**

14  ounces (400 g) rice stick noodles

3   tablespoons sesame oil

1¼  pounds (600 g) tenderloin beef, cut into thin strips

2   red bell peppers (capsicums), seeded and cut into thin strips

Serves: 4
Preparation: 30 minutes
Cooking: 25–30 minutes
Level: 2

You could also use: Chinese wheat noodles, tagliatelle

# NOODLES WITH BEEF & BLACK BEAN SAUCE

Place the noodles in a medium bowl, cover with boiling water, and soak until softened, 5–10 minutes. • Drain and set aside. • Place a wok over high heat. • When it is very hot, add the sesame oil. • Add the beef and stir-fry for 2 minutes. • Add the bell peppers and stir-fry for 2 minutes. • Stir in the black bean sauce and heat for 1 minute. • Add the noodles. • Toss well and serve hot.

14 ounces (400 g) rice stick noodles

3 tablespoons Asian sesame oil

1¼ pounds (600 g) tenderloin beef, cut into thin strips

2 green bell peppers (capsicums), seeded and diced

¾ cup (180 ml) Chinese black bean sauce

Serves: 4
Preparation: 15 minutes
Cooking: 5 minutes
Level: 1

You could also use: ramen noodles, linguine

# BLACK BEAN BEEF NOODLES

Cook the noodles according to the instructions on the package. Drain and set aside. • Place a wok over high heat. When it is very hot, add 2 tablespoons of oil. • Add the beef and stir-fry for 3 minutes. Remove from the pan and set aside. • Add the remaining oil and stir-fry the garlic and onion over medium heat until softened, about 3 minutes. • Pour in the black bean sauce, mirin, and green beans. • Stir-fry for 3 minutes. • Return the beef and noodles to the wok. Stir-fry for 1 minute. • Toss well and serve hot.

| | |
|---|---|
| 1 | pound (500 g) flat fresh egg noodles |
| ¼ | cup (60 ml) peanut oil |
| 1 | pound (500 g) fillet beef, cut into thin strips |
| 2 | cloves garlic, finely chopped |
| 1 | onion, thinly sliced |
| ¼ | cup (60 ml) Chinese black bean sauce |
| 1 | tablespoon mirin or sweet sherry |
| 5 | ounces (150 g) green beans |

Serves: 4
Preparation: 10 minutes
Cooking: 13–15 minutes
Level: 1

You could also use: tagliatelle

# STICKY BEEF WITH NOODLES

Prepare the noodles according to the instructions on the package. • Drain and refresh under cold running water. Drain again and set aside. • Marinate the steak in a bowl with the soy and sweet chilli sauces for 10 minutes. • Chop the ginger, garlic, cashews and chilli in a small food processor (or pound in a pestle and mortar) to form a paste. Set aside. • Heat a grill pan (griddle) or frying pan until very hot. Add the steaks, well coated in the marinade, and cook to your liking; 3–4 minutes each side for medium rare. Set aside to rest. • Heat the peanut oil in a wok or frying pan over medium-high heat and fry the cashew paste for 1 minute. Add the carrots, bell pepper, and a splash of water and stir-fry for 2 minutes. • Add the noodles and cilantro and stir well. • Serve the noodles with the sticky beef.

| | |
|---|---|
| 12 | ounces (350 g) cellophane noodles |
| 4 | (8-ounce/250-g) rump or sirloin steaks |
| 1/4 | cup (60 ml) dark soy sauce |
| 4 | tablespoons (60 ml) Thai sweet chilli sauce |
| 1 | tablespoon peeled fresh ginger |
| 2 | cloves garlic, peeled |
| 1/2 | cup (60 g) cashew nuts |
| 1 | dried chile, crumbled |
| 2 | tablespoons peanut oil |
| 2 | carrots, cut into matchsticks |
| 1 | red bell pepper (capsicum), seeded and thinly sliced |
| | Handful fresh cilantro (coriander) leaves |

Serves: 4
Preparation: 10 minutes
+ 15 minutes to marinate
Cooking: 15–20 minutes
Level: 1

You could also use: dried rice vermicelli, rice stick noodles

# STIR-FRIED BEEF WITH NOODLES & VEGGIES

**582**

Cook the hokkien noodles in plenty of boiling water. Refer to the package for the exact cooking time.
• Drain and set aside. • Place a wok over high heat.
• When it is very hot, add 2 tablespoons of oil.
• Add the beef and stir-fry for 3 minutes. • Remove from the pan and set aside. • Add the remaining oil and stir-fry the garlic over medium heat until pale gold, about 1 minute. • Add the asparagus and corn. Stir-fry for 3 minutes. • Return the beef to the wok.
• Add the oyster sauce, Shaoxing wine, and water.
• Stir-fry for 2 minutes. • Serve hot.

| | |
|---|---|
| 1 | **pound (500 g) hokkien noodles** |
| ¼ | **cup (60 ml) peanut oil** |
| 1 | **pound (500 g) fillet beef, cut into thin strips** |
| 2 | **cloves garlic, finely chopped** |
| 12 | **ounces (350 g) asparagus, trimmed and cut into short lengths** |
| 12 | **ounces (350 g) baby corn (sweetcorn), halved** |
| 3 | **tablespoons Chinese oyster sauce** |
| 1 | **tablespoon Shaoxing wine or sherry** |
| ¼ | **cup (60 ml) water** |

Serves: 4
Preparation: 10 minutes
Cooking: 14 minutes
Level: 1

You could also use: Chinese wheat noodles, tagliatelle

# MEE GORENG

Cook the hokkien noodles in plenty of boiling water. Refer to the package for the exact cooking time.
• Place a wok over high heat. • When it is very hot, add 1 tablespoon of oil. • Pour in the eggs. • Slide a wooden spatula under the eggs to loosen them from the pan. Shake the pan with a rotating movement to spread. Cook until nicely browned on the underside.
• Remove from the heat and cut into thin strips.
• Add 1 tablespoon of oil to the wok. • Add the beef and stir-fry for 3 minutes. • Remove from the pan and set aside. • Add the remaining oil and stir-fry the garlic, scallions, shrimp paste, and sambal oelek for 1 minute. • Stir in the kecap manis, stock, noodles, and beef. • Stir-fry for 2 minutes. • Add the cilantro, strips of egg, and peanuts. • Serve hot.

■■■ *Mee goreng is the name for "fried noodles" in Indonesia and Malaysia, where it is a common dish. Many different types of noodles are prepared this way. Sambal oelek is a spicy chile paste used to flavor dishes in many parts of Asia. It is available in Asian food stores or online, as is the dried shrimp paste. Kecap manis is a thick, Indonesian sweet soy sauce. It is available in Asian supermarkets and food stores.*

| | |
|---|---|
| 1 | pound (500 g) hokkien noodles |
| 3 | tablespoons peanut oil |
| 3 | large eggs, lightly beaten |
| 1 | pound (500 g) fillet beef, cut into thin strips |
| 2 | cloves garlic, finely chopped |
| 4 | scallions (spring onions), thinly sliced |
| 2 | tablespoons dried shrimp paste |
| 2 | teaspoons sambal oelek |
| ¼ | cup (60 ml) kecap manis |
| ¼ | cup (60 ml) beef stock |
| 2 | tablespoons coarsely chopped fresh cilantro (coriander) |
| ¾ | cup (80 g) coarsely chopped unsalted peanuts |

Serves: 4–6
Preparation: 10 minutes
Cooking: 15 minutes
Level: 1

You could also use: fresh or dried egg noodles, tagliatelle

# SPICY BEEF NOODLE STIR-FRY

586

Cook the noodles according to the instructions on the package. • Drain and set aside. • Marinate the beef strips in the chili oil, 3 tablespoons of the lemon juice, soy sauce, garlic, ginger, and Tabasco for 15 minutes. • Heat the oil in a wok or large frying pan over medium-high heat. Add the onion and stir-fry until softened, 3–4 minutes. • Add the beef and its marinade and stir-fry until the beef is lightly browned, 5–6 minutes. • Add the bell peppers, snow peas, corn, chile pepper, red pepper flakes, and remaining 3 tablespoons lemon juice. Stir-fry until the vegetables are tender-crisp, 3–4 minutes. • Add the scallions and noodles and stir-fry over high heat until well combined. • Serve hot.

14　ounces (400 g) ramen noodles

1　pound (500 g) lean beef fillet, cut into thin strips

2　tablespoons Asian chili oil

6　tablespoons (90 ml) freshly squeezed lemon juice

1　tablespoon dark soy sauce

2　cloves garlic, finely chopped

1　teaspoon finely grated fresh ginger

1　teaspoon Tabasco

2　tablespoons peanut oil

1　red onion, finely sliced

1　red bell pepper (capsicum), seeded and sliced

1　green bell pepper (capsicum), seeded and sliced

6　ounces (180 g) snow peas (mangetout), trimmed and chopped

1　cup (150 g) fresh or frozen corn kernels

1　red chile, seeded and finely chopped

2　teaspoons dried red pepper flakes

2　scallions (spring onions), sliced

Serves: 4
Preparation: 10 minutes
　+ 15 minutes to marinate
Cooking: 12–15 minutes
Level: 1

You could also use: hokkein noodles, spaghetti

# STIR-FRIED SPICY BEEF & NOODLES

Cook the noodles according to the instructions on the package. Drain and set aside. • Place a wok over high heat. • When it is very hot, add the oil. • Add the beef and stir-fry for 3 minutes. • Add the garlic, ginger, scallions, and chiles. Stir-fry for 1 minute. • Stir in the oyster sauce, soy sauce, and noodles. • Stir-fry for 2 minutes. • Toss well and serve hot.

| | |
|---|---|
| 1 | pound (500 g) flat fresh egg noodles |
| 2 | tablespoons peanut oil |
| 1 | pound (500 g) fillet beef, cut into thin strips |
| 2 | cloves garlic, finely chopped |
| 2 | teaspoons finely grated fresh ginger |
| 6 | scallions (spring onions), cut into short lengths |
| 2 | fresh red chiles, seeded and thinly sliced |
| ¼ | cup (60 ml) Chinese oyster sauce |
| 2 | tablespoons dark soy sauce |

Serves: 4
Preparation: 10 minutes
Cooking: 10 minutes
Level: 1

You could also use: tagliatelle, pappardelle

# PORK LO MEIN

Cook the noodles in plenty of boiling water until tender, 3–5 minutes. Refer to the package for exact cooking time. • Drain and set aside. • Place a wok over high heat. • When it is very hot, add the pork and five-spice powder. Cook for 3 minutes. • Add the soy sauce and cabbage. Cook for 2 minutes. • Add the noodles and cook for 2 minutes. • Toss well and serve hot.

1½ **pounds (600 g) fresh thin Chinese egg noodles**

1 **pound (500 g) ground (minced) pork**

1 **tablespoon five-spice powder**

⅓ **cup (90 ml) soy sauce**

½ **Chinese cabbage (wombok), finely shredded**

Serves: 4–6
Preparation: 5 minutes
Cooking: 10 minutes
Level: 1

You could also use: tagliolini, tagliatelle

# PORK GREEN CURRY WITH NOODLES

Cook the noodles in plenty of boiling water until tender. Refer to the package for exact cooking time. • Drain and set aside. • Heat the oil in a wok over high heat and add the pork. Stir-fry until browned evenly all over, 6–8 minutes. • Push the meat to one side, lower the heat, and stir in the curry paste, ginger, and chile. Stir-fry until incorporated, about 1 minute. Gradually add the coconut milk, mixing in with the meat. • Add the water, stir well to combine, and bring to a boil. Reduce the heat to a gentle simmer and add the corn. Simmer for 5 minutes. • Add the noodles to the wok with the mangetout, bamboo shoots, and scallions. Mix well and stir-fry until heated through, 1–2 minutes. • Garnish with the cilantro and serve hot.

12 ounces (350 g) round egg noodles

1 tablespoon sunflower oil

14 ounces (400 g) pork fillet, cut into thin strips

2 tablespoons Thai green curry paste

1 (1-inch/2.5-cm) piece fresh ginger, peeled and thinly sliced

1 small red chile, seeded and thinly sliced

$1^2/_3$ cups (400 ml) coconut milk

$^1/_3$ cup (90 ml) water

3 ounces (100 g) baby corn (sweetcorn), halved

4 ounces (125 g) mangetout, halved

7 ounces (200 g) canned bamboo shoots, drained

3 scallions (spring onions), trimmed and thickly sliced

$^1/_2$ cup (25 g) coarsely chopped fresh cilantro (coriander)

Serves: 4
Preparation: 15 minutes
Cooking: 15–20 minutes
Level: 1

You could also use: hokkein noodles, spaghetti, linguine

# FIVE-SPICE PORK WITH HOKKIEN NOODLES

Cook the hokkien noodles in plenty of boiling water. Refer to the package for the exact cooking time.
• Drain and set aside. • Place a wok over high heat.
• When it is very hot, add 1 tablespoon of oil. • Add the five-spice powder, garlic, and ginger. Stir-fry for about 30 seconds. • Add the pork and stir-fry until cooked, about 5 minutes. • Remove from the pan and set aside. • Add the remaining oil to the wok.
• Add the scallions and stir-fry for 2 minutes.
• Add the noodles, pork, and hoisin and oyster sauces. • Stir-fry for 2 minutes. • Toss well and serve hot.

| | |
|---|---|
| 1 | pound (500 g) hokkien noodles |
| 2 | tablespoons peanut oil |
| 1 | teaspoon Chinese five-spice powder |
| 2 | cloves garlic, finely chopped |
| 1 | tablespoon finely grated ginger |
| 1 | pound (500 g) pork fillet, cut into small pieces |
| 4 | scallions (spring onions), cut into 2-inch (5-cm) lengths |
| 2 | tablespoons hoisin sauce |
| 2 | tablespoons oyster sauce |

Serves: 4
Preparation: 10 minutes
Cooking: 15 minutes
Level: 1

You could also use: Chinese egg noodles, tagliatelle

# NOODLES WITH SPICY GROUND PORK

Cook the noodles in plenty of boiling water. Refer to the package for the exact cooking time. • Drain and set aside. • Place a wok over high heat. • When it is very hot, add the oil. • Stir-fry the pork for 4 minutes. • Add the garlic, ginger, and chiles. Stir-fry for 1 minute. • Add the laksa paste, fish sauce, brown sugar, and scallions. • Stir-fry for 2 minutes. • Add the noodles. Stir-fry for 2 minutes. • Toss well and serve hot.

| | |
|---|---|
| 1 | pound (500 g) fresh rice noodles |
| 1 | tablespoon peanut oil |
| 1½ | pounds (750 g) ground (minced) pork |
| 2 | cloves garlic, finely chopped |
| 2 | teaspoons finely grated ginger |
| 2 | small fresh green chiles, seeded and finely chopped |
| 3 | tablespoons laksa paste |
| 1 | tablespoon Asian fish sauce |
| 1 | tablespoon brown sugar |
| 4 | scallions (spring onions), thinly sliced |

Serves: 4
Preparation: 15 minutes
Cooking: 10 minutes
Level: 1

■■■ *Laksa paste and chiles vary in heat. Adjust the amount according to your taste. Laksa paste is available in many Asian supermarkets.*

You could also use: tagliatelle

# HOKKIEN NOODLES WITH PORK & SNOW PEAS

598

Cook the hokkien noodles in plenty of boiling water. Refer to the package for the exact cooking time. • Drain and set aside. • Place a wok over high heat. • When it is very hot, add the oil. • Stir-fry the pork for 4 minutes. • Add the curry paste and cook for 30 seconds. • Stir in the lime juice, fish sauce, brown sugar, kaffir lime leaves, snow peas, and chiles. • Stir-fry for 3 minutes. • Serve hot with the noodles.

| | |
|---|---|
| 1 | pound (500 g) hokkien noodles |
| 2 | tablespoons peanut oil |
| 1 | pound (500 g) pork fillet, thinly sliced |
| 2 | tablespoons Thai red curry paste |
| 2 | tablespoons freshly squeezed lime juice |
| 1 | tablespoon Asian fish sauce |
| 2 | tablespoons brown sugar |
| 4 | kaffir lime leaves, thinly sliced |
| 5 | ounces (150 g) snow peas (mangetout), trimmed and halved |
| 2 | fresh red chiles, seeded and very thinly sliced |

Serves: 4
Preparation: 10 minutes
Cooking: 13 minutes
Level: 1

■■■ *Kaffir lime, also known as makrut lime, is a member of the citrus family. The fruit is knobbly and bitter-tasting, and it is the leaves that are most commonly used to flavor food. If you can't find the lime leaves for this dish, it is okay to leave them out.*

You could also use: Chinese egg noodles, tagliatelle

# SATAY LAMB & NOODLE STIR-FRY

Place the noodles in a medium bowl and let stand in boiling water for 5 minutes. • Drain and set aside. • Place a wok over high heat. • When it is very hot, add 1 tablespoon of oil. • Add the lamb and stir-fry for 3 minutes. • Remove from the pan and set aside. • Add the remaining oil and stir-fry the garlic and onion over medium heat until softened, about 3 minutes. • Add the yard-long beans and stir-fry for 1 minute. • Stir in the coconut milk, satay sauce, and lamb. • Cook for 2 minutes. • Add the noodles and toss well. Serve hot.

| | |
|---|---|
| 1 | pound (500 g) rice stick noodles |
| 2 | tablespoons peanut oil |
| 1 | pound (500 g) fillet lamb, cut into thin strips |
| 2 | cloves garlic, finely chopped |
| 1 | onion, cut into thin wedges |
| 8 | ounces (250 g) yard-long beans, cut into short lengths |
| 1 | cup (250 ml) coconut milk |
| 1 | cup (250 ml) satay sauce, storebought or homemade (see page 574) |

Serves: 4
Preparation: 15 minutes
Cooking: 10 minutes
Level: 1

■■■ *Satay sauce is a sweet, spicy peanut sauce that is widely used in Indonesian, Malaysian, and Thai cuisines. It is available in Asian food markets and from online suppliers, or see our recipe on page 574). Yard-long beans, also known as snake beans, asparagus beans, or China peas, are the fresh beans from which black-eyed peas are derived. If unavailable, replace with green beans.*

You could also use: tagliatelle

# WARM BLACK BEAN LAMB & RICE NOODLE SALAD

602

Cook the noodles in plenty of boiling water. Refer to the package for the exact cooking time. • Drain and set aside. • Mix 2 tablespoons of peanut oil, the mirin, sesame oil, and brown sugar in a small bowl. • Pour the mixture over the noodles and toss well. • Mix the black bean sauce, the remaining peanut oil, and lamb in a medium bowl. • Place a grill pan over medium-high heat. • Grill the lamb on each side for 5 minutes. • Let rest for 5 minutes. Slice the lamb thinly. • Add the lamb and spinach to the noodles. • Toss well and serve warm.

| | |
|---|---|
| 8 | ounces (250 g) rice stick noodles |
| ¼ | cup (60 ml) peanut oil |
| 2 | tablespoons mirin or sweet sherry |
| 1 | teaspoon Asian sesame oil |
| 2 | teaspoons brown sugar |
| 2 | tablespoons Chinese black bean sauce |
| 1 | pound (500 g) boneless leg of lamb or lamb tenderloin |
| 2 | cups (100 g) baby spinach leaves |

Serves: 4
Preparation: 20 minutes
Cooking: 10 minutes
Level: 1

You could also use: cellophane noodles, tagliolini

# Index

## Baked Pasta

## Fresh Pasta

## SHORT PASTA